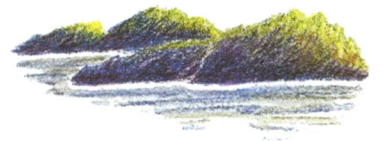

Home in an Island Garden

in pursuit of an artful life

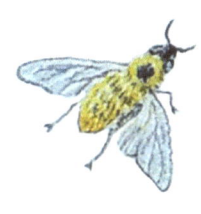 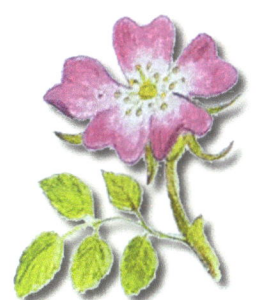 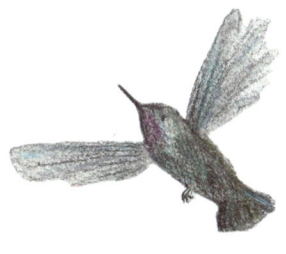

Nancy McDonnell Spaulding

Home in an Island Garden
In Pursuit of an Artful Life

Written by
Nancy McDonnell Spaulding

All art (including drawings, serigraphs, pastels and oil paintings)
are original works by the author.

First Edition
Copyright ©2021 by Nancy McDonnell Spaulding

ISBN: 978-1-7367911-0-3

All rights reserved
KDP Edition

No portion of this work may be reproduced or transmitted in any form or by any means, electronic or mechanical, including photocopying and recording, or by an information storage or retrieval system, without written permission from the publisher.

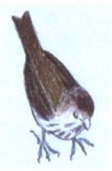

Fox Sparrow Press
Friday Harbor, WA

For Lewis,
Laurel and Heather

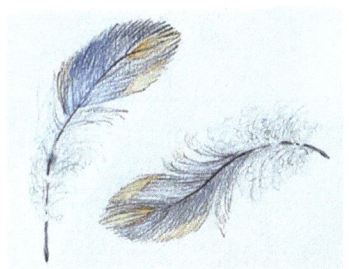

Table of Contents

INTRODUCTION - Islands of the Mind 7

ONE - We Were Drawn to an Island - 1978 13

TWO - Return of the Violet-green Swallows 25

THREE - Days Filled With Roses 35

FOUR - Building the Dome - 1979 47

FIVE - An Admiration for Bumblebees 55

SIX - Embracing Chaos: Our Early Island Years - 1979 to 1981 65

SEVEN - The Quail Diaries 75

EIGHT - A Merry-Go-Round - 1983 to 1999 87

NINE - The Garden in Winter 99

TEN - The Exuberant Season 109

ELEVEN - The Glories of Summer and Fall 121

TWELVE - Transformations - 2000 to 2008 131

THIRTEEN - Riding the Wild Wave of Time 141

LIST OF ARTWORK - Title and Medium 152

ABOUT THE AUTHOR 155

ACKNOWLEDGMENTS 156

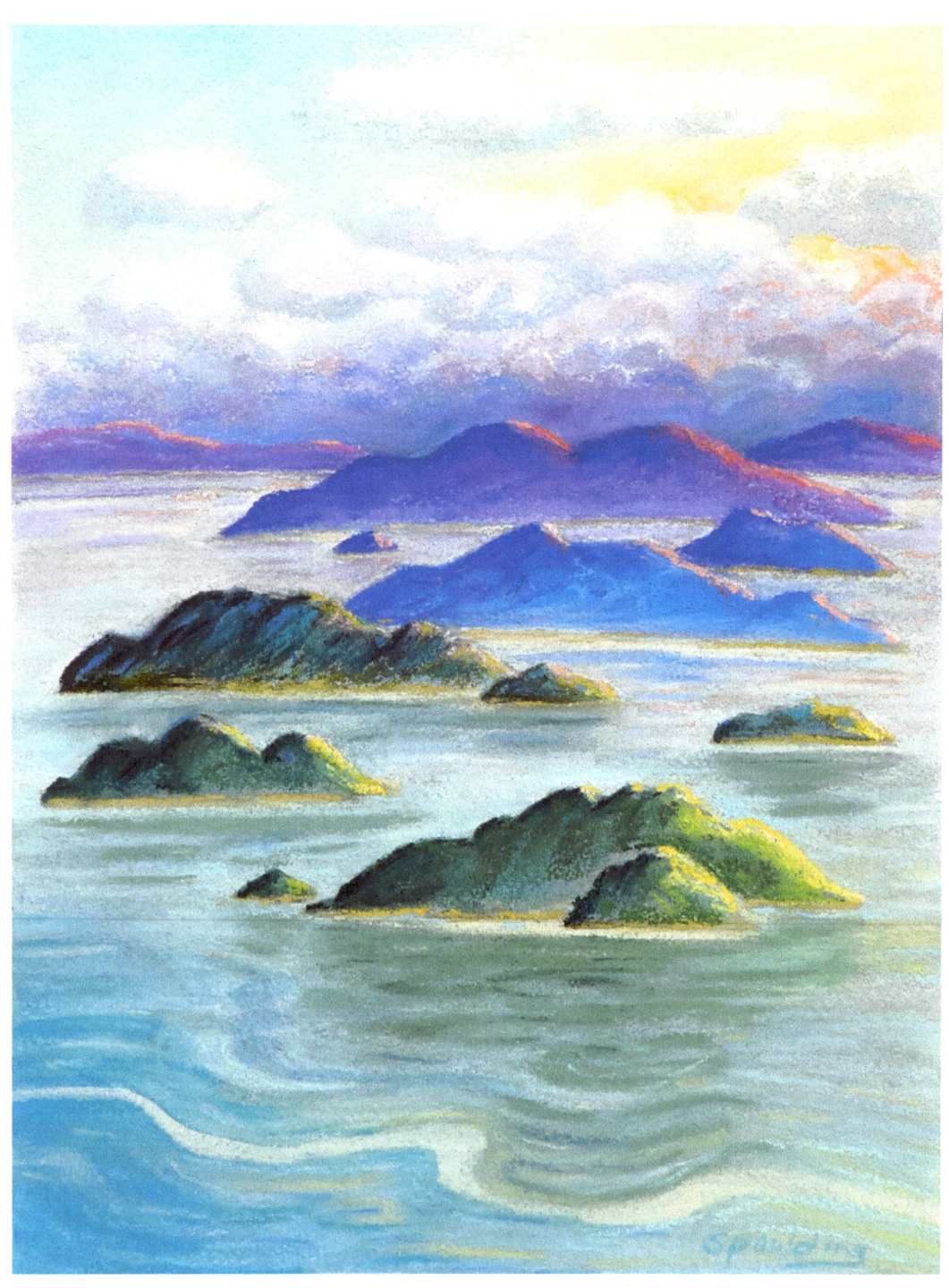

Islands of the Mind

Introduction

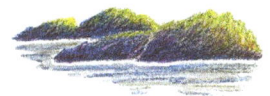

Islands of the Mind

The first island I fell in love with was a floating island. While growing up in Vermont, my brother and I often hiked cross country to a remote part of our farm where beaver had constructed a dam, creating a massive pond. Hidden in the brush at the edge of the black water was an old abandoned row boat. We claimed it as our own and used it to cross to mossy islands. With each footstep these mossy havens sank inches into the water, though the larger ones held us up as we sat in the sun exploring odd plants and insects. We watched the sundews' tentacled leaves ensnare unwary gnats and flies, while blue herons perched in a tall hemlock kept watch. Silently we awaited the slap of beaver tails on the opposite side of the pond. If lucky, we would see them swim and dive alongside their lodge to enter their den of heaped branches from under water. The memories of these things reside, gentle and wispy like a dream.

My second impression of islands also came during my childhood. Our family had spent a year in Spain where my father was employed designing runways for the NATO base at Rota. When it was time to return home, my mother, brother and I left ahead of my father so we could get back in the routines of school. We flew from Lisbon to Ganders, Newfoundland where it was necessary to stop and refuel. We were flying on a TWA four engine propeller plane, long before the age of jet travel. I remember deplaning, walking across the tarmac and into the large waiting room where the echoing clomps of the passengers' feet across the broad wooden planks of the floor announced our arrival to the big rustic terminal.

Once back on the plane and again on our way, it was my turn to sit in the window seat. In the night I could make out a chain of barely discernible, dark patches in the sea below. There seemed to be thousands upon thousands, never ending as we droned along. Gradually, the mounds of treed rock gathered the first glow of daylight, a light that seemed to emanate from the Atlantic itself, before any sign of the sunrise appeared. Mile after mile, island worlds drifted by beneath us, most devoid of human habitation. I watched enthralled, until we eventually landed in New York.

It occurred to me that though strung together in a tightly woven fabric of family and friends, we human beings were all living lives experienced only by ourselves. The geography of humanity was perhaps like that of islands.

The nature of small worlds set apart intrigued me. Landscapes defined by watery edges have always seemed a welcome place for repose and meditation. Like miniature continents on a scale that is easily grasped, islands are places you can almost get to know by heart. Yet for all their intimacy islands remain reticent, mysterious.

By their nature, islands are crossroads and stepping stones for travelers who have braved the sea. They are carved out by wind and time. From their edges, wide expanses of water and sky fill the soul. They provide distant outlooks on the world. They are at the mercy of weather, reappearing and disappearing in fog and changing light. Their isolation is unforgiving, yet tides and currents come and go, lapping their shores, bringing drifters: people, birds, seeds, wandering mammals and sea creatures, logs, shipwrecks, treasure and contraband and nowadays garbage. They are places in constant flux.

While cut off, islands have always been connected to the world by people who took to their boats and ventured great distances, be they Celts, Vikings, Polynesians, Greeks, or Phoenicians. Though many choose the isolation of their island homes, islanders are generally not hicks, or stuck in the mucks. After living on an island, it seems I have never been in a place where people travel so much.

Finding an island was not a conscious effort. While living in the desert southwest attending college, I met a young man, who it turned out, grew up in Vermont only thirty miles from where our family farm was. I had no intention of becoming attached to anybody, but that changed when I kept encountering Lewis hiding himself away in the university library, skipping his classes and writing poetry. We wanted the world to be a better place, As the war in Vietnam kept raging, Lewis decided to apply to the domestic Peace Corps, or VISTA, and to serve the country by volunteering to "fight the war on poverty."

I decided to apply as well. Shortly after getting married, we were both accepted. Off we went, living in ghettos, on reservations, and ultimately coming to Washington State where we fell in love with the green forests, the glacial peaks and the sea. After two years of service, Washington became our home.

Our first home in the Northwest was a small upstairs apartment along the Hood Canal. When not working, we paddled our canoe amid curious seals that looked like scuba divers rising from the deep; on closer inspection, dogs with whiskers and no ears. The peninsula was a fascinating place of enchanting rain forests, high mountains, sea and sky. It was a land of plenty, overflowing with berries, mushrooms, shellfish and fish. We lived on oysters and blackberry tarts.

The more enchanted we grew, the more exploring we did. We sometimes took the Coho ferry to Victoria from Port Angeles and as we crossed the wide straits of Juan de Fuca, we caught glimpses of the many island worlds that lay to the north. We also drove to Port

Townsend and strolled the streets of gingerbread houses, ate chowder and boarded the Washington ferry across Admiralty Inlet to Whidbey Island which lay to the east. There we explored windswept cliffs and cozy bays.

I often found myself thinking of my grandfather, Albert Brown. As a young boy he had immigrated with his family to Tacoma from Pilot Mound, Manitoba. They had traveled west to Vancouver and then traveled by steamboat from Vancouver to the South Sound, seeking a warmer climate and better educational opportunities. In those days it was impractical to travel the coastline by land as the forests were nearly impenetrable. As we became familiar with the inland sea I wondered what sights would have been familiar to the family and thought it interesting that I had come back to a part of the world that they had long since left.

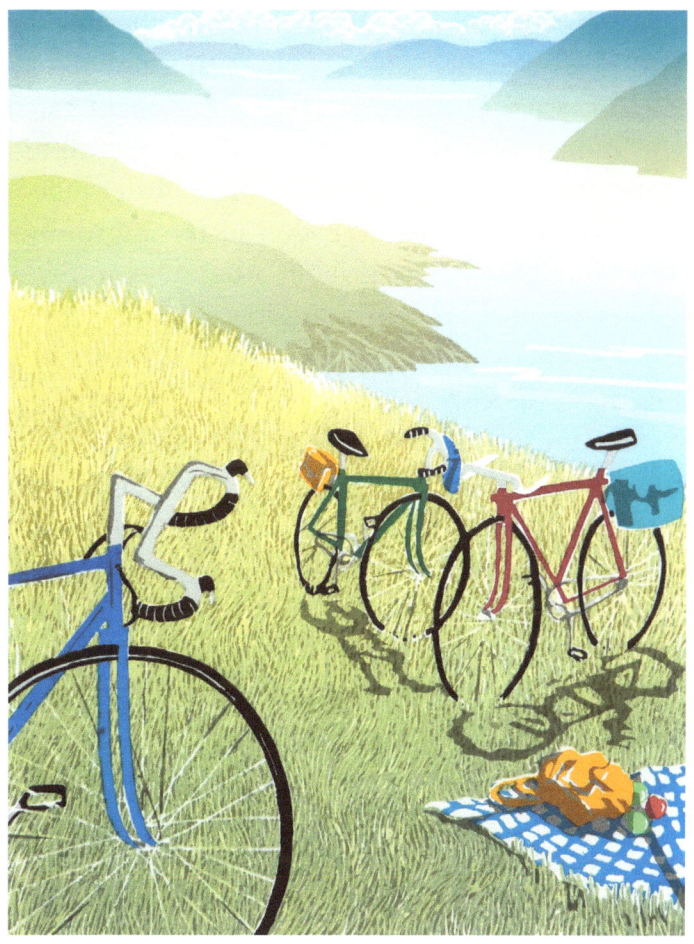

Bicycle Picnic

Lewis found a job that took us to a little town near the Canadian border. There we stayed for ten years, starting a family and searching for direction. We opened an art studio called *Silver Quill*. Lewis did portraits and pursued his photography. I began to sketch and paint and make small silkscreen prints. I didn't know where my endeavors would lead me. All I knew is that I had to make art.

When we had time off we explored trails in the North Cascades, sometimes taking our two girls, still very young, into the high country wandering past pristine lakes and through flower filled meadows. After reading a book called *For the Love of Some Islands*, the mysterious mounded hills that lay off the coast began to pull us in their direction.

Eventually we planned to tour the farthest island by bicycle. There was not much traffic in the mid-seventies as we rode along enjoying the varied landscape of the island, nearly twenty miles long and about half as wide. We stopped at many points of historical interest as well as the interesting marine labs we had read about and then journeyed on getting the feel of the place. Out on the west side of the island we pitched our little backpacking tent on the bluff of the county park there, then settled in for an evening.

We soon became mesmerized by the movement of the water below, flowing rapidly with a tidal change. Light of the setting sun gilded the upturns of the wavelets rushing past and the smooth patches of water were light catchers mirroring the sky above. Freighters thrummed by in the night, lights from communities on Vancouver Island twinkled across the straits and the constant lapping of water lulled us to sleep.

We awoke to fog. The chill of the morning made packing up and moving on more appealing than hanging about a sodden campfire. Cold and bedraggled, wearing socks as gloves, we peddled southward toward a beautiful lighthouse where we stopped for a break.

As the summer fog began to lift, the snow capped peaks of the Olympic Mountains began to appear, defining the peninsula where we had first become acquainted with Washington. A ribbon of fog remained out in the straits which obscured the base of the mountains. Water below us swept past the rocks where ribbons of giant bull kelp floated in patterns like Celtic knots. Anchored strongly to the sea bottom, the amber undersea forest provided a surface on top of the water where oystercatchers, gulls and terns were perched.

We continued to circumnavigate the island. By the time we reached the east side we pulled off at a field where farmers were haying. It was reminiscent of New England except that beyond the field lay a serene bay. Across the bay lay an island beyond, behind that island more rounded shapes of distant islands and foothills to the Cascade mountains on the mainland. Beyond the receding foothills we could see peak after peak culminating with Mount Baker in the north and the areas where we often hiked.

As we rested, we commented "Imagine living in this place!" Standing there by the road I felt happy and content as though my feet had found the ground they wanted to take root on.

Returning home, we carried the dream. I returned to my drawing. Lewis decided he too would like to try silkscreening. We began doing art shows.

Several years later when the time was right we went back to the island. We found a local real estate agent and told him what we were looking for. "We want to build a house," we said, "and a studio as we are artists." Also we added, "We would like a sunny location where we can have a garden." The kindly man looked through his papers and remarked that he thought he had something we might be interested in. He gave us a ride in his car a few miles out of town, heading south toward Cattle Point when he pulled off at the very farmer's field where we had watched the haymakers in the sun.

Remembering our bicycle adventure, we looked at each other in disbelief. "Yes," we said "we think this is what we have been looking for."

And so it was decided. We would move to a neighborhood of hundreds of islands, rock faces constellated, that arose from the depths of the Salish Sea and cradled life and kindled imaginations.

*The most beautiful thing we can experience is the mysterious.
It is the source of all true science and all true art.*

—Albert Einstein

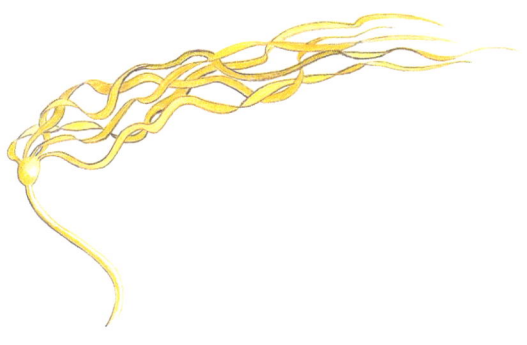

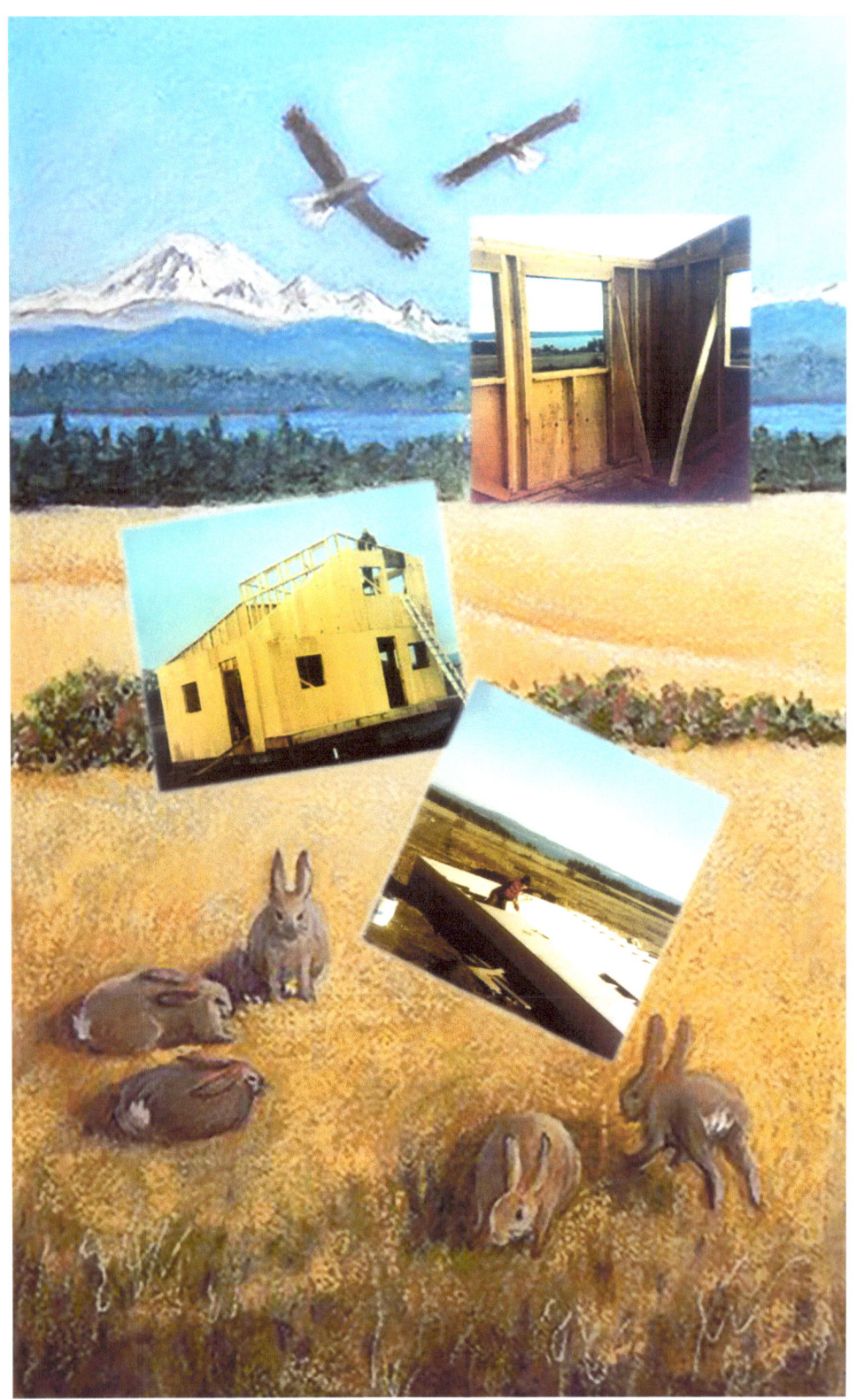

Building the Studio

Chapter One

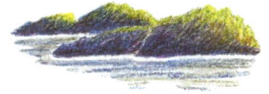

We Were Drawn to an Island
—1978—

I was in my early thirties. It was my birthday, and what a gift! We were here at last on the island and I was beginning to recover from moving day.

Our family had gotten up at four in the morning the previous day, excited to leave for our new home. Then we found that the borrowed truck in the driveway wouldn't start. Its shadowed hulk filled with our belongings was rendered useless with a dead battery. Hitched onto the back of the truck was the used travel trailer we had just purchased, also filled with our belongings. With jumper cables we got the truck started only to find that the lights on the trailer behind didn't seem connected properly.

Our friend who had volunteered to drive his truck with our trailer in tow, appeared just as we had given up hope for an early start. Fiddling in the dark with his help, we got the lights working with just enough time to catch the first morning ferry. As the truck and trailer pulled out of the drive, the four of us, our dog, our calico cat, and goldfish sloshing about in a bowl, all tumbled into our Volkswagen bus glad to be on our way. Then at the very last minute with all the commotion, Misty jumped out with a yowl before we could shut the door. She fled off into the darkness.

There was no time to look for the cat.

Already the truck and trailer were forging ahead in the darkness and we were in a rush to stay in sight. By the time we were on the freeway heading south I grew alarmed as the trailer ahead swung back and forth, its tail lights swaying from side to side. Our friend was pushing the speed limit and every time we rounded a bend the trailer lurched into the fog lane and then careened wildly back into our lane. As we drove along I couldn't help but imagine a tragic ending to our dreams before they had ever begun.

Checking in the mirror, our two young daughters sat silently upright on the back seat with eyes wide, peering into the darkness. We were all sick with worry about Misty but held onto the hope that she would wait for us at our old house until Lewis returned in a few days to pick up a final load of things stashed in the garage.

Once on board the ferry the October morning cleared, the sun rose into a sky of blue. We all stood on deck in the wind as we made that first trip to our new home, a little exhausted, a lot excited and sensing the unknown as the ferry plied its way across the wide passage and into the island world

We had not yet become islanders and were already feeling the constraint of a ferry schedule, a fact of life that would become both a blessing and a curse every time a transit to the mainland was planned.

If there was a simple way to move it had certainly eluded us. If there were doubts, it was too late to reconsider.

The following day, though, I never felt more alive. After months of deliberations our plan to make a life in a new place was becoming reality.

The small trailer was perched in our open field. We slept well in the tiny space cuddled in as on a family camping trip. I awoke very early and without changing position I looked out the window and watched the progress of the dawn. The light was entrancing as it trickled slowly toward us across the landscape. The Cascade Mountains grew faintly visible, delicately colored. As the light grew stronger, the mountains became silhouetted like a jagged crosscut saw, backlit by peach and topped with turquoise and blue. The atmosphere shimmered with depth and I sensed the space and distance as though I could reach out and break through it. It felt like the curvature of the earth was just within my grasp. Perhaps, I imagined, the whole universe was at my fingertips.

We are to live here I thought wondrously, on this piece of earth laid out before me, a farm where they once raised peas, solidly set on bedrock and cradled by glacial till, with a massive view to the world.

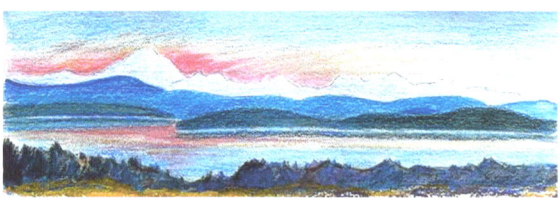

The first few days were packed with all the necessary steps of getting established in a new place. First was settling the girls into their new school. Any misgivings about what we had left behind we put aside as we dug in, and planned our strategies. How were we to proceed with the physical building of a place, dealing with the fact that most of our possessions were packed in a tiny storage unit, and figuring out how we would survive the coming winter in a flimsy little space with our children and pets?

A library book on building simple structures was our guide as we got ready to start our studio building. The studio would be built before our house as we would need to work and create, if we were to survive here.

The book said to put up batter boards so that when the man with his excavator came he would know where to work. We spent all day with tedious measurements, exacting where corners and walls would lie. When our man came he dug out our specified location and he dug out the batter boards too. We had some laughs about that. We would begin our measurements again and all would be well, but we never forgot the folly of our uncertain beginning.

As the days went by and we began laying block for our foundation, the children went off to school and afterwards returned to play and explore in the field, sometimes to sneak up on the wild rabbits.

We ate our suppers in the tiny trailer house and sat together in the evenings while watching the mountains and the sky, as darkness slowly swallowed us up. It would be a long time before we had any electricity to extend the light of day.

It was fortuitous that we had the light of a full moon those first days after our arrival. Our younger daughter Heather chanted "I see the moon and the moon sees me", a nursery rhyme her grandmother had taught her. She felt comforted that the same moon that shown on our old house was still shining on her in our new location. Personally, I found a similar comfort in that we could look out and see Komo Kulshan, the Indigenous name for the glacier peak, Mount Baker. That we were still under the mountain's watchful eye felt right to me.

Laurie and Heather and I began exploring every corner of the field. The land was covered by dried grasses, greatly overgrazed by rabbits. There were two large warrens and many more on the neighboring places. Where the warrens were located the earth was barren and riddled with holes. Passageways tunneled everywhere making underground booby traps. Even more hazardous were the two and three foot deep burrows that person could easily fall into.

Rabbits by the dozens were continually going in and out. Sometimes it seemed like the ground itself was moving, especially toward evening when their colony became more active.

At the bottom of the field where it sloped gently away to the east, we found sedges growing. There must be moisture I thought, but at the end of the dry summer and fall it was hard to imagine. Runways tunneled through the grass made by legions of field mice. A tiny shrew no bigger than my thumb scurried along the mouse trails and as we stopped to look the busily occupied creature scurried up over my foot, whiskers a twiddle and then off into the grass.

Along two sides of our land we found ditches where small willows, hawthorns and native crabapple trees were beginning to take hold. We also found native spiraea, reminding me of my Vermont childhood where we used to call it steeplebush.

We climbed onto both of the large rock piles that had been assembled on our land. It was fun to pick over the stones that have been stacked there over the years by those who had farmed here. We also explored a few large boulders parked randomly by glaciers that once covered this place. Sitting on the lichen covered surfaces we took stock of all that we could see. To the east beyond our property line, fields sloped gently eastward toward the water where a dark strip of firs edged the bay. To the west our field was edged by the county road and a broken down barbed wire fence. Bald Eagles and Red-tailed Hawks surveyed the rabbits' activities from above. I looked for other signs of life in the spacious landscape. It was empty, sunlit and windblown, but it filled our imaginations and seemed overflowing with possibility.

As the weeks passed by we settled into our new routines. The trailer was our glorified campsite providing us shelter from a life spent mostly outdoors. The school bus stopped by punctually every morning and the girls were off for most of the day. Lewis and I began work on our construction site as soon as they were gone. Though we never said as much to each other, I know we both had questioning moments. Could the two of us really pull off this building project alone?

With our measurements painstakingly reestablished, we moved forward laying cement blocks for the foundation. As we mixed mortar in the wheelbarrow, pulling the sand and cement mix back and forth with a garden hoe, I couldn't help but think of my days as a youngster helping my father with his various projects back at our old farmhouse in Vermont. I was his small assistant as he hammered, sawed, dug—always with sweat pouring off his brow.

My father had excelled scholastically in high school and been accepted to college just before the Great Depression. His father, the son of Irish immigrants, was proud of his achievements but told him it would be wise to learn something of the trades as well. The result was that in spite of graduating as a civil engineer, he had learned much about bricklaying, electricity, plumbing and other practical skills. In truth, as I look back, my father always seemed happiest when he was physically involved with a project be it building, gardening, fiddling with cameras, preparing for birding trips, or baking cakes! I felt confident that with his wisdom behind us that we would both be fine.

We were beginning to meet our neighbors who often dropped by to check on our progress. We found the island was a welcoming place. One neighbor brought me a hammer that he didn't need any more, small and easy for me to swing. Others brought fresh bread or cookies.

A family across the road had a big long haired collie named Champ who came down the hill and over to visit us nearly every day. He seemed to fit right in as he took therapy for his old arthritic bones by lying in the sun warmed dirt of our construction site. He liked our companionship and company of our pets. Tristan, getting up in years himself, was a great dog and true family member. Lewis and I had picked him up on our travels long before Laurie and Heather were born. He was a flop eared collie/shepherd mix we had gotten as a puppy for five dollars from a New Hampshire farm. We heard the ad on the car radio as we were driving through and stopped. He went everywhere with us. When each of the girls were born, he took on the responsibility to be their guardian and constant companion.

Misty, who had been successfully rescued by Lewis weeks ago, accepted Champ's presence too. With feline independence she prowled around the fields and caught mice. She had discovered her own entryway into our trailer, coming and going through the small opening made for the electric hook up, and finding hideaways in the far recesses of the kitchen cabinets.

When the school bus delivered the girls home at the end of the day, all the animals headed up the driveway, a sort of welcoming train. Champ would lead the way with his repetitive deep questioning bark, looking back always to see if Misty and Tristan were trailing along behind. They always were.

The family in a farmhouse up the hill had us in for meals and we were in awe that a home could be so comfortable after our weeks in a trailer with no electricity and getting our water from a hose.

Most everyone reached out in support though there was one neighbor down the road who was offended by our arrival. I think he considered us riff raff. Perhaps it was my bell bottoms jeans and long hair, Lewis' long hair, or perhaps the VW bus and the old trailer which he might have thought were permanent blight to the landscape.

We discovered that there was a nursery on the island and we went out to explore. It was hidden down a lane through a woods by a little lake. We found that they had apple trees and we bought a Northern Spy, what we hoped would be the beginning of an orchard. I was happy that now we had three garden plants on our property! The apple tree was added to the two old fashioned roses I brought from our old place on the mainland.

By mid-November our luck with pleasant fall weather had come to an end. Storms came through regularly delivering driving rain and relentless winds. On one such day we had stopped work anyway to get ready for an art show in Bellingham on the mainland near our old haunts. Scheduled the upcoming weekend, it was our first show since our move to the island.

The sky that morning was a warning, a blood red strip between mountains and the grey clouds overhead. The girls left for school and we immediately got to work. Lewis drove down to our storage unit where we had stashed our artwork and frames and glass. We switched our personal clutter out of the trailer and into the bus and then moved the framing operation out of the bus and into the trailer. Within the cramped space, shoulders bent over the small kitchen table, we managed to prepare enough inventory for the show. Before the girls got home again we made the switch again, putting all the art in the bus and our personal possessions back in the trailer. With the bus loaded and ready to go early the following morning we settled in for a hot supper of what we called "trailer soup", books and schoolwork. The wind and rain continued.

I thought we must certainly be crazy. As the winds grew stronger in the night and the trailer rocked in the wind, I remained wakeful and prepared mentally for being out of touch with Lewis for the next several days, isolated with no car.

Lewis left early in the morning and shortly after, out of the blue, the OPALCO truck from our island power company drove in to hook up our electricity. It seemed a magical transformation had taken place and only wished I could have had some way to give the news to Lewis. The girls and I spent the week-end inside as the storm raged, but it was more comfortable with power. A small transistor radio kept us somewhat up to date with the wild weather and news. The Northeaster that had brought bitter winds to the islands and our vulnerable trailer abode had also delivered wind and snow to the mainland where Lewis was driving the bus around in the icy drifts.

When headlights turned into our drive late Sunday night, how glad we were for his return. He, in turn, was amazed to see lights glowing from our windows as he approached. We traded news. Somehow he had managed to make some good sales during the show in Bellingham. And somehow we had all managed to keep warm enough. It had been a huge effort as we crossed some major hurdles, all good reminders to us of what we were trying to accomplish. Building had consumed so much of our attention and energy throughout the fall that our artistic goals had all but disappeared. I hadn't realized how lost and empty I had been feeling. There was something worth striving for after all.

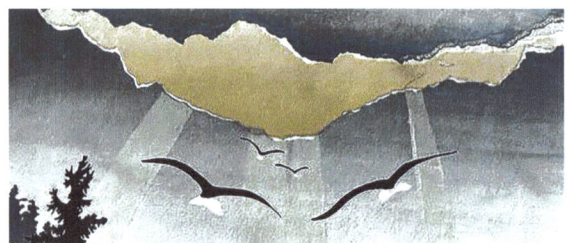

December wore on with more inclement weather. Often the rain kept me awake at night as it pelted down on the metal roof so close to our heads. When we had moments of clearing and promise of sunshine, we made use of the time working outside. Invigorated by being so close to the land, we would often stop to catch our breaths and to admire the stark winter boughs of the Garry Oaks on the ridge against the sky, or the billowing clouds and the wild waves in the bay to our east. All the colors of the spectrum combined to create a dazzling white on the heads and tails of the eagles almost always soaring somewhere above. "Sky!" I often felt myself saying with exhilaration.

We made progress on the studio with a subfloor now covering the foundation and around the periphery. Walls appeared, defined by two by fours. Being able to use power tools was a big improvement. When the weather allowed, we worked furiously to complete a floor for the upstairs section of the studio where my working space would be. With the cold weather, the trailer seemed to become smaller and smaller for the four of us. Consequently we were compelled to work harder and harder, driven on by the excitement of the emerging structure.

When we had completed the walls upstairs we were gratified. Everything felt solid, level and square. The shell of the building was so pleasing that I was wild with excitement to see what the finished space would be like. When evening came and Lewis was resting and the girls occupied with homework I slipped outside into the darkness for some fresh air and to keep company with the Great Horned Owls who watched from the trees across the road, replacements for the diurnal birds of prey.

I climbed up to the studio platform where we had worked all day and stood still listening to the night. Clouds had rolled in obscuring stars that had shined so brightly earlier. The night was very still except for the continued hooting of the owls. I felt the wonder of a comforting darkness encompassing me. Far off to the west the lights of Victoria on Vancouver Island reflected off the clouds. In the east several illuminated patches of cloud revealed where several mainland communities lay tucked in below. To be able to see but not to be able to reach those places conjured up feelings both wistful and grateful. This is what it is like to be on an island, I thought. I am a person removed, invisible in the night.

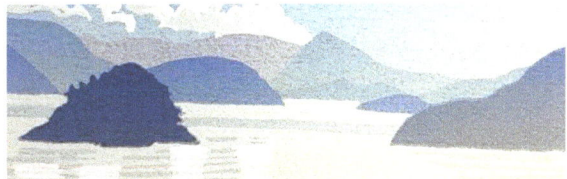

In mid December another major storm came through. I remember it was a Saturday afternoon. We sat huddled in the trailer hoping it wouldn't tip over with us inside as the gusts became gale force winds. We looked out the window, speechless as the large radial arm saw on its metal stand began moving across the studio deck towards us. The tarp we had used to cover it had come loose and turned into a sail, driving the heavy mass forward until it skidded off the decking, hanging itself up in the dirt a few feet away, and finally tipping over onto its side like a beast, deceased.

The following day we heard that a new house under construction just up the road had its newly erected walls all blown in. We were grateful that our building was now beyond that point and that we had made it through the storm without a major disaster.

When the storm finally cleared we were treated to a bright winter full moon. I went for a walk through the fields in the silvery light. Misty followed along through the frosty grass. When I got down to the ditch I looked back at the shadowy form of our studio standing firm in the night. The roof was not yet on, just walls and window openings. It looked strangely wondrous, like a basket filled with moonlight.

We spent Christmas in the trailer with a branch of hawthorn covered in red berries for our tree. We took Laurie and Heather to town to see the arrival of the Christmas Ship from Victoria. Santa Claus was onboard with treats for all the island children. The offerings of simple toys wrapped in pretty paper were like gifts of gold in our state of minimal living. How beautiful we found the lights of the boats in the harbor reflecting so many colors in the black water and dark night. It was a moment of much gratitude. When we returned home to our hawthorne branch we were filled with warmth and happiness.

By January even greater progress was made. We had a roof and a fireplace installed. One sunny day I swept out piles of sawdust and brought in some small furnishings. We were all so stir crazy in the trailer it felt good to spread out. I knew we were breaking all the rules, to be living in a construction zone, but it felt so luxurious.

My parents had sent a little porcelain cocoa pitcher at Christmas that I set out on a pretty cloth over an upturned crate. It looked so cheerful that it made us all smile. Incongruous as it was with the rustic surroundings, it signaled that there might possibly be a more civilized life in our future.

We moved ahead with insulating the walls. As we worked, the children took their sleeping bags up to my studio space where it was comfortably cozy and smelled sweet and woodsy from new lumber. It would be a new sleeping space for all of us as it was nice to get out of the musty trailer. Until the house was built though, it would have to remain our headquarters for cooking and plumbing.

Heather was the first to make drawings in the upstairs space, amusing herself in having room to stretch out in. I knew my time would come!

With more time spent in the upstairs, I found that my studio felt like a ship's wheelhouse and that I could be sailing out over the landscape laid out before us, master of my destiny.

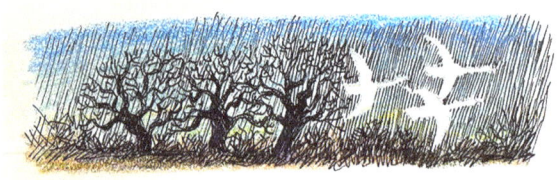

Winter days were often beautiful. One day four Trumpeter Swans flew directly overhead as we were working. Eerily luminous against an equally white pearlescent sky, and flying so low we could hear the whoosh of their graceful wings; they passed overhead, sweeping the sky with their slow, considered strokes. Their bugle calls pierced the stillness of the morning.

As they disappeared over the crest of the ridge to the valley beyond, so suddenly gone, we were left wondering if we had seen or heard them at all.

One day there was a Bald Eagle down near the ditch with its prey. Laurie slipped on her boots and was out the door in a flash. "I am going to see how near I can get," she said. We saw her circumnavigate the field and creep along the neighbor's line like a sleuth until she was just behind the eagle on the other side of the ditch. She looked so small and the eagle so big, nearly as tall as she. With wings that stretch to eight feet and standing somewhere close to three feet tall, the bird was impressive. It never moved. Laurie silently worked her way back to the trailer, proud of her achievement.

Champ came to live with us permanently. His family was going back to Seattle and hoped we would take him. He was already with us most of the time and we gladly welcomed him to the fold.

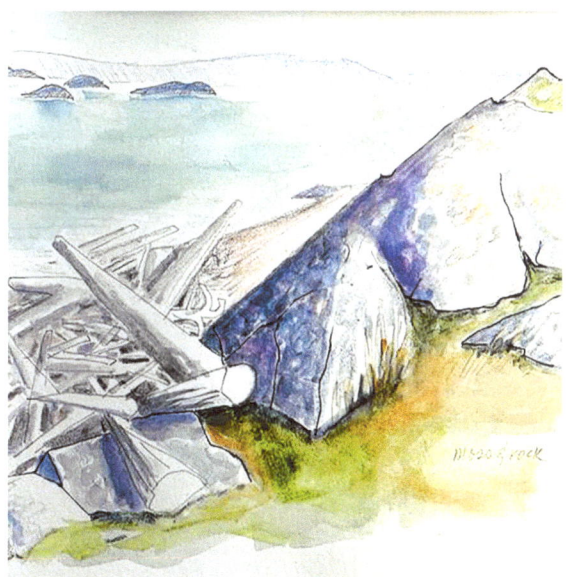

One weekend in late January we decided to take time off and head for South Beach, just three miles down the road. It was refreshing to get away from work and invigorating to wander around the coves and clamber over the rocks. We saw otters and seals and golden blankets of winter grass, silky in the winter sun; nearby a bleached bone in a bed of green moss. The air was piercing and briny. Drift logs were strewn on the pebble beach. We all entertained ourselves with our own discoveries and left for home satisfied.

We went home by way of town to get some treats, chips, pie, and chocolate as we are all incessantly hungry all of the time. While in town I used a pay phone to make a call to my mother and father, far away and so out of touch.

Finally home again we discovered we had locked ourselves out of the trailer, still our kitchen headquarters. After much ado, Lewis took out the whole latch as we were so desperate to get out of the cold. Until we had time to repair it, we had to keep the door shut with rope with the hope that no big winds would arise.

The studio progress took a big leap when Lewis installed windows: real glass windows which he then trimmed out. It is hard to describe the deep appreciation I felt at that moment after living for weeks and weeks in a place where opaque plastic covered the openings. Looking through the clear panes brought tears of joy to my eyes.

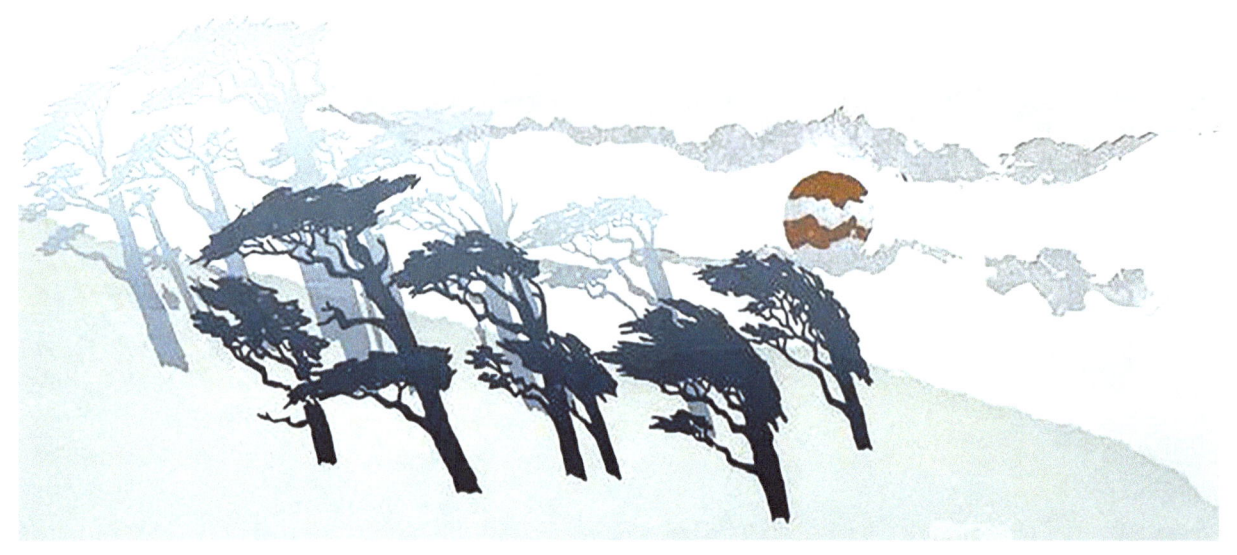

Ah windows! A word from Middle English meaning eye to the wind.
That seemed very apropos to where we found ourselves living.

The eternal sound of the sea on every side has a tendency to wear away the edge of human thought and perception, sharp outlines become blurred and softened like a sketch in charcoal.

—Celia Thaxter *Among the Isles of Shoals*

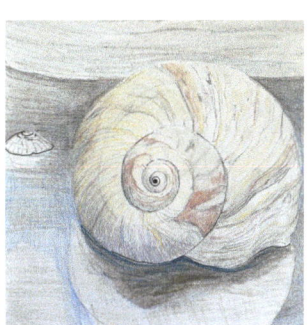

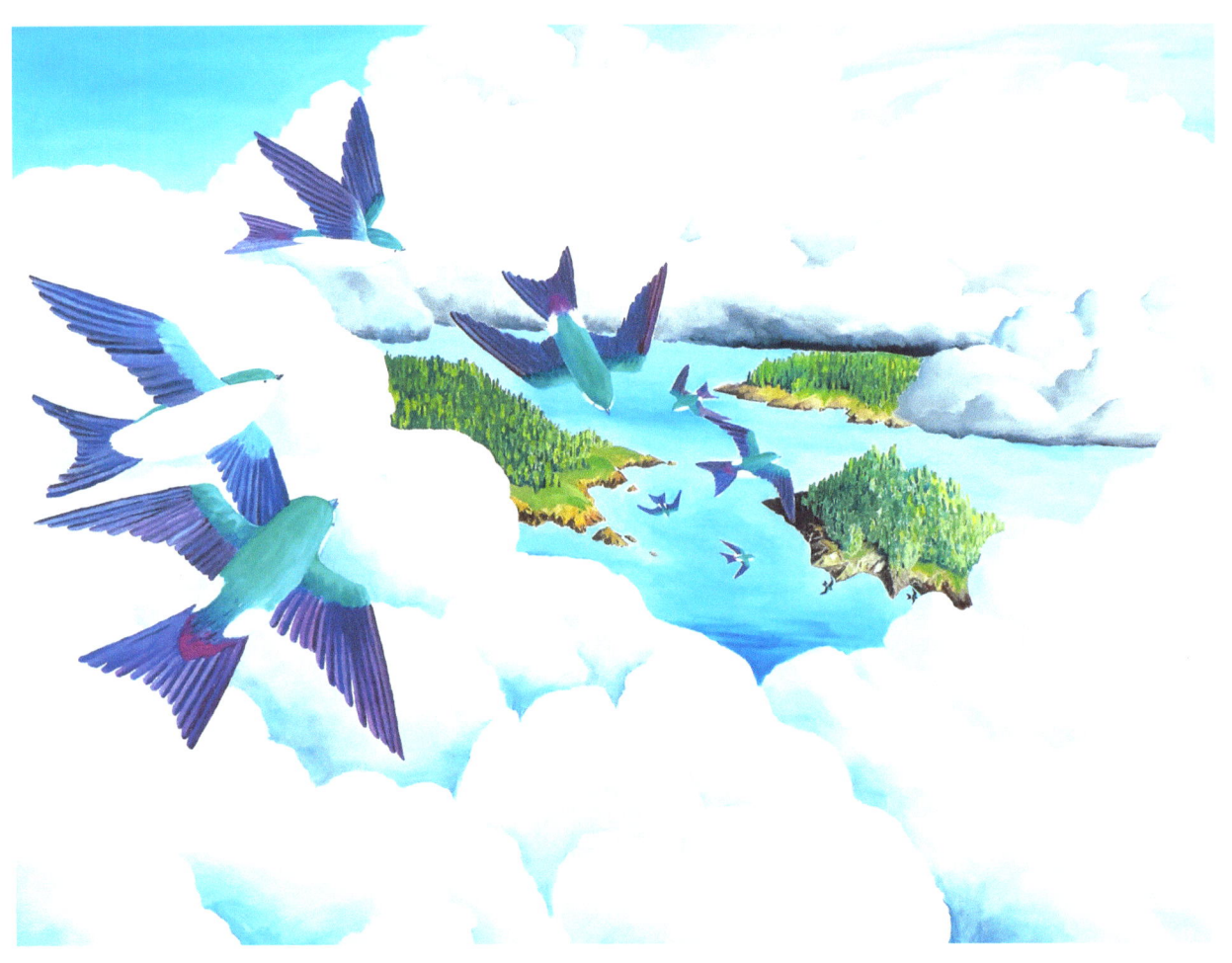

Violet-green Swallows Return to the Islands

Chapter Two

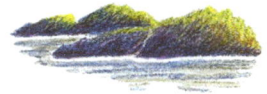

Return of the Violet-green Swallows

As years went by and life evolved for us on the island, we became immersed with the patterns of life around us, distinct to every season. Each year we added more to the garden, and more attention was given to what was happening outdoors as the pressures of building relaxed.

The return of swallows to their northern breeding grounds became and remains my favorite rite of spring. No other event seems to hold quite the same ebullient and free flowing joy as that moment when we first spot them above our patch of garden and apple treed field. Who seems more joyful is hard to tell, the swallows or me.

With the colors of an aurora borealis, valiant birds in hues of teal green and purple ply the skies with graceful acrobatic wings. By the thousands, swallows fill the air with an unrelenting urgency to travel north from their wintering places as far south as Central America. They will travel in large social groups as far as two-hundred miles a day. They will forage on insects along the way. Finally they will home in to their northern range with an innate trust that their breeding ground awaits.

 Barely discernible at first glimpse, I listen for their distinctly fluid notes as they circle over to inspect the terrain below. I follow their flight in and out of the atmosphere above as they disappear and reappear into the blue. It is a long awaited moment of elation and always seems to mark the real beginning of spring.

Every year after spring equinox I go though anticipation anxiety. What if the swallows don't come back? During the past year, what perils did our birds have to negotiate on their long migration south to Mexico and Central America and back again? What sort of world did they find in their overwintering place? Did they find welcome and equal affection from people where they spend the winter? Clearly our little spot on the island is deeply connected to communities on the other end of their migration. Wouldn't it be nice to say hello and share stories? I find myself wondering, wishing I knew more.

We have been fortunate that over time on our tiny piece of island, we have had four species of swallow nesting here: Barn, Tree, Cliff and Violet-green.

Cliff Swallows tried to start a colony under the eaves of my upstairs studio. They built long tubular mud nests. They were successful for a couple of years though eventually they gave up the location. We were not sure why.

During the first years of gardening here, Tree Swallows often took up occupancy in the birdhouses we had up for offer. Their beautiful iridescent teal blue backs and snow white breasts were striking. They sang in liquid, cascading notes as they perched on fences or shovel handles. I have been disappointed they have not come back. There do not seem to be as many tree swallows on the island these days and the ones that do come here tend to nest on the higher hills of the west side.

We built a small barn a few years after our arrival. We made it from stones in our field and logs from the beach to accommodate a pony for Heather, but swallows liked it too. We have hosted a continuous population of Barn Swallows ever since that I follow with great interest every year. For over thirty five years there has been at least one nest on the same beam over the doorway. The resident pair usually have two clutches each summer and by the end of summer there are generally a dozen or more fledglings that join their parents, patrolling our orchard and garden. Their presence is gratifying, and delightful, as with the Violet-greens.

The Violet-greens and the Barns usually arrive at our place in late March within a week or two of each other. The Violet-greens come first. After being spotted now and then in the neighborhood, it is a special day when they descend to our level and swoop along the south studio wall checking out the place, as though making sure everything is as they remember it. Generally the day is bright with sun. I stop everything I am doing. I call out to Lewis, or if he sees them first he calls to me, and we go out to watch. Their dark pointed wings swim gracefully downward, spiraling in their descent and now and then their agile airborne bodies flip to reveal a flash of white or deep metallic green as they close in on our studio.

These are the valiant survivors of an arduous journey covering three thousand miles or more, wingbeat by wingbeat. I am always sure it is our same birds, or if not the same pair, at least some of the offspring from last year's nest. They act with a certainty of where they are. They announce their arrival with cheerful enthusiasm, meant no doubt for themselves, but I like to think it is for us too. Crows can recognize individual people's faces. It seems only logical that the swallows know their old nesting spot and who we are as well.

A first Nesting Box and a Beginning

When the swallows come back in the spring, I am always reminded of the first year we came. Our studio building was so new we hadn't yet painted the exterior plywood. We were outside working when the Violet-greens arrived and were drawn immediately to our building site. The south facing wall caught the sunlight and warmth and as we lingered there to warm ourselves, the birds flew back and forth repeatedly. Laurie, in fourth grade at the time, was really excited by their arrival. Since her birthday was coming up, Lewis decided to make her a birdhouse that we could attach to the wall.

The day of her birthday we presented her the house. She took it outside so that Lewis could put it up right away. We all trailed her out to the studio deck where she set the house on a bench while Lewis rummaged around for the proper tools. At that very moment, out of nowhere, a swallow flew down and lit upon the birdhouse, as though it had been waiting all the while to take possession of it. He called out cheerily and his mate swooped down to join him. The two sat and chattered away, as though discussing the new nest box. It was a moment of wonder for all four of us, connecting with the wild birds.

When the house was installed on the wall a short while later, the birds began going in and out with purpose. It was the beginning of our first season with Violet-green swallows. We have all felt a personal connection with them ever since. It was fortuitous that Laurie's birthday coincided perfectly with their nesting season.

Since then we have been compelled to provide them nesting boxes every year. In return they eat insects, sing, and add immeasurable beauty and interest to our days.

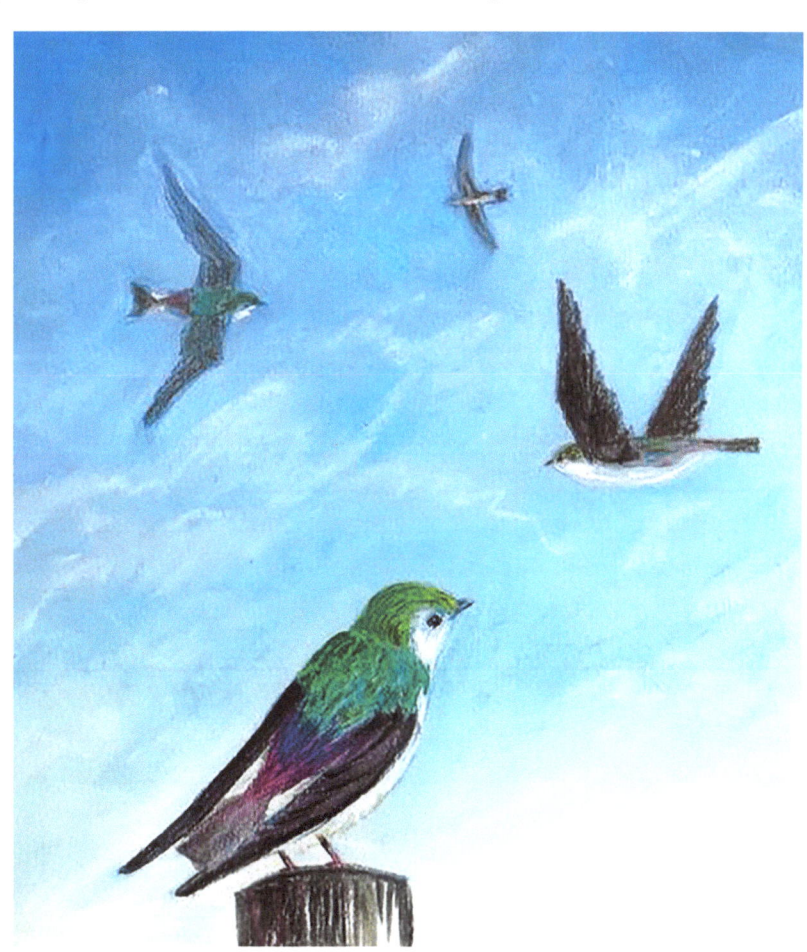
Violet-green Swallows

Over time with trial and error we have learned that it is important not to put the nesting boxes up too soon, even though the swallows seem to look for them. Other birds, such as the aggressive non native English Sparrows, may try to take over. When that happens we have often taken the house down again for awhile, or as in one year I gave the bottom of the box a sound thumping with a broom handle when the sparrows were inside. Their inspection of the box was quickly cut short as they couldn't fly out of the little doorway fast enough. They never returned.

The swallows seem to take a few weeks to get used to their northern range again as they regain their strength. They gather together in wetlands where there are lots of insects to forage upon. Females arrive later than the males, at which time they regroup to find their mate or align with another. Swallows are monogamous seasonally and that would suggest they engage in new courtships every year. Perhaps if both adults of a pair survive their migration they may choose to mate again.

When they show up at our place with an interest in starting a nest, they fly back and forth along the eaves inspecting the tiniest of gaps and when the houses are up they begin to stake claims.

Since there is often more than one pair hoping to win the house the competition gets fierce. We started putting up two houses. Still, only one pair ever dominated the wall and control of both houses. We never were sure which house would be chosen as a nest site. It seemed to vary from year to year. Since they wanted more space between nesting sites, we put other houses out around the garden but Violet-greens have never chosen those, opting either for the wall or going off into the trees or checking out our neighbor's offerings.

One might think that a nesting box on our studio wall above the deck where we sit in the sun would be an unwise idea. Violet-greens are fastidious birds. Try as you might, you will never find a dropping below the birdhouse. As part of their survival strategy, any sign of their presence is kept minimal. It appears that they fly as far as the orchard to defecate. They keep their nest box clean in a similar manner. Violet-green Swallows have a handy built in diaper system that allows the parents to clean up expediently after the young. Excrement is produced in a little fecal sac. This clever biological solution to cleanliness allows for easy removal. From time to time, if you are watching closely, you will see the parents fly out of the nest with a little white membrane in their beak that they carry far away for disposal.

For years we have placed our deck chairs right under the house and never once has an unwelcome gift fallen from above into our hair or onto our picnic lunch or books or papers.

I am always happy when the swallows begin nesting on our studio building because the nest box is on the same level as my upstairs studio windows. Even when concentrating on work, I am still aware of birds coming and going from the box. In my periphery, wing forms slip past me and my concentration is happily broken. If I stop to look at just the right moment, I catch the metallic gleam of the male's teal green head which blends into the feathers of his back and violet purple rump. Two distinctive pearly white side panels just above his tail wrap around to join his white breast and chin. The female is more conservatively dressed in a greenish brown to purplish brown jacket, though she too is slightly iridescent when observed closely in the right light. My upstairs windows are the perfect vantage point. Her breast and neck are a dusty white, but all in all though subtle, she is still a beauty.

Spring after spring the birds have come and every new season seems to play out in a unique way. The birds have become my subjects in art and admiration. I have begun to see them as individuals as well as representatives of their species. Between April and July we share space and time together, a four month span that moves along quickly and is always too soon over.

Nest Building and Families

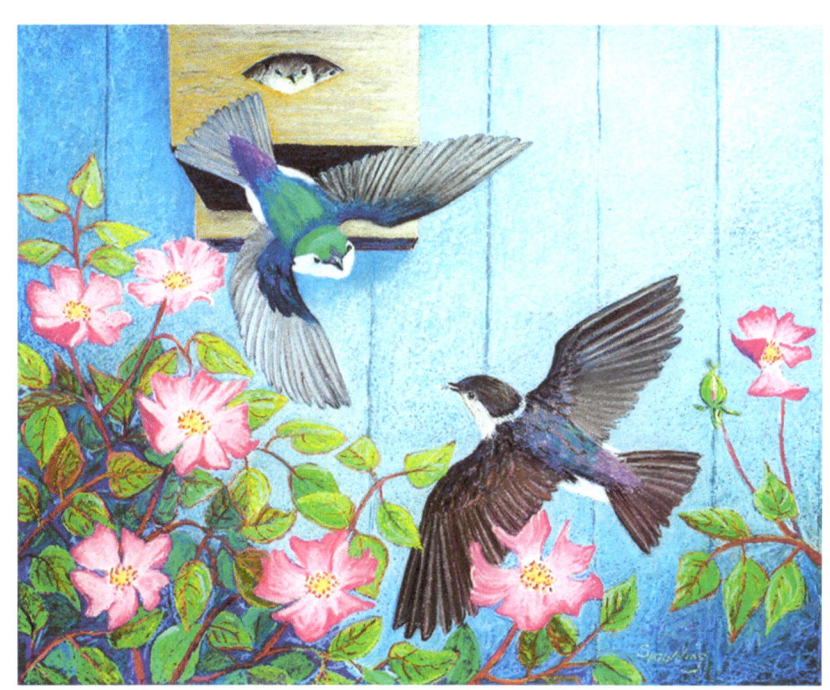

Changing Places

Once they have selected their nesting site their effort goes into nest building. While we are working in the garden or perhaps stopping for a coffee break on the deck, we watch the swallows fly in and out and quickly returning with long pieces of grass and stems followed by an odd assortment of feathers with which they line the grass made cup. Sometimes they seem to need more advanced engineering skills to get their objects through the small hole, but they persist pushing and pulling big bits through the entrance and succeed in finishing up in five or six days. From then on we don't see as much of the female as she spends more time inside. She will lay one egg a day until she has four to seven, and then she will begin to sit and incubate them so that they will be ready to hatch at the same time.

The incubation period lasts about twenty days at which time the chicks begin to hatch. We can usually tell when this excitement takes place because the parents launch off on a foraging frenzy. How hard they work providing food for their offspring!

On early summer mornings I have seen them already at work as soon as dawn breaks. At our latitude the sun rises at four in the morning in June. I have often stayed up reading in our window seat until the last of twilight in June, nearly ten o'clock. The swallows are still going in and out for one last bug patrol. The feeding regimen gets more and more intense as the little birds grow. At one week old we begin to hear the first tiny peeps which get more insistent as the birds get bigger. By the time three weeks have past, the new family is ready to fledge. I always hope to be around to see the new family fly out for the first time. For days their heads have been stretching out of the round doorway watching their parents, craning to be the first open mouth to receive food. With more maturity they begin to lean out and look around, taking in a larger picture of the world. Their eyes follow us as we walk up and down the brick walk.

When they are ready to fly, one at a time they lean way out of the doorway precariously balancing at the edge, their shoulder-like scapular feathers coming into view. They seem balanced between assessing the risk and evaluating their own new prowess, before suddenly taking the leap and flying away with an unexpected adeptness. When you see it happen it takes your breath away. As soon as one fledgling is gone another head fills the hole and the next bird follows the same steps, until also daring to launch. Usually they all fledge within minutes of each other, flying off with their parents into high firs nearby. Some families return to the house for a few more nights. I have seen them come back in final minutes of twilight to slip silently into the house, the youngsters negotiating the perch-less entry as easily as their parents. In some years, when they fledge, it is the last time we will see them so closely in our midst until another year goes by.

One year a youngster simply wouldn't leave the house. It took two extra days of cajoling from the anxious parents before their last one would dare to join its siblings who by now were circling and diving and beginning to catch their own suppers. Finally he was ready and launched. The adults appeared to be so patient and proud.

Often during this process, in the excitement of the moment, the Barn Swallows join in to watch the show. There seems to be a social understanding between these two species, as they often seem to answer to each other's calls. I think they enjoy keeping watch on one another and their prospective territories.

One mysterious spring, the Violet-greens stayed for two extra weeks. They had had an unusually chaotic start to their nesting season as there had been two pairs fighting for the nest more intently than usual. Finally calm returned and all seemed well. One morning though, as I passed between the house and the studio, I noticed that an egg had been thrown out of the house where it had smashed on the deck below. It was pure white with a yellow yoke just like a chicken egg, but jelly bean sized. I wondered what was going on. The next day another egg met the same fate. Something was really out of sync. Another odd development was that the parents started bringing in nest material again. This stage should be over by now, I thought.

Then the usual rhythm seemed to fall in place once again. The female continued quietly sitting in the house and the male perched on the ferrule atop the outdoor umbrella, singing his lilting song, announcing his presence all around the garden. We began to hear telltale peeps and two weeks later two chicks fledged. We waited and watched but there were only the two. Were these two youngsters part of the clutch of the two smashed eggs? While the parents were busy with these two out on the wing, they were still bringing food into the house where, we noted, there was still peeping. Every day we expected to see more youngsters fledge, but two entire weeks went by.

We kept watching, hoping that we would be around to see what happened. Fortunately I was in the studio one morning when there was such a commotion I ran downstairs and out into the sun. Swallows were coursing back and forth against the studio wall, the parents, the two juveniles, the Barns and their first family of five, all chirping and creating quite a stir. I had thought they were notes of alarm, but then I realized that the birds were in a state of excitement. The remaining Violet-green chicks were finally leaning out of the box ready for flight. All the birds seemed to be encouraging them.

Lewis and I took a break and watched until five Violet-greens left the box to join the others. What an achievement! The beleaguered and devoted parents must have been ecstatic that their long effort was finally over. They had inadvertently raised seven chicks this season, in two overlapping clutches. They had been delivering meals all day long for five weeks.

One can theorize over what may have happened. I tend to think that some misfortune came to the first female and the male had found a new mate to carry on with his brood. The second female, upon moving into the much desired birdhouse could have tried to destroy the eggs that were not her own. Somehow, two had been spared.

Our daughter Heather saw another scenario. How could the parents miss two eggs in the nest if they were trying to get rid of them, she queried. Perhaps they had started a clutch and two eggs weren't viable. Those they got rid of, but with only two eggs left, perhaps the female was stimulated to lay more.

Whatever the science behind it, it was a complicated season which left another unsolved mystery to ponder.

Recently we had a year when the swallows started to nest but were discouraged by house wrens that got into the house and threw out all their nesting material. This was a new development in our neighborhood and not a welcome one. I thought we had lost the swallows for the season, but two pairs remained nearby in the firs along the north border of our property. I had not been aware of any nesting by swallows in nearby trees here in the past, though tree cavities are Violet-green's natural preference. Of course, there were no trees when we first came. Now that they have become so mature, enough to provide nesting cavities, new patterns are likely to emerge. The Downy Woodpeckers and Red-breasted Nuthatches in our trees would have had old nesting holes that swallows could now make use of.

I was disappointed not to have the swallows closer in the garden that summer, but by July I was amazed to see a group of twenty or more flying over the nearby orchard and sometimes over the raised beds in our vegetable garden. They stayed for several weeks flying together, chattering, performing their acrobatic flights, gliding and fluttering searching out insects on high. Being thus rewarded, in the end I realized that perhaps they had been even more successful in the trees and more families had grouped together.

Regardless, we will still put up our nesting boxes. I was happy that the year following the wren debacle, a pair of Violet-greens was willing to take up housekeeping on the studio wall again.

Each year we continue to enjoy their behavior and to learn more about them as we keep watch. Certainly the returning birds are offspring or possibly adults from previous years. Though they only have a fifty percent chance to live longer than a year and a half, if they are fortunate they could live seven years or more. Though birds usually seem very familiar with the place when they return, sometimes returning birds are more reclusive which makes us wonder if they are new to this nesting spot or first year adults with less experience.

With climate change, pressures on land everywhere, and more and more insecticide use, I worry. Every year as the planet tilts us back to longer days and winter is forced back into hiding, we will continue to anticipate the metallic flash of violet and green, miraculously appearing overhead. With long awaited joy, we will hope that the small offerings we provide in our garden will tip conditions in the swallows' favor during their stay in the north.

William Leon Dawson ornithologist, comparing the Violet-greens to Tree Swallows for whom he had already "lavished all his superlatives and accolades," said "What shall we do for the Violet-green Swallows? Let us simply call them children of heaven."

1923

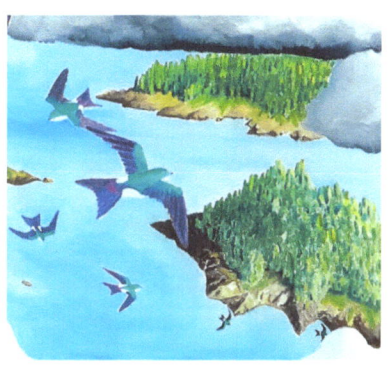

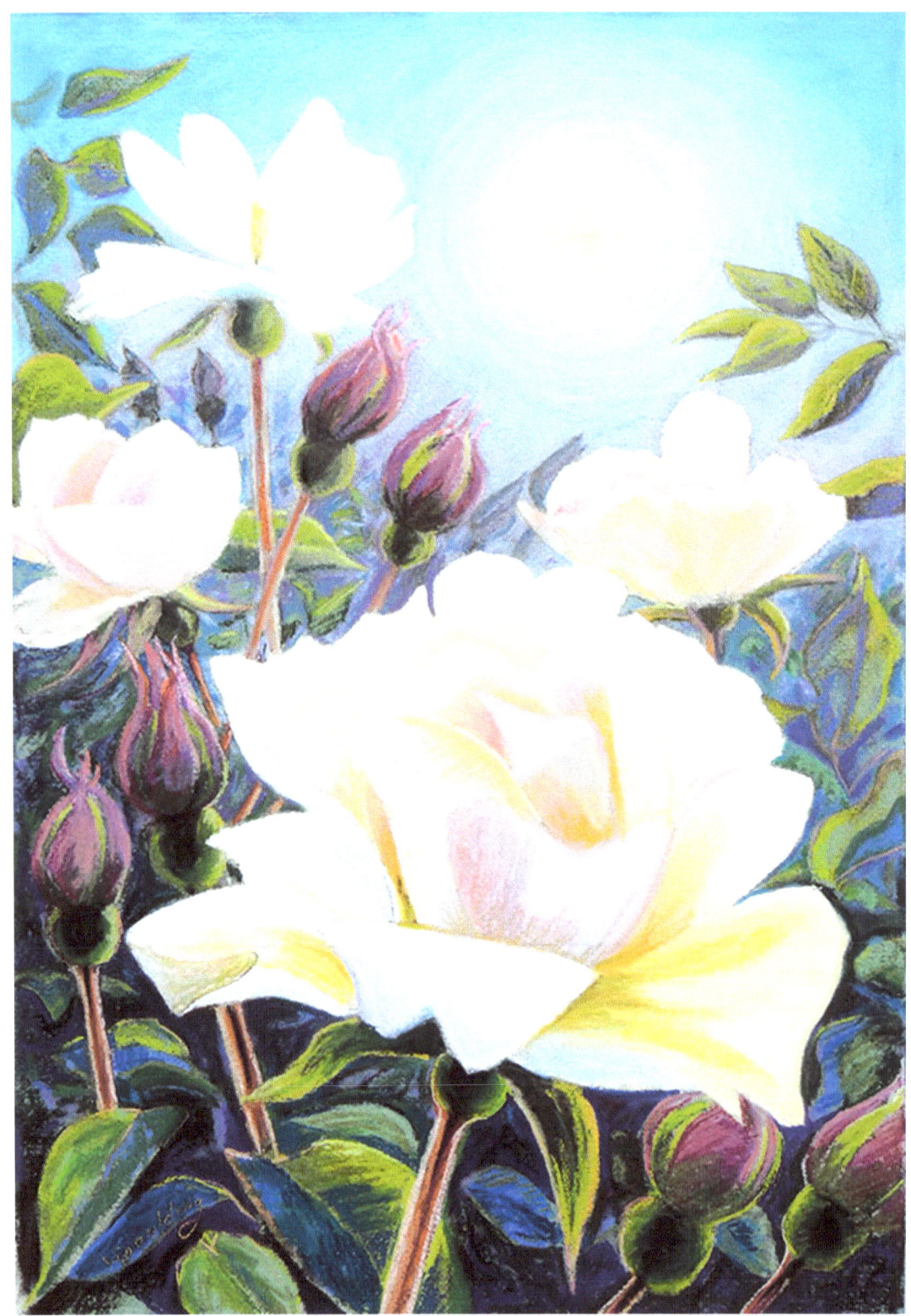

Moonlight Rambler

Chapter *Three*

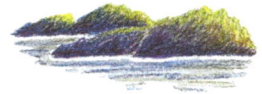

Days Filled With Roses

For millennia, wild rose species have graced the northern hemisphere of our planet. With attributes of beauty, scent and healing, these plants have charmed human beings for eons. The attraction to roses has led people to cultivate them wherever their paths have crossed.

I have always had fond memories of my father's desert rose garden. He fussed over his collection of fifty or more Hybrid Tea roses. They were set out in little circular wells that could be irrigated easily in the dry Southwest. Often he delivered bouquets of his beautiful flowers by bicycle to our neighbors. I loved my father and his delight in gardening but the same passion for roses never came over me until I discovered roses of a very different sort.

When Lewis and I came to the Pacific Northwest we spent a lot of time hiking. I loved the wildflowers in the high country and in the lowlands as well. Wild roses thrived in this climate and I found the native Nootka Roses attractive in their simple form and lovely scent.

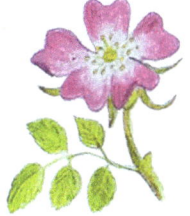

Long before moving to an island, our family had gone for an outing to Fort Casey State Park on Whidbey Island, where a lighthouse towered over the edge of the Salish Sea. Bunkers were built into the hill where cannons were stored during Second World War. While the others explored the historical sights I chose to walk down a grassy aisle, carved through the acres of wild rose bushes that covered the bluff above the beach. There I became hidden in thickets. The path was downward sloping and faced out over the Straits of Juan de Fuca. Across the inlet lay the Olympic Peninsula, where mountains gleamed with brightness that day, their snowy caps protruding out of white cumulous clouds. It was difficult to differentiate peaks from sky.

Directly in front of me, the straits opened out to the Pacific Ocean. To the north were little emerald islands, one behind the other, fading into the distance. Their receding ridge lines disappeared into the billowing clouds along the northwesterly horizon, beckoning toward infinite places in the far beyond.

I felt completely alone in the vast space. It was silent, and everywhere was the scent of rose. This ethereal stage lifted me out of myself into a sense of timelessness. That feeling was so profound, I never spoke to anyone about the experience until years later.

My Curiosity For Roses Begins

When we first settled in northwest Washington in the late sixties, we lived in a little town near the Canadian border. Our aging landlord persuaded us to buy the circa 1890 two story clapboard house that we were renting. Still in our twenties, we hadn't felt ready for such a commitment, but it made sense financially so we bought it.

The house was on a small corner lot. Other than a very tall Silver Poplar tree out front, there was little other landscaping, except two old shrub roses. These were roses such as I had never seen before. They were large bushes, a bit rangy in winter, but when spring arrived, the canes became laden with leaves and flowers, charming in every way. The exquisite blossoms were so highly perfumed, they simply stunned me. I had never known roses to be so aromatic.

Though the two roses were very distinct from each other in many ways, they had several similar traits which I noted. They were highly scented, they grew in the form of an attractive shrub, they seemed to thrive without care, and they bloomed only once a year, in June. Both were reminiscent in form and scent of the wild Nootka Roses that lined the roadways, except the blooms were multi petaled, not simple five petaled flowers. What were these mysterious plants that grew in our yard and where did they come from?

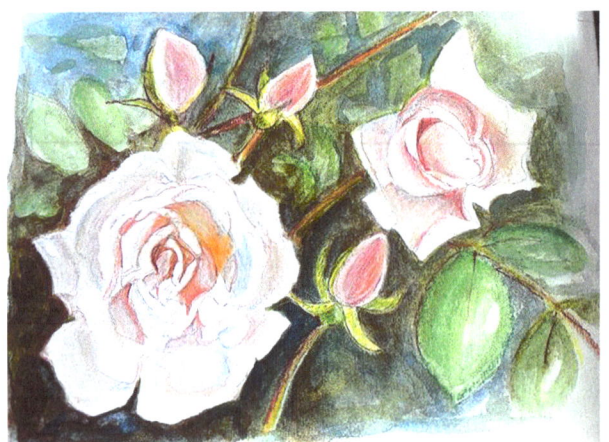
New Dawn

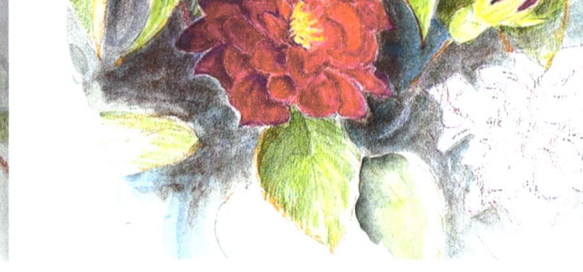
Tuscany Rose

My search led me to the local library where I soon discovered the world of old fashioned roses, often called heirloom or heritage roses.

Because their history goes back centuries before records were kept, we may never know the complete story regarding their origins. We do know that wild roses occurred in the Middle East, Europe, Northern Africa, Asia, and North America. The categories of heirloom roses, and in fact all roses that we know today, would have evolved from these species roses. At what point did the flowers become multi petaled or when did color changes occur in the blooms? Were these changes naturally occurring mutations, and to what degree would people have been instrumental with their development, propagating them over time for their uniqueness?

There is much mystery regarding the earliest gardeners of roses, but early frescos reveal that Greeks and Romans grew them hundreds of years B.C. As I walk past my plants in my garden today, I take delight in the revelation that these very roses are carrying genetic material from those ancient gardeners' collections. I imagine people as long as forty centuries ago, walking the hillsides and mountains discovering desirable plants. As very early plant hunters, they dug up their treasured finds and carried them back to their abodes. Imagine what they might have to say if we could talk to them today.

My roses seemed to have early origins. After looking at many possibilities in old gardening books, the deep red rose looked like the early Gallicas portrayed. It could possibly be a descendant of The Tuscan Rose, reportedly cultivated in Europe as early as the 1400s. The Tuscany Rose was one of the Gallica roses originating in the Eastern Mediterranean region, brought to France by the Romans where it became so successful Linnaeus mistakenly thought they were native there and named them Gallica roses

The pink rose seemed to be most like Dr. W. Von Fleet, a popular rose developed at the turn of the century in the United States by a man of that name. The rose was marketed widely in 1910 by Walter Von Fleet, a hybridizer of many American classics. The Dooryard Roses, as they were called, were bred to be vigorous and tough, and to provide carefree beauty for homes of hardworking families across our vast countryside. Though this rose's history turned out to be much more recent than the Tuscan Rose, its parentage included a native wild rose of the American prairies which I found intriguing. If my lovely pink rose had historic connections to an early American rose grower as well as to our native prairies, I was delighted. The unique look of the cupped, pearl-pink rose and the dates involved all made it seem very possible.

When we started to remodel our old house, we found the insulation under the walls was made of lath and old newspapers, yellowed with age. The pages were all dated in the 1890s. Perhaps the early inhabitants had planted the red rose when the house was new? Tuscany roses could have come west by wagon on the Oregon trail. Records show that families brought roses west with them amongst their most prized possessions. Once in the West roses could have been reproduced by cuttings. New Dawn could have been added after 1910.

When Lewis and I decided we would move to a five acre field on an island, I dug up clumps of the backyard roses to take with me. I began to dream of surrounding myself with a garden of old fashioned roses. I had become acquainted with two heirloom roses. Already they had captivated me with their beauty and stories of their past. These roses seemed to hang on to enough of the wild to satisfy me while being romantic and generous in their flowering.

As we built our studio and house, I kept my two roses in pots for awhile. We were all roughing it. They had to fend for themselves with minimal care. It was a year after our move that I finally had a little place fenced in for them where they were protected from rabbits and deer. Once in the ground, the two roses began to thrive in spite of our barren and over-grazed landscape.

In the seventies and early eighties finding sources for old-fashioned roses was difficult. There was no internet to aid with searches. The bibliography in one of the books I had been reading listed three nurseries in the United States. Two of these were west of the Mississippi. I wrote to them both asking for their catalogs, placing a first class fifteen cent stamp on an envelope and waiting patiently for a reply.

In due time, I received a small pamphlet from *High Country Gardens* in Denver. It was printed on pale green, mat paper stock, with lists of their collections and varieties. Simple, one color pen and ink illustrations decorated the pages. I poured over the new found information for hours on end.

There were shrub roses, climbers, species roses, and rugosas. The nursery recommended choices for theme gardens, such as cottage gardens, historic gardens, or wildlife gardens. I began making lists.

My lists began getting longer when I received the second catalog from *Roses of Yesterday and Today* located in Watsonville, California. Their catalog was larger and contained some black and white photos, but mostly text, to describe for their rose offerings. The wrap-around cover, however, was printed in bright color, each year a new illustration showing an opulent bouquet of thirty or more roses, differing on front and back. Inside the first page of the booklet was a parchment sheet that could be laid over the front and back covers so that the name of the roses would fall over the pictures of them. This novel approach was helpful and entertaining, as well as an economical solution to expensive color reproductions in those days. Time and again I would read the catalog, then wrap the parchment over the cover, enabling myself to gradually learn the names of roses and what they looked like. I began to imagine which roses would be suited to our island location.

The names of rose categories were like poetry: Gallicas, Albas, Centefolias, and Mosses, Musks, Damasks, Bourbons, and Hybrid Perpetuals, Noisettes, Polyanthas, Spinosissimas, and Rugosas! I wanted to become acquainted with them all.

A Rose Garden Begins

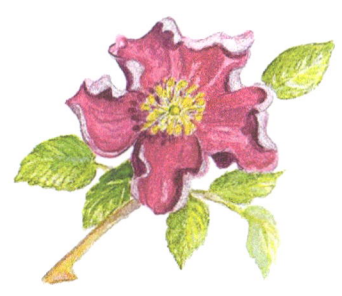

By the spring of 1982, I was ready to place my first order for Rugosa roses. They seemed a good rose to start with as they closely resembled species roses and would blend naturally with the landscape. I hoped they would make a lovely barrier between our garden fence and the orchard. Rugosa roses were developed from species roses native to Japan. I picked out seven varieties ranging in color from deep cerise to soft pinks and a white. The citrusy, deeply veined leaves and the big rose hips appearing in the fall, I have found to be added delights Now decades old, the hedge provides cover for birds, nectar for pollinators, and is loved by bees and me.

After the hedgerow of Rugosas proved to be a success, and my two initial roses continued thriving, I felt encouraged to continue collecting. Still, creating a garden in a wide open field was daunting. I had plenty of room for my plant choices, but I needed to place them in ways that were both artistic as well as suitable to their needs. Happily, the size and heartiness of old roses made them a good choice for creating barriers, hedges, centerpieces and garden rooms. I hoped by their nature they would become a garden.

Climbing Roses were what I chose the second year: Eglantine, New Dawn and Alchymist. Eglantine or Sweet Briar is a species rose native to the British Isles. It looks much like our native Nootka rose, but is more of a climber and is much thornier. It bears lovely pink roses which become the reddest of rose hips in the fall. It, like the rugosas, blended in perfectly with the natural surroundings and seemed appropriate for an island setting.

New Dawn is a most popular rose to this day. This rose was a sport, or natural mutation of Dr. W. Von Fleet. It was very much like the rose I brought with me, but had the advantage of being a repeat bloomer. It was one of the first heirlooms with that attribute. New Dawn was discovered in 1923, one year after Dr. Walter Von Fleet had passed away. Because of its scent and everblooming flowers, it became highly valued and developed for the market in 1930 when it became the first patented rose in America.

The Alchymist rose is a remarkably hardy climbing rose that became available to gardeners in 1956. I chose it for the ever changing color of the blooms, a trait that earned it its name. Because one of the parents of this rose was Eglantine, the sweet briar, I knew it would be hardy.

We planted the Alchymist to climb up into a cherry tree along the edge of the garden. The wonderful strong rose canes grew twelve feet or more up into the tree and the blossoms cascaded down over the boughs along the garden fence. The gorgeous flowers buds were very large in groups of four or five. As they opened up, the flowers appeared creamy white along the edges and pale yellow in the center, but as the flowers aged, their color grew deeper, magically becoming peach washed with raspberry with highlights of yellow remaining. Blossoms five or six inches across, made up of forty-one petals in quartered rosette pattern, offered a lovely fruity rose perfume.

The Alchymist is said to have one blooming period in early summer, yet it seems to bloom for weeks on end. When the cherry tree became sickly and had to be cut down, our Alchymist quickly adapted to a trellis for support and though does not grow as tall as it did in the tree, it continues to produce lovely big flowers year after year.

Adapting to change is important for gardeners and their plants. Severe weather is often threatening, be it summer heat and drought, or winter cold. When we had a northeaster one winter, many favorite plants were lost including my first New Dawn. The temperatures dropped in twenty four hours from a benign fifty degree rain to nearly zero degrees as sixty mile an hour winds pummeled our islands. The tall climber suffered splits along the base of its canes where it had frozen so suddenly. Eventually it had to be removed as the only surviving part of the plant was the root below the graft. That root produced a different rose altogether. Since that year, I decided to only purchase hardy roses grown on their own roots to avoid those unsatisfactory surprises.

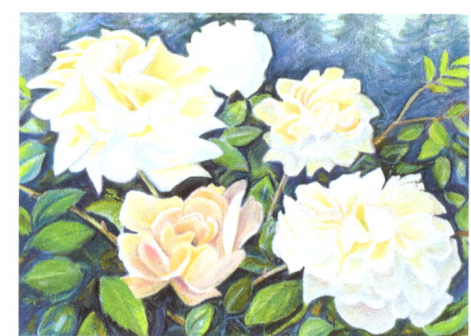

Alchymist

Fortunately in the late eighties, more sources for old-fashioned roses were available, as many gardeners were choosing to grow them. A new nursery with hundreds of heirlooms, all on their own rootstock, turned out to be nearby in Oregon. I was delighted to be able to find so many of the roses I had dreamed of planting, grown on their own roots. I continued to add these to the garden, happy in the knowledge that they would most likely be survivors should we be faced with stressful weather or climate conditions.

A Garden Landscape Evolves

Soon we had enough shrubs and climbers to provide sweet scents and color all around our new buildings. A garden with structure was beginning to form as the plants grew.

In the beginning my focus was only on collecting and planting roses. As time went on I realized I needed to include other plants to make the setting look more natural and inviting. I had only a haphazard collection of wildflowers and herbs which nestled in nicely among the shrubs and climbers. I had little knowledge of landscaping other than of landscapes that called to me in my art and wanderings. It was apparent that more thought was needed to create an inviting garden environment.

Always open to new passions, suddenly the world of columbines, foxgloves, poppies and delphiniums, and all plants "cottage" began to entice me. My Cornish friend Amanda, both gardener and artist, introduced me to varieties of primulas I had never seen before as well as campions and Ladies Mantle. All my gardening friends had favorites I was eager to try. The spaces between the roses filled with an ever growing variety of perennials and flowering plants. A place to lose oneself in was gradually evolving.

Lewis began designing and constructing fences, trellises and arbors to give some vertical structure to the garden design and much needed support for the roses. He enjoyed this aspect of gardening as he designed and created benches and hideaways where a person could find refuge amid all the varied plants forms being introduced. We were having fun.

I had wanted my rose collection to include as many varieties as possible, but after some disappointing losses I decided to only plant those that were adapted to the terrain and climate where we lived. Fortunately, we lived in a setting very hospitable to the majority of rose types.

My heirloom roses from antiquity included the Tuscan Rose that I brought from our old house, and the Apothecary Rose that I added later. Also called Red Rose of Lancaster, The Apothecary rose grows as a short well rounded shrub which during its blossoming period becomes a mound covered with fuchsia-red semi double flowers. The flowers are deeply scented and said to be the only rose that will keep its scent indefinitely after the petals are dried and ground. Because of the loose form of the flowers, the stamens are readily available to foraging pollinators. Large Tiger Swallowtail butterflies visit frequently. As I walk past, I love to remember that The Apothecary Rose was well established in Europe, particularly France and Italy, during the Renaissance.

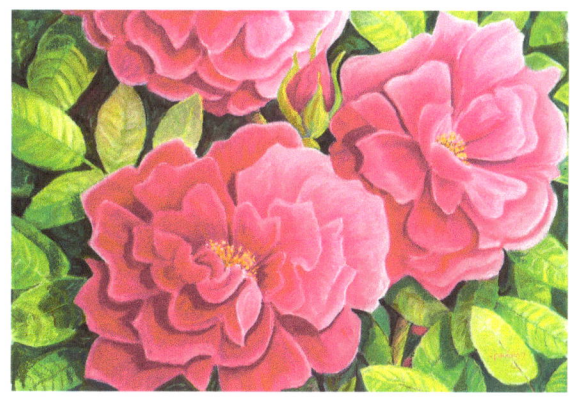

Red Rose of Lancaster

Albas were another group brought to Europe by the Romans. As the name suggests, the color range of this group is primarily white, with a few that are light pink. They are the hardiest of roses and include some of the most deeply scented blooms supported on canes bearing pleasing blueish green leaves. The Albas seem to thrive in sun or partial shade and were thought to be popular during the Renaissance period, likely depicted in Botticelli's *The Birth Of Venus*. The alba in my garden, The White Rose of York, is a handsome plant with tall eight foot canes that reach skyward with grace. When laden with white blossoms it is especially lovely by moonlight.

I collected two Moss roses, so named for the fascinating mossy structure adorning the sepals and stems, noticed mainly when the flowers are in bud form. Dark red in color, they are both three to four feet tall and offer sweet blooms in early summer when they blossom. They are gentle and unobtrusive additions in a border. The loosely arranged petals of the flowers are reminiscent of a soft worn fabric whose dye is slightly faded, yet you never want to part with it.

In 1985, I ordered two Damask roses of ancient origin which I chose for their history and their legendary scent. They have been heartily performing ever since. Madame Hardy is a cherished rose for her unique blossoms of white or slightly pink flowers, tightly formed in what is called a quartered style. Four circular patterns of petals surround a green eye in the center of the flower. She smells divine. Every year when Madame is blossoming, I take my drawing pad out to the garden to sketch the flowers yet one more time, as I lose myself in the pleasure and wonder of her fine design.

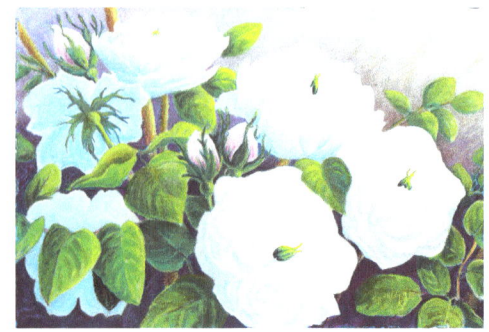

Madame Hardy

The second Damask is Isphahan. Every June I stand before this giant rose, bearing its clusters of three inch, cupped, very double pink flowers in clusters of twelve or more, feasting my eyes on its opulence and breathing in the heavenly scent. This rose has also been called Pompon des Prince, originating in Persia, taken to Turkey in the Middle Ages, and arriving in Europe in the thirteenth century. The Turks distilled its petals for perfume and made rose water, which they used as a flavor in nougat and marzipan. Being in the presence of Isphahan is like taking an exotic journey: Rosy pompoms, curvaceous, decorative, fluffy flowers that were deemed suitable for royalty.

In the evening in summer we often sit on the blue bench beneath the arbor where Isphahan grows. The tall canes rise twelve feet or more into the air with the support of the lattice, arcing outward and down nearly to the ground creating a massive mountain of flowers which has become entwined with honeysuckle. The bench, in the grotto created beneath, looks out to the opposite side of the arbor where other climbers grow. As the sun lowers in the west, it renders the leaves of Trier and Climbing Paul Lede translucent, their roses ride the air, petals shimmery, illuminated. We sit with books, or eat our supper, and watch the hummingbirds.

One of my favorite roses purchased in the mid eighties is Constance Spry. This rose was marketed as a shrub rose at the time and described as growing four to six feet tall. Constance immediately exploded beyond her bounds, but in a delightful way. This rose was planted against our barn constructed of driftwood logs which the canes happily climbed upon. The flowers were beautiful large, pink cup-shaped blooms, like a cabbage rose, and had a spicy scent of myrrh.

I had chosen this rose because I learned that it was named after a true English heroine. Constance Spry was a floral designer, amateur rosarian, and educator who lived in England mid-century. During WWII she risked her own safety, traveling to France to bring roses back to England, saving valuable specimens from the ravages of war.

I was a surprise to learn that the rose Constance Spry was the first of the English roses bred by the rosarian David Austin. As his first success, he had shown it to Graham Thomas, another famed gardener instrumental in advancing the resurgence of old roses, who was

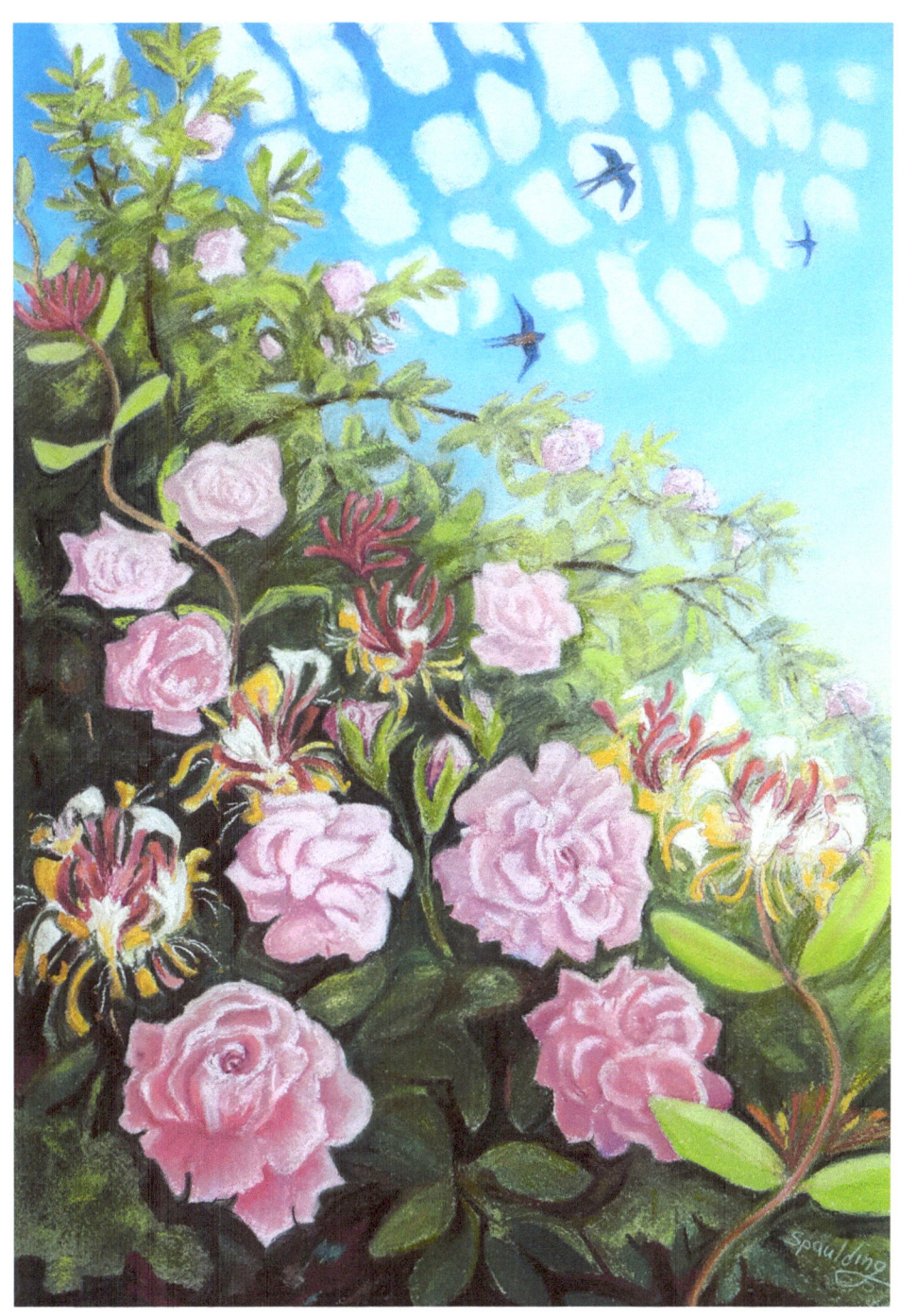

Summer Dreams with Isphahan

also a prominent nurseryman. Together, the two men named the rose and Graham Thomas marketed Constance Spry as a Shrub Rose. David Austin had not yet advanced to become the renowned rose breeder and originator of a whole new category of rose, the English Roses.

The English Roses have brought wonderful new choices to rose lovers. I was not aware of them until the late nineties though David Austin had been working to develop new varieties since the 1950s. By breeding the modern tea roses with older heirlooms he was able to combine all the loveliest attributes of old roses, scent, form and heartiness, with the repeating bloom and wider range of color available in modern roses. Of his "new race of roses" David Austin has said "they are the most fragrant roses of all time, not excluding the old roses themselves. English roses are in fact the new old roses, if I may be forgiven for that apparent contradiction in terms."

The English Roses are the perfect complement for my older varieties. Even as my garden space runs out I will never run out of enticements. Happily, The Shropshire Lad, Sweet Juliet, the Generous Gardener, Gentle Hermione, Abraham Darby, The Ambridge Rose, Charlotte and Miss Alice reside in the garden now.

One of the joys of having a garden is the element of surprise. I love to discover "volunteers" in the vegetable garden or in the border beds. While not always desirable, sometimes wonderful things appear. Because we have been here so long, two mysterious roses have emerged and matured from the germination of errant rose seeds. I would imagine birds eating hips could distribute such seeds. One of these roses appeared in the field, an unusually robust Nootka Rose with distinctive Rugosa traits. The other appeared right in the garden along the border between 0Red Rose of York and a wild Nootka that refused to be weeded out. The result of that cross is a massively resilient bush covered with highly perfumed, delicate, pink, double blooms on very thorny stems. The two unique new shrubs are delightful additions, both adding amazement to the process of gardening.

It has been satisfying to create such a large garden. I have taken on what generally should require a staff of several and the backing of much more than the income of a street artist. On the other hand, I have become acquainted first hand with plants I have read and dreamed about. I have reveled in working amongst them. Lewis has built fences, gates, benches and arbors and I have dug and weeded, seeded and potted. Our refuge is not always well tended, but it is always a place where we feel happy while creating a haven for birds, creatures, and people. I have learned that a garden is never a finished thing but always a constant evolving, a playing out of plant growth and seasonal change, influenced by our actions or lack of the same.

As in the first years of our garden, the roses reign and continue to create an aura, a sense of beauty and life throughout the property. I can go among them and disappear, just as I did on the cliffs of Whidbey Island many years ago. In my imagination or in a reality I don't really understand, the roses have given me a window into space and time itself.

Oh no man knows what wild centuries roves back the rose.

—Walter DeLa Mare

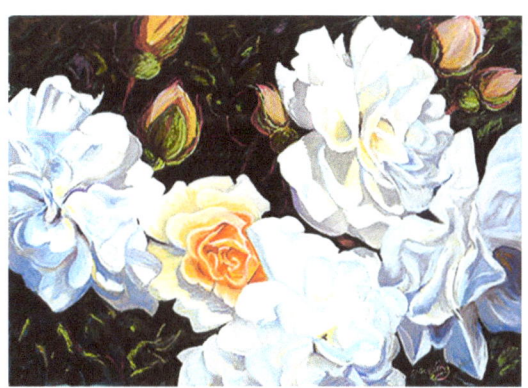

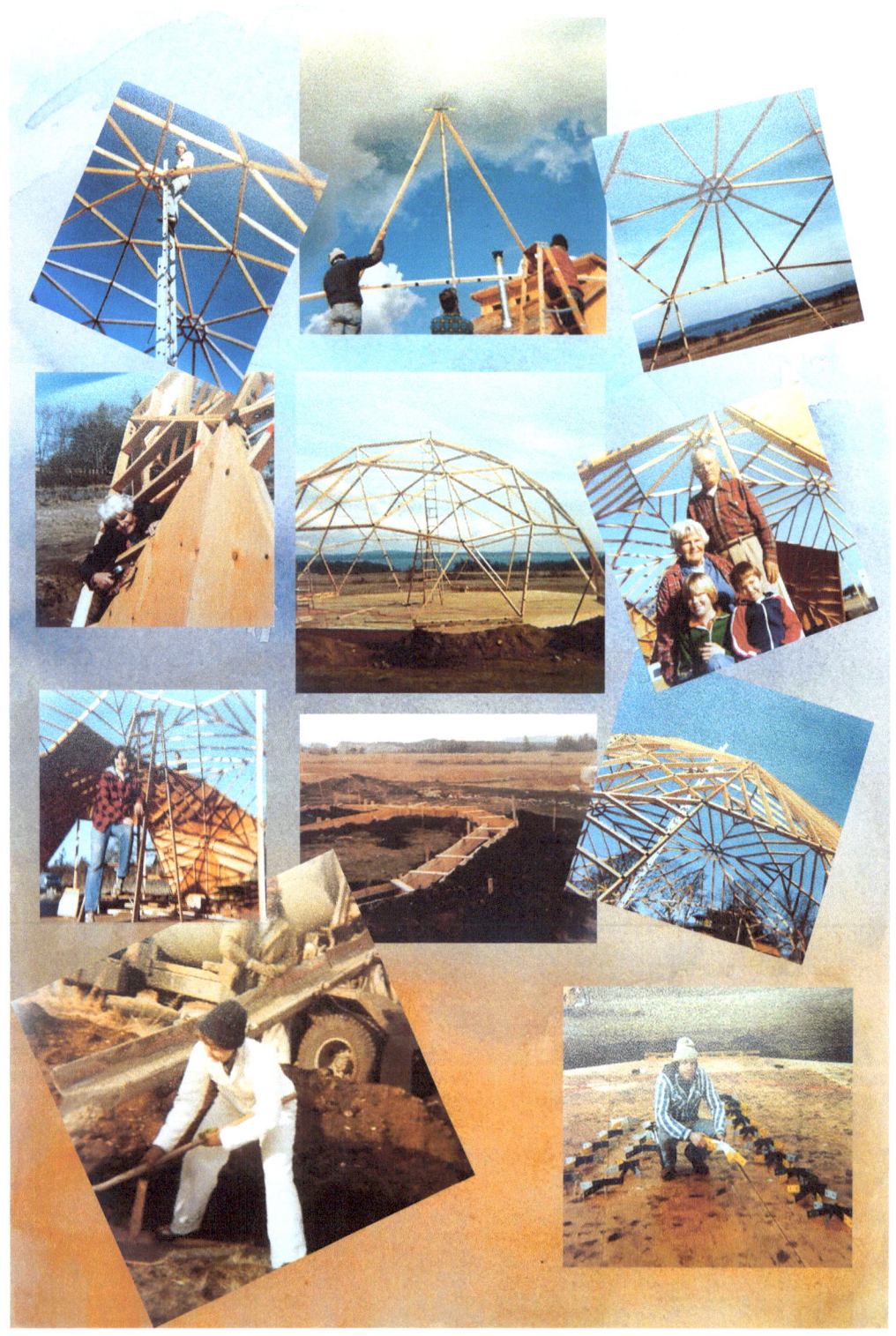

Dome Construction

Chapter Four

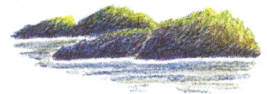

Building The Dome - 1979

By January the studio was closed in and cozy, though not finished on the inside nor painted on the outside. It was a tight, water and windproof shelter and we were grateful for it. We slept upstairs all in a row in our sleeping bags. The little Baby Bear cast iron stove kept us toasty.

Insulating the studio's interior and the readying downstairs print room kept us occupied most winter days. With the addition of a few more shelves and work tables it would be usable. It was critical that we find creative time amid the chaos and we needed a space to work. Our summer shows would start in a few months time. Funds from the sale of our house on the mainland wouldn't last much longer. For extra security, Lewis had signed up for some smaller winter shows at malls and exhibition halls in the urban areas around Puget Sound. I, in the meanwhile began to work on new designs with hopes of getting a lot of silk screen printing accomplished before the craft fair season began.

We felt exhausted from the demands every day brought. It was unbearably hard to wrap our minds around the idea of constructing another whole building, as soon as February. We knew we needed to forge onward especially for Laurie and Heather who had no space to call their own. It wasn't fair to make them camp like this with no end in sight. The luxury of having a home dangled ahead of us like a sweet, juicy carrot.

Our prefabricated geodesic dome, constructed in the San Francisco Bay area, was scheduled to arrive in early March. With just two month before its arrival, we were obliged to start building the foundation before it came. Hadn't we just been down this road only weeks ago?

Back to measurements again and working outdoors, we felt pressure building. The circular foundation needed to accommodate our dome which was forty feet in diameter. If it hadn't been for the stark and sometimes startling beauty surrounding us, I don't think I could have continued on.

While plotting out the circular trench, to find relief from shoveling, I looked at whatever was going on in our field, over the water and in the sky. In a season of wind, distant flocks of crows tossed about like flakes of ash let loose from a chimney. Bald Eagles rode the currents, close enough to catch a glint of light in their golden eyes. Gusts ruffled their feathers as they soared past.

As we worked I compared ravens and crows. Deep throaty chortling and comic guttural sounds generally announced the arrival of a raven. When in close proximity to their smaller cousins, it became obvious that they were considerably larger. They had thick beaks and big boat tails. If a pair of ravens happened to fly over they often tipped their wings, dipping and trading places, as though flying along in a continuous nod to each other.

Our foundation began to take on the appearance of an ancient monument to some deity, or cryptic writing for peoples of another time. Neighbors were interested. Were we building a swimming pool, they wondered?

When the wooden forms around the circular foundation were finally ready Lewis ordered a load of cement. On yet another cold and clammy day the truck arrived and began to pour the thick grey mass into the trench. Lewis and I moved the cement along with our shovels. The crew stood watching as they directed more and more cement down the chute. It was heavy and I could barely keep pace. Dressed in Lewis' old moving man overalls, panting with exhaustion, I must have been a sight. I am not sure why the effort didn't kill me.

At the end of February there was a solar eclipse. The day started slowly as though time were standing still. We stopped to watch. The dismal cloudy morning became more dismal and dark as we approached totality. Unexpectedly there came a break in the clouds. Laurie and Heather rushed to get the pinhole cameras we had made around the dinner table the night before. There was just enough time before the clouds rolled together again to catch a quick peak of the sun's slender crescent cast against the studio wall, for the moment all that was left of our energy star.

As light slowly returned and the day eased into normalcy, we sat in the trailer eating hot soup. It was time for a rest and to contemplate.

My mother and father appeared at the end of the day having made the late afternoon boat. We hadn't been expecting them for another day, but they had made record time on their drive north. They were both lovers of the open road and always had been. I don't know how many solo drives my mother had made back and forth crossing the country from Tucson to New England, or how many forays she took exploring Arizona on her own. I remembered the many drives she took with my brother and me when we were kids, sightseeing and traveling to old haunts she wanted us to see. She was intrepid.

My father was an adventurer too and felt excited that our family seemed spread all over the map, "doing things," as he said. He was the kind of person who when he could, made every day an adventure, noting the humor in it, or the wonder. He had suffered a disability during World War II, before I was born. When serving as a commander in the Navy he contracted a near fatal case of pneumonia. Thankfully he recovered, but for the rest of his life his legs were left with ulcerated sores that never healed, a side effect from the massive doses of penicillin he had been given. I knew he lived with pain on a daily basis, but he never ever spoke of it.

It was important to both of my parents to be with us to help with the raising of the dome. We shouldn't have been surprised by their early arrival.

March arrived and our camp site expanded by two more people. As we sat and planned the excitement was palpable. We talked about practical things like what would be nice for supper and then how tall we would build the block foundation wall to support the dome. My father advised building a short or pony wall across the middle as the span was too long for the timbers. We talked about nature, weather and of Buckminster Fuller.

Buckminster Fuller, a twentieth century visionary, was an architect, engineer, philosopher and original thinker. He has been called one of the last great transcendentalists, carrying on the tradition of thoughtful knowledge seekers, writers and humanitarians of the 19th century. Emerson, Thoreau, the Alcotts and his great aunt Margaret Fuller come to mind. One of his many inventions was the geodesic dome. He said "When working on a problem, I never think about beauty, but if the solution is not beautiful, I know it is wrong."

We loved the concept of a geodesic dome, a structure built of triangles that formed pentagons and hexagons, stacked one upon the other to create a sphere. The result was the strongest of buildings, also economical. It enclosed a specified space with one third less materials than a traditional structure would require. Winds would roll off its walls. It would be easy to heat. It seemed sensible, futuristic but at the same time rooted in the architecture of many Indigenous peoples around the world.

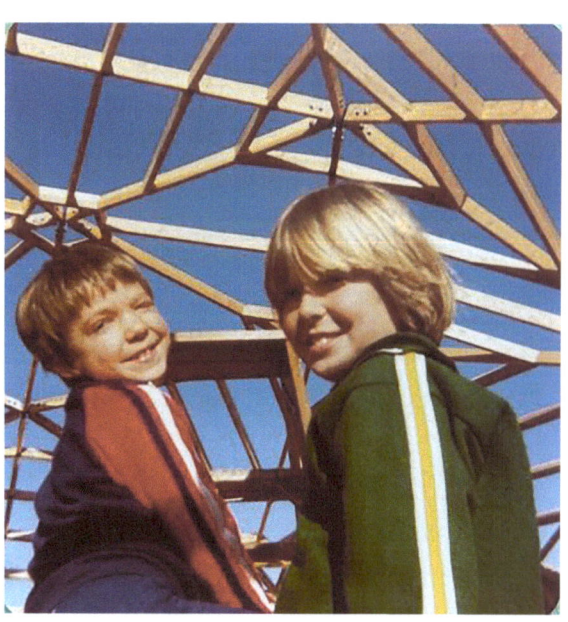

Dome Inspectors Heather and Laurel

We thought of Yurts, Hogans, Igloos and the round and wheelhouse designs of the Celts and Picts. We thought of Roman and Greek temples that were places of balance and harmony. We hoped to create a space where we would nestle into the landscape and feel part of the land that we were living on.

The four of us began to lay blocks for the first course of the foundation and finished two thirds of the circle in one day. Two extra pairs of hands made everything go faster. By three days the second course was all but done. My father with his surveyor's level checked our progress, keeping us on track. At night we all piled into the studio to sleep and we felt satisfied by the work we had completed.

The first springlike day arrived and it was exhilarating. An early fog cleared out by mid morning and the sun actually felt warm for the first time since fall. The thermometer we had attached to the studio said sixty degrees. Birdsong rippled forth from the hedgerows. Everyone felt ecstatic except for Lewis. He had to go to Seattle for a mall show we had scheduled. He would be stuck inside for five days with other artists, hoping to attract the attention of passersby who were in the mall to shop for something else. Still, it was the only thing going at the time of year. We helped him pack up the bus, regretted that he needed to go and wished him well. Any bit of success with the art side of our lives would be good news.

My mother and father and I continued on laying the last of the blocks. Then the next day they both came down with colds and I had a tremendous sense of guilt. We decided to slow down and focus on our visit not our work.

In the midst of our break the much anticipated news came.

Unable to reach us by phone, a truck from the local freight company drove in to see if we would be home the next few days as a big shipment was due to arrive. The dome was getting closer! We were relieved of its whereabouts and anticipated the arrival. When the chorus of spring peepers filled the night air, the frogs seemed to express wild abandon and urgency that we felt also in the moment.

Just as promised, a flat bed truck pulled in to our little compound on Friday, mid afternoon. They took a pallet off the truck with a hoist and set it down in the driveway. We stared at it and wondered if this could possibly be the whole shipment. A rectangular cube measuring about eight by six by six feet did not look big enough to construct a house.

The exterior plywood was precut into triangles and the kiln dried two by fours were wrapped in a tidy bundle. On top lay an array of metal hubs that would hinge the triangles together. Separate from the package was a five gallon metal bucket filled with nuts and bolts and looking a bit like an afterthought balanced on top.

Not sure whether to be alarmed or mystified, we pondered what sort of situation we had gotten ourselves into.

My father, engineer, builder of bridges, highways, water purification systems and runways all around the world, was undaunted. The fact there were no directions included with the collection of materials was equally unconcerning to him. The lumber was all color coded, what could go wrong? As he was as positive about the construction as ever, I felt my excitement returning.

We waited for Lewis' return so didn't work on anything until the following Monday which dawned with a big red sun illuminating the grey, just like Monet's *Impression, Sunrise*. The weather was toying with us, being springlike one moment and bitter cold the next. Equinoctial storms, my mother said, though the first of spring was still a couple of weeks away.

It stayed foggy until noon. Mom, Dad and I worked to finish the sills around the dome foundation. When the sun came out at lunchtime we stopped for a picnic lunch. By the end of the day we were quite tired. Making supper in close quarters, I cut my hand on a knife, not seriously but enough to warn me that I wasn't in the best form. In the evening we listened to owls while waiting for Lewis' return. Finally we gave up and went to bed. He drove in moments later.

Over coffee, the next morning Lewis caught up with the progress we made when he was gone, and we listened to tales from the mall. The weather kept flip flopping so we cleaned up around our building site and then retreated inside resorting to food, cheese and cinnamon rolls. Granddad and the girls decided to make a cake. At some point something went awry and Laurie decided to run away from home, at which time she became the imaginary Mrs. Bunny and did not become Laurie again until half way through supper. We all played bingo after dinner and Heather fell asleep before she went to bed.

Finally the grand clear day we had been hoping for, arrived. Dad and Lewis got to work finishing the joists that spanned the diameter of the dome and became supports for the floor. My mother and I worked to devise a small garden plot which would have to be fenced eventually. We saw two butterflies which seems miraculous: a Tortoiseshell and an Admiral. There were most definitely swallows high overhead and a red tailed hawk made circular patterns while riding the updrafts like a sublime mobile. We began to feel quite elated by what lay ahead. There was so much to learn about our land as spring approached bringing new life.

As the sun set that afternoon it dropped into a mist forming sun dogs, a parhelion. Pretty rainbow patches on either side of a veiled sun, adorned the sullen sky.

Later, the Great Horned Owls began calling into the night and when the moon rose, it had a big ring around it where it too was flanked by iridescent patches: moon dogs! Mom predicted another change of weather. It has been changing constantly, so from what to what?

Meteorological effects predominated our psyches each day as we attempted to move forward with the decking as quickly as possible. We watched moonsets in the oak trees and sunrises through fog in the east, streaming bands of gold turning to deep, deep red. Sailors take warning. The temperature dropped considerably but we soldiered on. With about two thirds of the floor done we ran out of material. A break was called for so we went to the beach and found beach logs to make fence posts for the garden.

Cold wet weather continued. With the progress we had made and with the calendar running out for my parents' stay, we could wait no longer. The time had come for dome raising day! With the four of us, it went up quickly, like magic almost. The positioning of the first tier of pentagons was determined by where we had decided the windows and doors would be. The precut lumber and metal hubs went together like a giant tinker toy set. We were able to get all the way around the circle before the day was over.

We celebrated with dinner in town. When we got home, the sky was clear and we all stepped up onto the dome platform and watched the stars through the open triangles of our upward reaching walls. We all went to bed feeling a deep sense of accomplishment.

March 17th arrived and was meant to be a celebratory day, my father's birthday, a day he lets his Irish twinkle show. We finished up the dome hexagons and the final top pentagon. We were working high on ladders supported by construction itself which by then was gently turning inward to create a hemisphere. It seemed to take hours of adjusting and tightening, spider manning about, before getting the last connectors to snap together. When at last the final hub clicked into place the structure became solid and firm, the integrity of the dome had been accomplished. When we quit, my poor dad was exhausted and couldn't seem to get himself warm as we settled around the fire. Birthday celebrations were cancelled. We piled him with blankets and fixed broth.

The next day my father was very sick with a chest cold, high fever and weakness. We decided we should call a doctor at the clinic in town. The trailer was turned into his recovery room.

We all felt miserable and the cold wind added insult to injury. The rest of us continued to work fitting the two by fours into the now upright pentagons. The kiln dried lumber was so hard it was nearly impossible to nail into. We checked frequently on our patient who was eager for the latest reports with our progress.

The first day of spring arrived, the week of stormy weather finally abated. My father got out of bed for the first time in days and began occupying himself with his Chinese language books and with working through various plumbing puzzles for Lewis to tackle at a later date.

The sunshine and fresh air felt so good we waited outside until the school bus stopped for Laurie and Heather. Leaf buds were swelling on the little fruit trees we purchased last fall which surely meant a resurgence of good things to come. Then it was back to work on our beautiful hemisphere which was becoming more ornate in pattern as all the two by fours were nailed in place, twelve inches apart in every triangle. Sky, drifting clouds, flying birds were all framed by delightful geometric shapes.

One day we were able to spend the afternoon in shirtsleeves up on the ladders, Lewis, our spider man, in the highest places. The placement of the exterior plywood sheathing was progressing rapidly and by the end of the day we were nearly done. My mother helped hold boards in place as we hammered, and with a hammer in hand herself, she too, drove nails where she could. Quickly we covered triangle after triangle.

The space and sky, visible through the patterns of the dome structure we had constructed were so appealing it seemed regrettable to cover them over. Now as the pentagons and hexagons became a roof we saw that the overall shape embraced us in a comforting way. We had carefully chosen the openings that would remain as windows and skylights and we began to see the resulting space that would define our home.

At that point it was time to stop and consider together what we had done and enjoy the last couple of days before our travelers would depart. We had had a few scares but my father and mother were glad they had come.

When the morning of departure came, we helped them to gather up all their possessions. There is a different aspect to leaving this place, so unlike anywhere else I have known. Because we are dependent on ferries and at the mercy of their schedule, when it is time to board the moment is decisive, unforgiving. I find there is a deeper sense of parting and sometimes melancholy. It was at least comforting that they had a beautiful spring day to start their drive south.

We were glad to get back to our own routines, to have our own crazy, independent lives back, but there was an emptiness. When I heard several days later that our travelers had reached home where they could rest and recover, then I relaxed.

Their help to us had been immense and in spite of the hardships, they rallied and embraced the adventure of our moving to the island. That kindness and generosity will always be with me.

In Retrospect

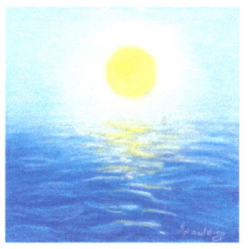

With all the years that have passed, I wish that I had focused more on the moment during those hectic times. We were so caught up in daily routines, survival, balancing our creative lives with rearing our children as we continued to work toward our dreams. Many opportunities simply escaped us.

I am glad I didn't know that to the day almost, ten short years after the dome went up, we would lose my father. I am sure that I went a whole year without smiling after he was gone. It certainly felt that way. One day when I looked into the mirror I saw that my face looked old and drawn like a stranger's. Then one day in another spring, I found myself laughing and took notice of it as though it was something foreign, coming from someone else. I was surprised by the sound of it, awakened by the familiarity of it, and overcome that newfound joy had come to find me after being so long gone.

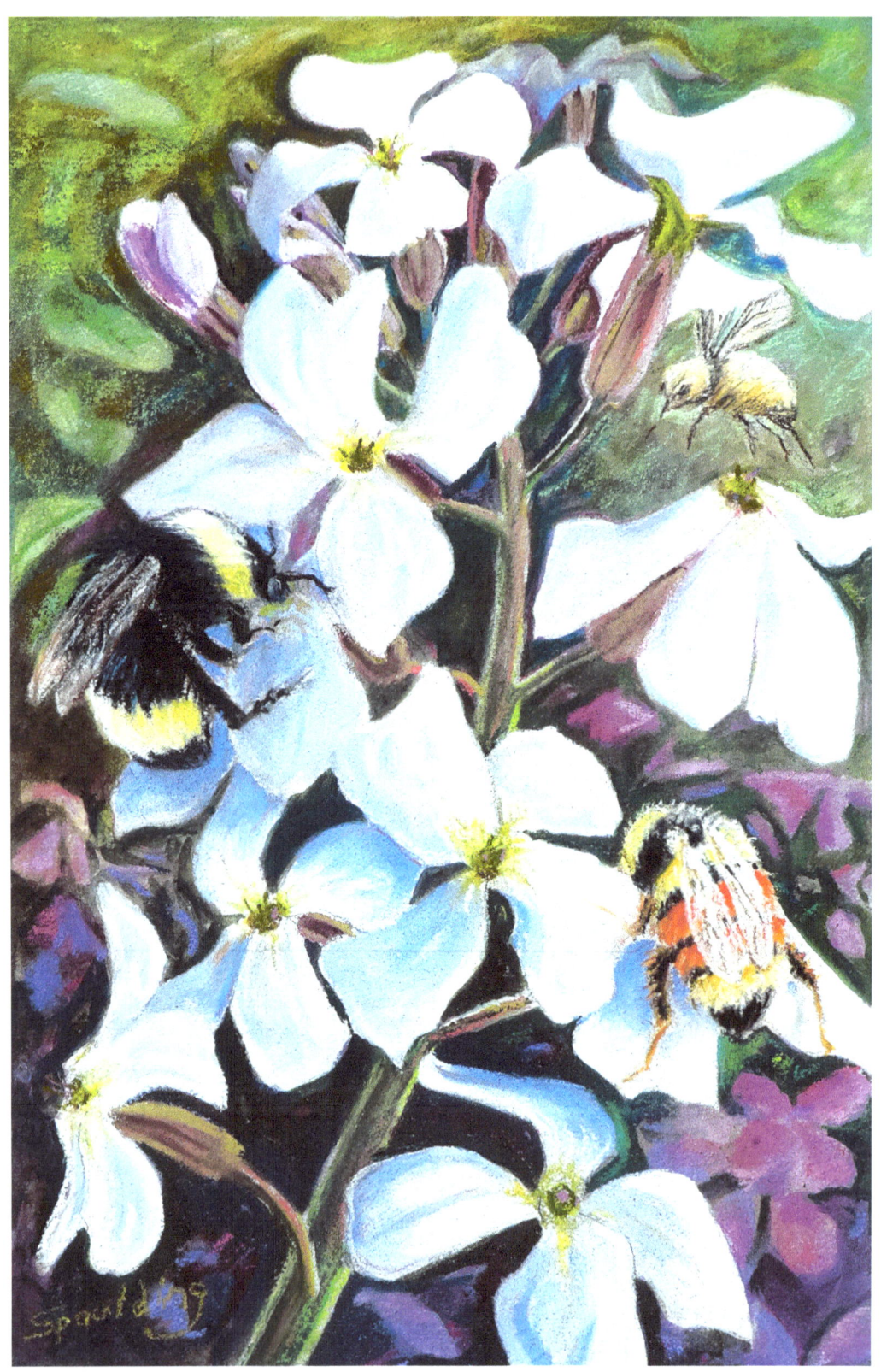

Bumblebees on Dame's Rocket

Chapter Five

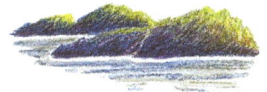

An Admiration for Bumblebees

One mid-April morning, I decided to tackle the blackberry roots that had begun to sneak under the fence as they invaded my herb garden. The area, shaded in early spring by both a plum tree outside the fence and an ornamental pear inside the fence, lagged a bit behind the rest of the garden. I still had time to get it weeded before the onset of warmer weather.

I sent the shovel deep into the ground and loosened a large knob of blackberry root, easing it out of the dirt. Then I stopped in dismay as I noticed a large bumblebee in the shovelful of earth. She was big like a beetle, all black but for a creamy yellow face, a shoulder scarf of the same yellow edging the front of her thorax and a yellow abdominal band. Her fur was matted down and the sleepy creature barely moved. "Oh no," I thought, "could I have destroyed this queen bee's nest?"

I had been seeing many bumblebees of her kind, as well as other species, already out foraging in sunnier areas of the garden where native huckleberry, native currant, rosemary, heathers and a number of azaleas and rhododendrons were in full bloom. That observation made me think that this bee had probably started a nest. Momentarily, I rethought what was before me. I questioned if she was a bee at all, with her slicked down fur from her underworld sleep. Minutes later she looked more familiar as she fluffed herself out and began to move about in the leaf litter on uncertain legs.

I contacted fellow islander, Thor Hanson, field biologist and author who lives not far down the road. "The slow bee" he assured me was a queen, her species commonly called yellow or white faced bumble bee. "You found her in what entomologists would call her hibernaculum, where she dug down last fall to sleep away the flowerless winter months." He added, "Though she may have preferred a little more rest, with all this nice weather I'm sure she warmed up and will be just fine."

That was great news. I had watched her rustle down into the sticks and leaves when I left her. Now I wondered if she would she build a nest somewhere in the garden? I thought about the winter months we had just escaped from. While we cuddled inside with our fire, our fleece and our books, this bee and the other queens were biding time in their underground hideaways, managing to keep dry and warm as they waited for spring. Because she had chosen a dark shady corner, my April discovery was later than the other bees I had been observing.

A hibernaculum, from Latin "A tent for winter quarters" is a shelter where a creature can hide-out out or hibernate for the winter months. The bees' winter home is a tiny chamber several inches below the ground's surface, reached through an entrance tunnel and just big enough for her to curl up in.

We find ourselves rooting for her when we learn that bumblebee queens are the only ones in their clan to survive the winter. After all the workers have lived out their lives by the end of summer's warm weather and after each fertile female has mated with a stingless male, for whom that ritual is his only function, each queen crawls into her winter den. She bears the responsibility for the survival of her tribe, carrying their genetic code in her future eggs. I have read that the doorway of her home faces north so she won't waken too soon by the warmth of fickle winter's sunlight. She needs to avoid its lure which might pull her out into a cold winter world where she could be caught unaware and perish. Only when the sun reaches a certain angle with approaching spring, will she come out into the world again after her winter sleep.

I have wondered about this timing. My garden is on the 49th parallel, far enough north that the sun's angle seems very low until March. Yet in February if we have several days of sunshine, I have spotted large bumbles out gathering warmth. Apparently their little doorways have seen enough light that they feel safe enough to greet the outdoor world. That is usually how I feel too when we get a stretch of mild weather during winter in the great Northwest. I am eager to be outdoors. Hugging the Pacific Ocean, we are fortunate to experience some warmth in winter that makes us feel the presence of spring long before the calendar arrival, but we can be fooled. Perhaps then the temperature is as important as light in the queens' awakenings. It could be that she is ready to gamble, with hope that a few of the earliest flowers have begun to bloom, available to give her nourishment and strength.

I gamble too. Should I remove the mulch from tender plants so that they can see the light and start to grow? Should I think about planting a few hearty seeds? The risk is often worth it.

I have been watching bumblebees on our property for many years. Over time, with the coming of each spring I have become more and more curious about their private lives. Since making the island my home in the late 1970s, I have had numerous encounters with them as I work in the garden. We have seen many kinds come and go, some populations burgeoning in a particular year and perhaps disappearing the next. The world is not a particularly safe place for our foraging friends. We hope our garden will provide a small haven for them in our neighborhood at least!

As spring and summer comes to the garden, fields and nearby hedgerows, I discover the bees working the flowers for nectar and pollen. Some of the formidable furry fliers are heavy enough to weigh down the blossoms they land on. A large bee or queen can be nearly as big as the tip of my thumb. Some bees are as small as a fly and most are about the size of a jelly bean. My eye is immediately drawn to their color and patterns. I find it interesting to keep track of how many kinds there are, noting the variety of design. My little field notebooks are filled with sketches and the number of bee portraits in my photo collection increases every year. The big blacks with the white band, the butter yellow, the yellow with the orange stripe are some that fill the pages.

It isn't obligatory to know the scientific names of bumblebees as a gardener, but it is rewarding to notice what goes on in the space you have created, who is present or returning or perhaps missing in any given year. Observation is key to art and life, I say to myself, as year after year I continue to hone those skills. Focusing on bees is a great way to integrate with the garden and train your eye as you follow these active, colorful, hard working insects from flower to flower. I do wish I knew who they all are. If you learn nothing else about their names, it is certainly worthwhile to at least know their genus, Bombus, so apropos to their nature.

Bombus is a word derived from ancient Greek meaning to buzz or hum. Indeed, a perfect description for a bumble bee. To me the sound and use of the word in the modern sense also connotes a behavior of zipping about, and that describes their behavior too.

As more flowers are established in my garden, I have come to notice many more kinds of bees. There are over four thousand species of native bee in North America. Of those there are forty-six species of bumblebee. On our island seven species of bumblebee have been observed and considered common. Three others are considered rare and yet three more could possibly be found in our area. I am relatively confident that over the years I have observed all seven of the more common species that inhabit the island here in the garden. I am pleased by this as it confirms that I have managed to create habitat that is safe and attractive to them.

The bees love spring bulbs as they come into bloom. They are attracted to all the fruit trees which blossom early. They love our native huckleberry, wild currant and dandelions in spring, busily collecting nectar and pollen, assuring that the new broods of workers will thrive and prosper while pollinating my plants as they go along. The spring bloomers are soon followed by the long sequence of ornamental flowers and vegetables which progress through the summer and finally into the fall.

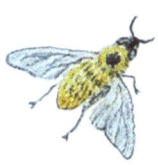

Late summer is a busy time for bees with lavender, mallows, rampant marjoram and oregano as well as the few zinnias in the vegetable beds. Recently in late summer I noticed some unusual bees that didn't appear to belong to any species I had seen earlier in the season. As Thor helped me to identify some of the "bumbles" in my photos, he pointed out that two of my pictures were of drones. I was really surprised by this news. I had read about male bees hatching out at the end of the season: stingless bees who were hatched to mate with a future queen, completing the cycle of the colony. I never expected to actually catch sight of a drone or manage to snap a picture of one. I was excited to have more of the bees' life cycle revealed to me through my continued looking.

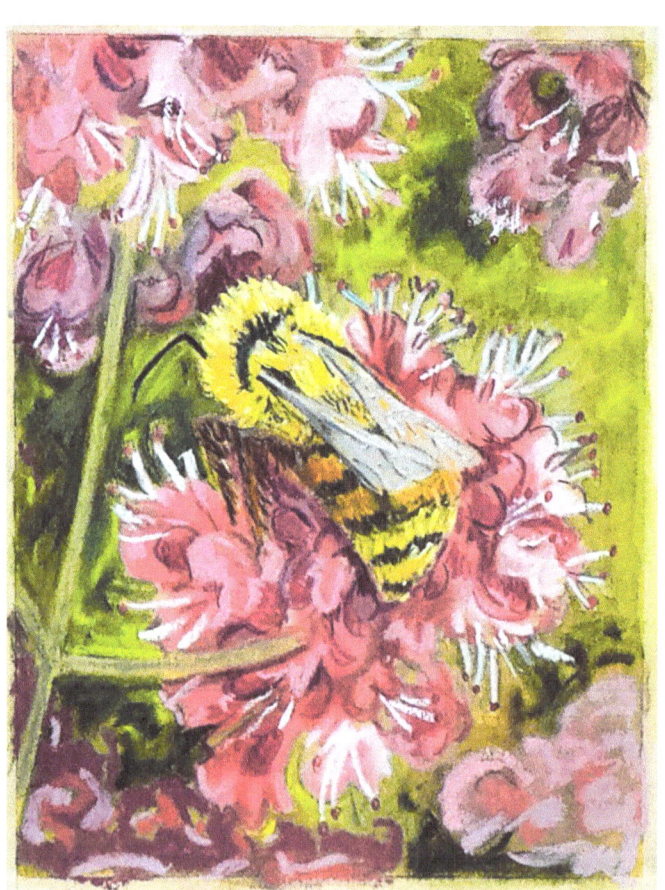

Drone on Marjoram Blossoms

Though curious where they may reside, I have only discovered nests a few times over the years. Bumblebees belong to a much smaller social unit than honey bees. Beginning with one, the queen in spring, and increasing population with each successive brood, a bumblebee colony is likely to be composed of fifty to two-hundred individuals at most. They manage to be quite secretive and like to remain hidden. They are clever and never approach their doorway directly to keep predators away from their underground dens. They are not as likely to be aggressive as honeybees.

For several years we had a variety of very large bumblebees inhabiting the garden that were distinguished by large fiery orange abdomens. They appeared early in spring about the same time as the rufous hummingbirds. The orange red iridescence of the hummingbirds caught our eyes flashing through the garden and so did the furry rouged brightness of the bees darting back and forth.

The orange bees were more aggressive than most which took me by surprise. They took possession of their favorite plants when they came into bloom and became territorial as they foraged during sunlit hours. The lovely ceanothus, covered in sky blue blossoms, became impossible to walk past. A path and garden steps went directly beneath its boughs. I found myself abandoning that route and taking the long way around the potting shed to get to the section of garden that lay beyond.

One late summer evening I was weeding near the ceanothus long after the bees had retired. In an effort to support myself as I reached for some weeds at the back of the hard to manage bed, I put my foot on a rock in the retaining wall that Lewis had built near some descending stone steps. My weight loosened the stone and ones around it. Immediately a large bombus came buzzing out and circled around me. "So this is where they live," I thought to myself as I began to back off. The bees had cleverly chosen an advantageous spot, deep in the wall, just feet from the ceanothus.

I thought by stepping back a bit the bee would also retreat, but it was still unhappy with my presence and not yet deterred in its effort to chase me off. I stepped backward again. The bee circled my face one more time and grazed my lip lightly, leaving me with a small red line, a reminder that I could have been stung outright. Did it graze me with its stinger in the midst of flight? I wasn't prepared for a sting on the wing and was grateful that this nest apparently had only one sentinel on guard duty.

As the summer wore on, I treated the big orange bombus with much respect. I left the weeds in that section of the garden until late summer. I put up a warning sign for passersby and let the bees live their life with as much privacy as they needed. They were a strikingly beautiful bee, bright and velvety looking, pretty enough to pet, should one be so foolish.

The second nest was also an accidental discovery but it was an entirely different experience. One summer day I was weeding under my big old Shrub Rose, the venerable old Gallica which we had nicknamed The Mother Rose. Because she grows on her own root this rose has a tendency to spread. I was crawling about underneath, pulling out handfuls of grass that had taken over under the tangled canes. In yanking out a large clump, a big spray of tiny bumble bees shot up in the air like a fireworks display. It happened so suddenly I had no chance to retreat. A sudden panic overcame me as I endeavored to back away on hands and knees. The bees paid absolutely no mind to me however. These little ground nesters were all in a dither about the disarray I had caused while apparently blaming no one. Up and down they went, a little forlorn fountain. I could almost hear them saying "Oh dear, Oh dear, Oh dear."

Ever since I disturbed their nest and replaced it as best I could, the little bees have been a favorite of mine. They seem to be the smallest kind of bumble bee that we have around here. They are colored pale yellow, almost cream, with subtle black stripes. They are often found in the herb garden working busily. I always keep a look out for them when summer comes, feeling that the garden is not complete until their presence has been noted.

I love to hear the hum of bees in my summer garden and to watch them foraging, gathering both nectar and pollen which, like honeybees, they carry in "baskets" on their

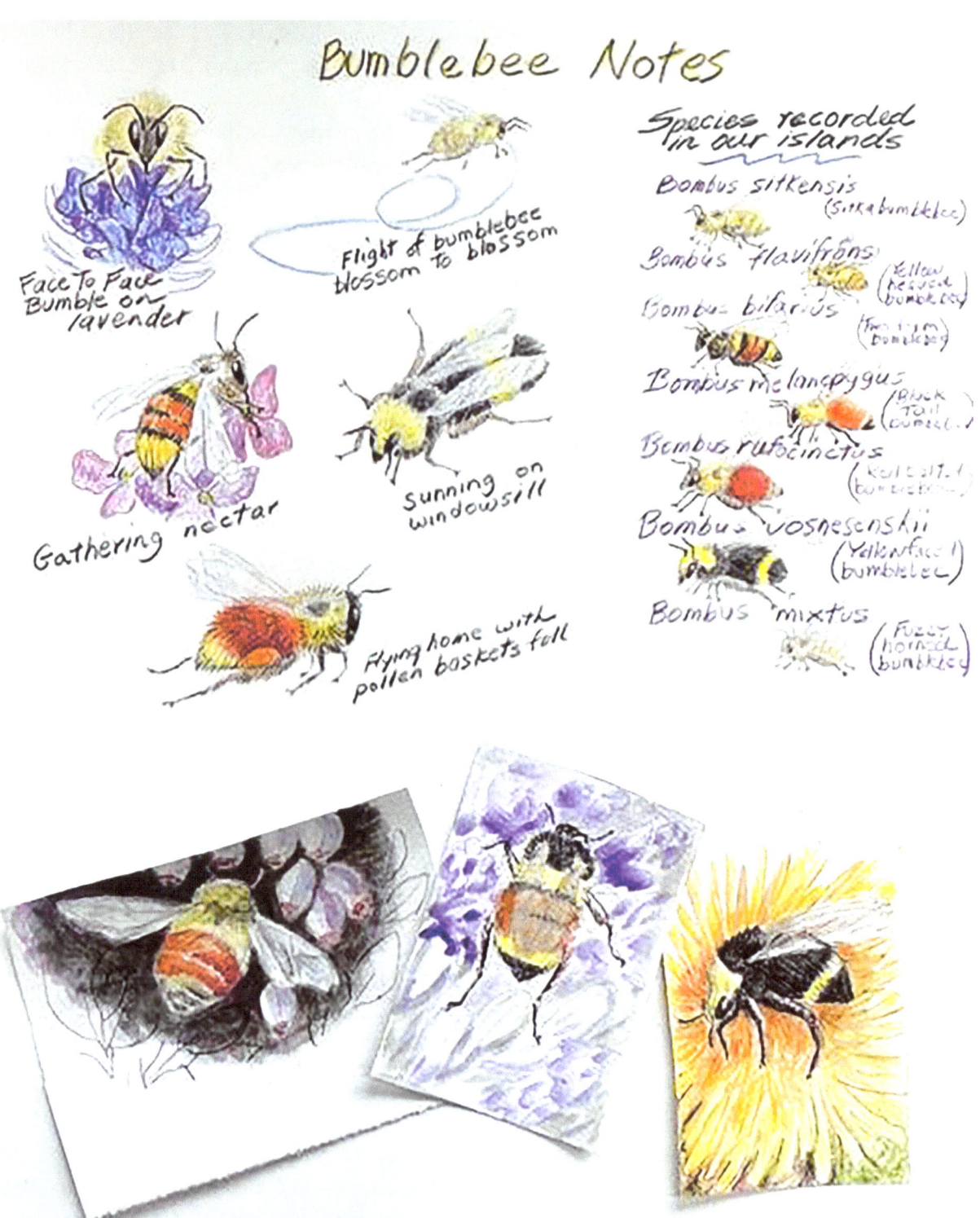

Bee Notebook

hind legs. Sometimes after they have been working hard you can see the large oval shapes of orange or white sticky pollen attached to the hairs on their hindmost legs. This cargo is occasionally massive enough to weight a bee down somewhat as they fly off with purpose to their nests.

The buzz of bees has come to be an essential sound in the garden and an important part of its make up. This dimension is not what a gardener generally thinks of when creating a garden. Thoughts are primarily on visual aspects, all the wonderful plants to grow and their placements. It is only after the plants have begun to grow and intertwine that the meaning of creating habitat becomes apparent. A successful garden, it turns out, is a mingling of visual, olfactory and auditory pleasures.

I discovered another thing about bees one fine spring morning. I had gone out to enjoy the early sunlight one May morning when the orchard was in full bloom. The apple trees were glorious, crowned with pinks and whites. I was hoping to catch sight of a bluebird as there had been sightings in the neighborhood and we had a pair interested in a nesting box the year before. I was lingering and dreaming my way along, enjoying the perfection of the morning. Newly opened blossoms pulled me toward them, seeming to beg me to stop and smell their perfume.

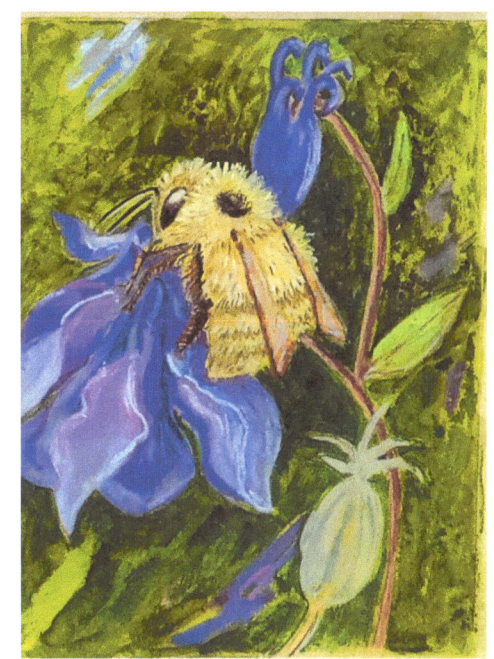

Little Bumble on Columbine

Next to the flowering stems, on a curled apple leaf facing the sun, was a bumblebee and a dew drop. The bee was mid sized with butter yellow hairs and a slender black stripe. At first I thought the bee was sunning itself, but then as I watched, I could see that she was busy taking a bath. She used her front leg to pick up a bit of water from the dewdrop and then she combed her fur. This she repeated until her entire body was bathed. I watched with enchantment. Even our insect friends go about the business of washing and tending to their physical being. I had never thought of this aspect of being a bee. This tiny creature seemed just as full of a sense of self as the rest of us!

We love the bees for the benefit they give us in pollinating our plants and aiding in the production of our fruits, vegetables and flowers. Whatever would we do without them? Their importance to the world cannot be understated. Our lives depend upon them! Living in their presence, I understand these things, but there is more yet to their gifts. Their intense industriousness, their varied beauty, their magical fairy wings coursing back and forth throughout the day, and their ultimate self sacrifice for their colony, these are things most inspirational and wondrous.

Once I saved a bee trapped in the upper skylight of our beach log barn. I discovered the big lemon colored worker going back and forth banging against the window repeating its action over and over again. Bees, like hummingbirds caught in upper story windows, seem unable to look down where their point of entrance had been, or where their exit could be, so strong is the pull of light through the glass.

My daughter Heather arrived for an afternoon visit and found me in the garden perplexed. She was soon equally dismayed about the bee stuck in the upper story. Using a jar to entrap it was of no use as we couldn't reach that high. Soon however, we devised another method of rescue. The garden was filled with Hesperus just then, the tall sturdy stemmed wildflower also called Dame's Rocket. Reminiscent of phlox but of the mustard family, its large heads of lavender white and cerise, sweetly scented blooms seemed effective for our plan. We tied a large sturdy stock in full bloom to the end of a rake handle and thrust it upward toward the now exhausted bee. It managed to land upon the flower and ride it downward as we lowered the rake carefully. When we exited the barn, the bee stayed on the flower which we stuck in a flower bed where it stayed and drank nectar until it eventually flew off with renewed strength.

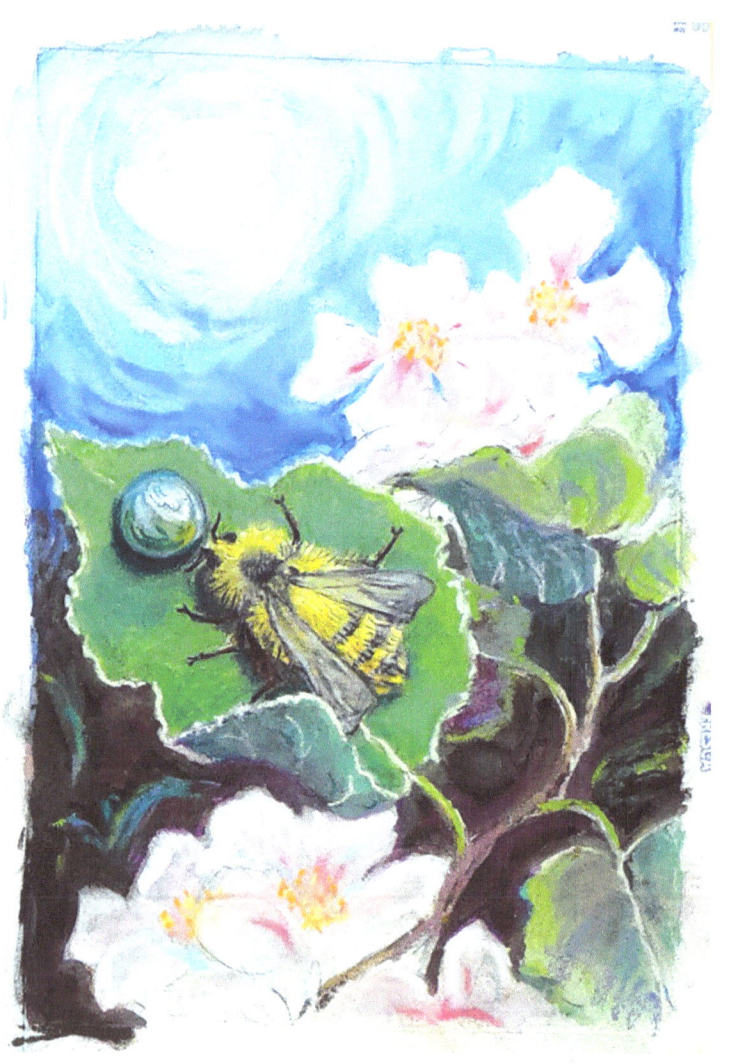

Bee With Dewdrop

A random act of kindness to a bee! It was a small gesture, but one that filled our afternoon with pleasure and satisfaction. Ever since that day, we have used the 'flower on a pole concept' to rescue numerous bees and hummingbirds trapped in high interior spaces around our place.

*The happiness of the bee and the dolphin is to exist. For man,
it is to know that and wonder at it.*

— Jacque Ives Cousteau

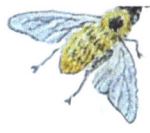

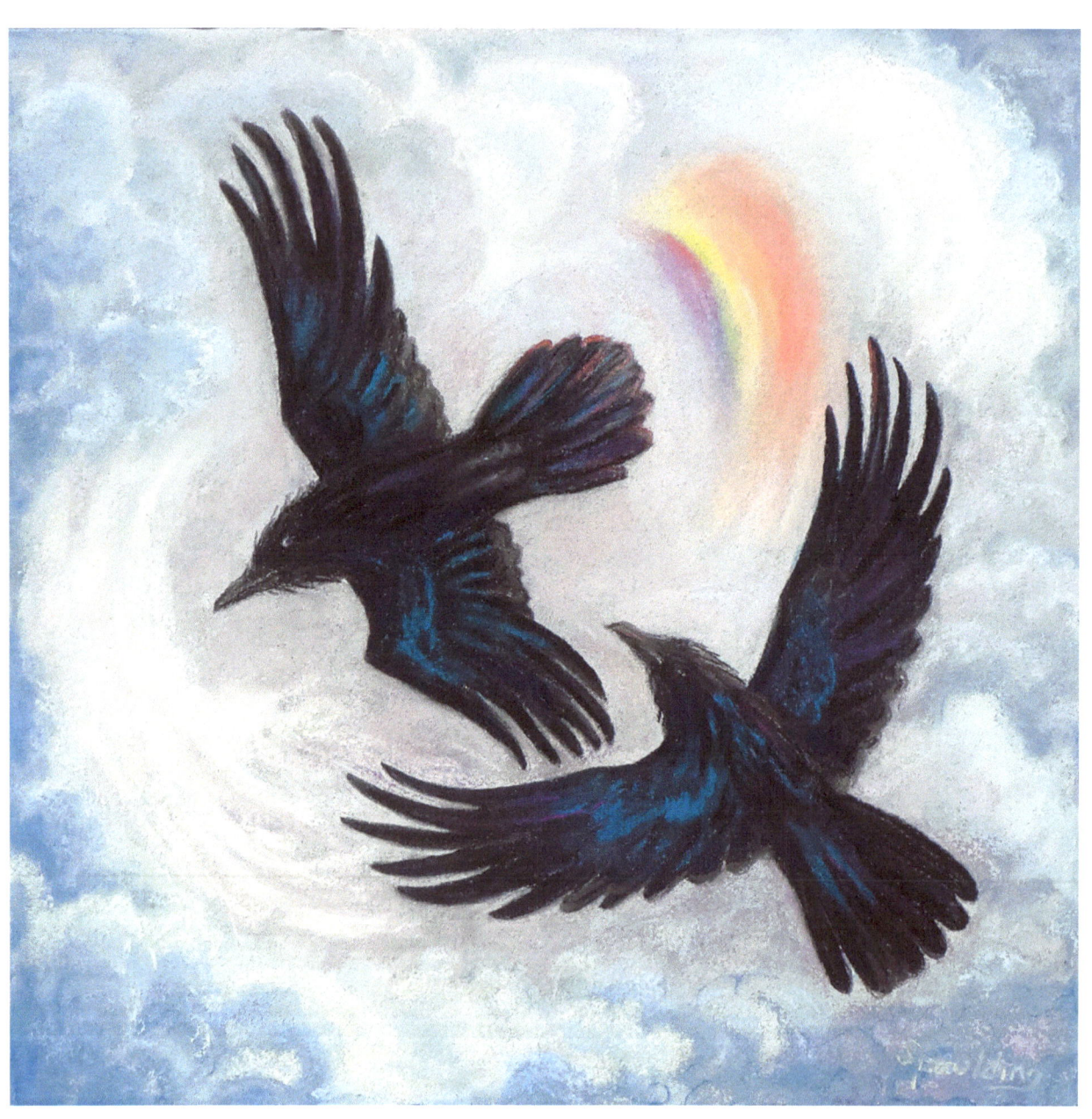

Ravens With Sundog

SIX

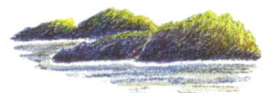

Embracing Chaos: Our Early Island Years
1979-1981

By the time we got to April, I thought everything would be so much easier. It wasn't. I struggled to keep warm in the studio as I worked on new silkscreen prints. Days continued to be damp and chilly. Our little stove heated the front of the studio but our print room required ventilation as it was a little too far from the stove to get the benefit of its warmth.

Working outdoors was a continual slog. Putting a shake roof on the dome required a big learning curve. It seemed to be taking forever. The roof of the dome included its walls, making the area we needed to cover enormous. Not only that, each pentagon or hexagon had to be finished as an entity in itself with a hip along each edge to avoid future leaks from one tilting surface to the next. Fitting the shakes to the unconventional shapes involved custom cutting for almost every piece.

I carried shakes up the ladder to Lewis, where he would measure and mark them. I took the marked shakes back down and made the cut on the radial arm saw and then delivered them back to Lewis. "Just call me Grover" I said, thinking of Sesame Street, as I scurried back and forth. It was tedious work. Neither of us were moving around enough in the breezes which meant that we constantly became chilled. One day my hands were so cold I broke down and cried. We only finished one triangle on our first day of roofing. As I projected forward, the task looked hopeless. We completed two the next day and felt a faint glimmer of success.

We both had a very healthy respect for the radial arm saw. In fact I was horrified by it most of the time. We both remembered keenly my father's words "Gee, if I had a saw like that, I would attach a little tin cup on the side for my fingers when they came off." His droll humor made the point. He didn't ever need to say more than that! We were exceedingly careful.

Gradually, we got much more adept at what we were doing and moved along faster. It helped that days were getting longer and warmer too.

By May, all the shakes finally in place, except where we would put in skylights. We were finally able to shift gears, working on art as well getting outside where the first job we tackled was rabbit fencing around our new little vegetable patch.

In mid May I finished up one new image, *Curve of Beach* just as we began to get inventory ready for the University Street Fair in Seattle. I was excited to get out and see people again. I missed both the artists we had gotten to know on the circuit and customers who were so upbeat. It was our first big fair of the season and the idea of the upcoming stimulation seemed exhilarating after our long island winter. Lewis, who had been off to a number smaller shows, was not quite so eager.

We had arranged for Laurie and Heather to stay with our next door neighbors whom we had gotten to know quite well. Besides being a welcoming neighbor, Dodie was the school secretary. After seeing that the girls were happily situated, Lewis and I slipped away with our load of art taking a late afternoon ferry which enabled us to get to the city by early evening. We had arrangements to stay with a friend whom we hadn't seen for a couple of years and were looking forward to reconnecting. We had known her as a newspaper reporter and looked forward to catching up with her and her new life.

We found her apartment easily, not too far from University Avenue. She lived upstairs on the fourth floor. As we visited over dinner, I happened to look out the window and noticed how the street below was roiling with Friday night activity. We watched from above and wondered if our VW bus and its load of art would be safe over night. Liz offered us another glass of wine and we began to laugh at the likelihood of kids breaking in and hauling off heavy boxes of silkscreened contraband. Who in the world would want it? More than likely, we realized, we had been away from city life so long we had become a bit paranoid.

We spent two busy days on the Avenue. As I had remembered in years past, the fair was a mad frenzy, crowds working their way down the street celebrating the first warm weather of the year. We were entertained by an array of characters manifesting a broad cross section of cultures and dress, as well as some rowdy souls best kept to a distance. We were not disappointed in who we saw by the way of friends and collectors and made new contacts as well. So much stimulation worked in my favor and my mood was high.

When the show closed on Sunday we disentangled ourselves from the fair as quickly as possible, joining the ranks of artists, like ants on steroids, chaotically dismantling their booths and loading their vehicles with wares and gear. We were able to reach our evening ferry which we boarded in gratitude, getting home in time to find Laurie and Heather bubbling over with all the things they had done in our absence: hearing a jazz band, going to a play, and being taken on a sail! Our neighbors had gone all out. Our first time leaving them had gone well.

A few days after we got home from Seattle, the big skylight we had ordered for our dome arrived. It wasn't what we were expecting. Instead of a six sided hexagon it was a fit for one of the triangles within the hexagon. We were going to have to rethink the entire design. In the meanwhile the plastic over the large opening would have to stay there awhile longer. We shifted to another project. Wiring.

As we mulled over how to resolve the skylight situation, life went on. There was a continual flow of building life, art life and social life.

Sometimes other school moms in the community dropped by with friends of Laurie and Heather, picking them up or dropping kids off. Having children in school definitely was pulling us in to the community.

I never forgot the time, a few weeks after our arrival on the island, when Heather didn't come home on the school bus. Laurie hadn't seen her after school and didn't know what happened to her. I drove back to the school worried as could be, and asked Dodie at the office if she had any idea where Heather could possibly have gone. "There was a Brownie meeting today, I am not sure where, but I bet she went along with the other girls," Dodie nodded with a smile. Her complete lack of concern kept my alarms at bay. "They should be all going home about now though," she concluded.

Being new to the island, I wasn't sure what to do or how to connect with anybody. I began to drive around town guessing where the Brownies might have met. Sure enough, coming down Nichols street, along came a vehicle loaded with kids and a mom in the driver's seat with a smile that lit up her whole face. She seemed to intuit who I was. Heather hadn't been able to explain to her how to find her own house but up to that point was having way too much fun to care. We were all soon laughing with relief to have made the encounter! Mystery solved.

One spring day while taking a break outdoors in the sun, a raven flew over us with something in its claws which it dropped in the driveway as it continued flying on. The falling shape hit the ground and bounced. I saw that it was a baby robin which was stunned only momentarily as it quickly righted itself and ran amazingly fast on its spindly legs. It hid in a patch of brush along the edge of the road. It didn't take but a minute for both parents to arrive. In moments they were all across the road where there was a thicket of Nootka rose bushes. We left them and went back inside confident the youngster would be taken care of until it was able to take flight. Another strange episode observed!

When we had time to dig a few holes again we added a number of new apple trees to our fledgling orchard. Lewis found several varieties we had hoped to add: Chelhalis, Spartan, McCoun,, King and Yellow Transparent. Getting them started right away seemed wise.

Lewis had been working on tiles in our kitchen, finishing the counters and putting in sinks. We decided how we would complete the skylight and moved forward to install the triangle, filling in the rest of the hexagon with roof except for two smaller horizontal openings for windows below. It turned out to be a blessing. The huge opening we had envisioned would have turned our home into a hothouse.

June came and it was beautiful. Often I simply couldn't concentrate while up in my studio. A nesting pair of Bald Eagles often slipped past acting out an aerial ballet, softly calling to echo each other. Often they seemed to float, rising higher and higher, drifting with the air currents. In the east cumulus clouds billowed over Mount Baker and the Sister Peaks, stretching upward in a tower of blinding white and casting shadows of dappled grey across the far landscape. As bright as the eagles' tails in the blue sky, white sails slipped by in the channel.

There was never a lack of inspiration. Only the lack of time for creation.

Everyone was glad it was summer. One day while Lewis was gone to see what he could sell in Leavenworth at *Art In The Park*, and while Laurie was off camping with a friend, Heather and I scrubbed the floors. We still lived on plywood sub flooring. As the boards were tracked with footprints from months of work and living rough, we wanted to get them as clean as we could for the company that was soon to arrive. Two sets of friends were coming from the mainland to investigate our adventure and give a hand with the final plumbing left to finish up in the dome.

When everybody arrived a few days later our place looked a lot cleaner. It looked like a happening with three Volkswagen buses parked in our drive. The Rogers, our friends from college days, came over from Anacortes where he now taught high school science. No sooner had Hal said hello than he grabbed his plumbing tools. He and Lewis got right to work. The children headed for the field and became absorbed in building forts in the rock piles.

In the evening our friends from Missoula pulled in with their two daughters. The six children had a slumber party in the shell of the dome, giggling in the dark. Their sleeping bags were spread over the floor. There was no water, no furniture, no insulation, no power, just a wonderful big round space that comforted in the dark.

We adults all sat in the trailer where we sat late into the night, listening to the last murmurs of the kids. We talked about life, hopes, dreams, growing organic vegetables and fruits, making natural dyes and dehydrators. Then almost as an afterthought, we got down to plumbing, the job that lay ahead of us.

The next day a serious effort was made on pipes and connections though we managed to take time out for the beach. Our friends, the Lees, had brought wonderful homemade flatbread and big luscious cherries from the Okanogan Valley which we savored throughout the day.

A couple of days later, before our friends departed, we were able to turn on the water. Water, miraculous water! It filled the pipes and poured out of the faucets. Everyone got drinks and we all laughed at the wonder of it.

We had hardly caught our breaths from the lovely visit and accomplishments we had made, when we began to work on wiring. My father had left explicit directions on what we needed to do. Progressing from the work he had done on an earlier all too short summer visit, Lewis continued to string wire. I became the handyman helper. We worked sporadically as time allowed us, With six art shows scheduled during the rest of the summer we both worked on art, and filled up the rest of the dreamy long days with time in the garden and activities with kids and friends.

The first fair was on Mercer Island and as it was one of the smaller ones, we decided Lewis would go down and do it by himself. The weather had been hot and I was worried his sales might not be worthwhile. By the end of the weekend, anxious to know how it came out, I stayed up late waiting for his return. He drove in around eleven looking rather sheepish. It was still not completely dark and when I looked out at our bus in the driveway I saw there was no booth tied to the top.

It seems that in his rush to get out of town Lewis had forgotten to secure our lovely cedar panels. As he picked up speed merging into freeway traffic, the entire stack slid off onto the pavement. He immediately pulled off to the shoulder hoping to retrieve them before any traffic came along but as he stood beside the road, a large semi barreled past smashing every single panel, turning our entire booth into a stack of kindling.

After the Mercer island show we had four shows back to back: Langley, Bellevue, Anacortes, and Coupeville. Lewis had to take time out to construct another booth as well as keeping on top of matting and framing and keeping up with some new work. We were under pressure every day and the month of August flew by. Even so, we were left with good memories when summer ended, ready to settle back into our home in the field.

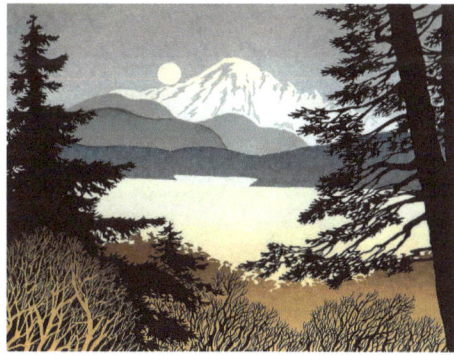

When another October came around it was hard to comprehend that we had been here a year. It was a a landmark worth celebrating. We were in high spirits thinking of all we had accomplished and baked a cake. It felt good to relax in our cozy unfinished space. I watched a pair of Marsh Hawks (Northern Harriers) coursing along our fence line, monitoring the ditches, and gliding over the apple trees. Life was good.

A few days later, electricians, Rex and John came by to put the final touches on our wiring. John, kindly and efficiently, had managed to nab the county electrical inspector who dropped in while they were finishing up. Our project was passed! With the electricity turned on, it truly was time for a celebration.

We had met Rex first at an art show in Everett. The show was so slow, all we did was hang out and get to know the other artists. Rex was selling pottery for his brother Rick, an island artist with whom we would become good friends. The brothers had grown up on the island and were a pair of jesters that had us going when we first met them both together, each pretending one was the other. Later, Rick got us involved with the Island Artisans group which had a co-op in Friday Harbor. We loved Rick's wild stories of his days growing up in the sixties when his father was the Game Warden here.

With wiring done I felt a lot more secure for winter as we finally could move forward installing the insulation. As I felt a lot more relaxed. I began to allow myself more studio days and finished several silkscreen prints that fall, including *Beach Logs*.

By Thanksgiving the inside of our dome looked like the interior of a silver ball bearing with the insulation finally done, but no wall or ceiling covering it. We were surrounded by silver foil, but we were going to be warm!

One day an old truck rattled in and a couple of gangly characters hopped out. They were dressed as though from another era, like people from a Dicken's novel. Quixotic with angular faces, they had noticed we still had a number of rabbit warrens on our place. They were licensed falconers from over east of the mountains, and wondered if they could try hunting on our land with their ferret and hawk.

In the past I had turned away hunters with guns as I didn't want shooting so close to our house, but this was intriguing. Even though the girls caught baby bunnies for pets from time to time, we were living close enough to the rabbits to know how often they were taken as prey. There was a huge population of rabbits on the island.

We agreed. The fellows went to their truck. One of them brought out a beautiful red tailed hawk wearing a hood. The other man had a mailbox. When he opened the door of the box, out came a long, lean and furry ferret. They explained that when the ferret was freed to weasel down the rabbit holes, the hawk would be released to catch rabbits that would come out on the run. It sounded like there would be a lot of action.

The ferret went down the hole and disappeared. We waited. The hawk flew up to the top of the electric pole on the other side of the road and it waited. The afternoon wore on and when two or more hours had passed, the two men decided to give up the effort and to round up their creatures. "The ferret is old," they explained and probably decided to take a nap down the rabbit hole.

It took a while to coax the hawk to fly down from the pole, which was eventually accomplished by holding a chunk of raw hamburger in a gloved hand. The hawk took its time looking over the terrain from its high perch at the top of the pole. When he finally decided he was ready to come down, he came with a flourish of broad wings and russet tail. After his hamburger snack, on went the hood over piercing yellow eyes. He complacently went back to the truck on the arm of his owner.

It took longer to wake up the ferret, but eventually it came out, sleepy eyed, and slipped into its mailbox den. Before the truck pulled out and away, we were given a big crate of apples from their eastern Washington farm. We enjoyed the apples for weeks.

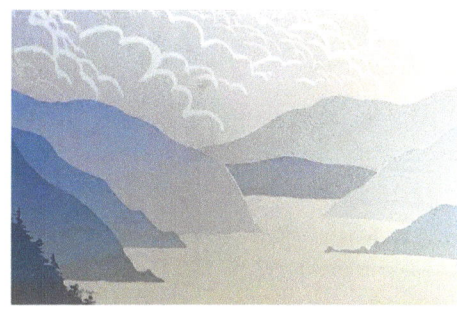

The winter passed more easily than our first year on the island, as we had less physical stress from building and being out in the elements. We were able to do more work on the creative side. However by March our savings were all but depleted. Lewis applied for an early spring show east of the mountains in hopes of getting us through. We had to order picture frames to get inventory ready to sell at the show and to our dismay it arrived C.O.D., wiping out the last of our funds.

When Lewis pulled out of the driveway he had barely enough cash for the gas needed to get to his destination. He had left me a twenty dollar bill in case we needed anything before his return. I was quite forlorn as he disappeared, wondering when I would see him again. With no cell phones and no credit cards back then, isolation felt much more real.

Several days later, Lewis showed up with enough cash to keep us going for a couple more months. It was some kind of miracle. We could breath easily again for awhile.

In May, 1980, we once again began the big show season with the University Street Fair. Saturday, the first day of the show, we had a splendid day. So many people were out and about, parading around in summer garb and buying up and down the street like fish on a feeding frenzy. We were feeling high being in the midst of it all.

On Sunday morning we celebrated with a breakfast at Julia's, a little bistro along Lake Union that served huge platters of scrambled eggs and tall glasses of freshly squeezed orange juice. Feeling energized for a busy day ahead, we headed back to our booth on the avenue feeling lucky that sunny warm weather was again forecast. By ten A.M., as the fair was opening, a vibrant crowd was already out enjoying the morning.

Only moments later though the spell was broken. News rippled up the street that brought everything to a stand still. Mount Saint Helens had erupted.

In those days before the digital era, communication was not so instant. Officials came walking up the street with megaphones telling the crowd to disperse, go home, especially if you were south of the city as I-5 could be closed at any time. All thoughts were turned to the mountain. What had happened, what was still happening and how best to get out of the city.

Mount Rainier had blocked the sound of the eruption for those in downtown Seattle, so we missed it. Just a little farther west unblocked by the mountain, the sound traveled up the Puget Sound basin. In the San Juan Islands many heard the sound of a big bang. When we finally got home our neighbor told us that the sound was so loud his first thought was that perhaps a big truck had careened into his garage.

Island life drifted along in a gentle rhythm, and we adjusted to it. In the off season the solitude was good. We watched the seasons come and go. We noted beauty when it appeared, bounty when it was given, lean times when they came and always held doggedly onto the idea that we could make the dream work.

A March moon was full on the spring equinox. My mother, who kept track of all things celestial, reminded me that this would not happen again for one hundred years. Frog choruses were so loud, the clammer pulled me into the bright nights to witness. The damp earth smelled sweet with new life.

We came to know an old time islander named Gareth who insisted in taking us to meet a couple she thought we should know. They had arrived on the island about the same time we had and were in the midst of starting a restaurant business in town called the Cannery House Restaurant. We were delighted to meet Frank and Susan and frequented their sandwich shop often. Frank asked us to hang our serigraphs (silkscreen prints) on the walls. That was the beginning of a long friend and business relationship.

In the spring of 1981, I mentioned to Frank how much I wanted to get out and see Yellow Island which was recently purchased by the Nature Conservancy, and to go hopefully when spring flowers were in bloom.

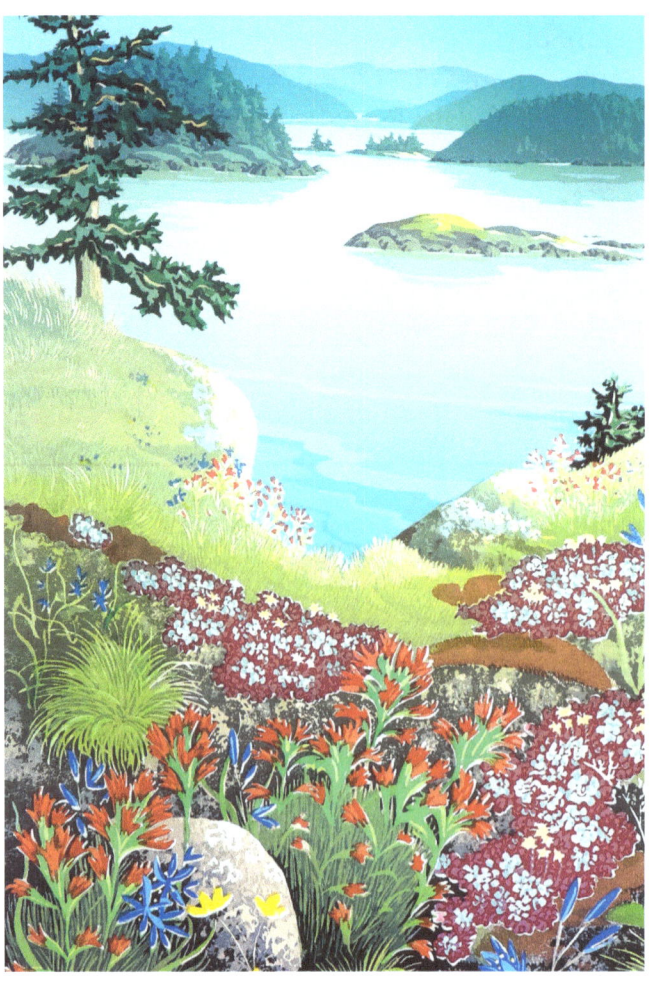

The next thing I knew he had arranged a trip. It turned out that he knew a fellow who had been a caretaker on Yellow Island when it was owned by the Dodd family who originally homesteaded there. Hal, not to be confused with our friend from Anacortes, was anxious to have a chance to get out to visit Yellow Island again.

Hal lived on a 1938 antique wooden boat that he had restored and kept anchored in the harbor. The boat's name was the *Gateless Gate*.

We met downtown at the Cannery House early one morning in the beginning of May. Frank gave us steaming cups of hot coffee while he packed up the lunch provisions, packages of the restaurants specialty sandwiches: The Lopez, The San Juan, The Orcas, and

The Shaw all which he made special on huge hoagie rolls. When ready, we headed down to the docks and boarded the *Gateless Gate*, filling the cozy cabin to the brim, five of us around a little wood stove, complete with steaming kettle.

It was an overcast morning, typical for early spring. The waters of the harbor and outer passage were a perfect mirror for the soft grey clouds and green treed shorelines. It took less than an hour to make our way up the channel and cross the opening of Wasp Pass where we anchored off Yellow Island.

Once on the island, Hal showed us the original homesteading cabin, tiny, snuggled into the rocks with ceilings so low it looked to be built for hobbits. It is where caretakers still stay and where he once lived.

We roamed the paths that circumnavigated the small eleven acre island, through lush meadows of flowers. As the sun came out the brilliance of color was remarkable to behold. Rufous Hummingbirds and bumblebees darted about in happy profusion. Primary colors of yellow, blue and red shimmered in the otherwise world of subdued greens, blacks and silvers. The tiny trails were barely discernible in places where masses of Camas Lilies, Indian Paintbrush, Western Buttercups and Field Chickweed grew tall, until the way opened out to rock faces covered with lichens and stonecrops, blooming. I have rarely ever seen such dense patches of flowers unless perhaps on hikes through alpine meadows.

The day was a trip to paradise and my head was filled with beautiful images, beauty that would sustain me for a very long time.

With Ordinary Talent and Extraordinary Perseverance
All Things Are Attainable.

—Thomas Fowell Buxton

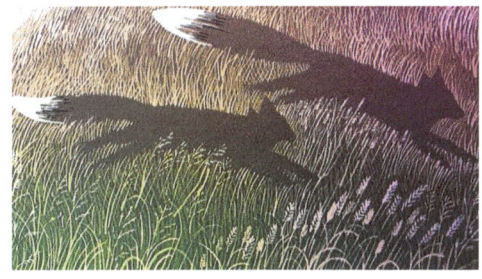

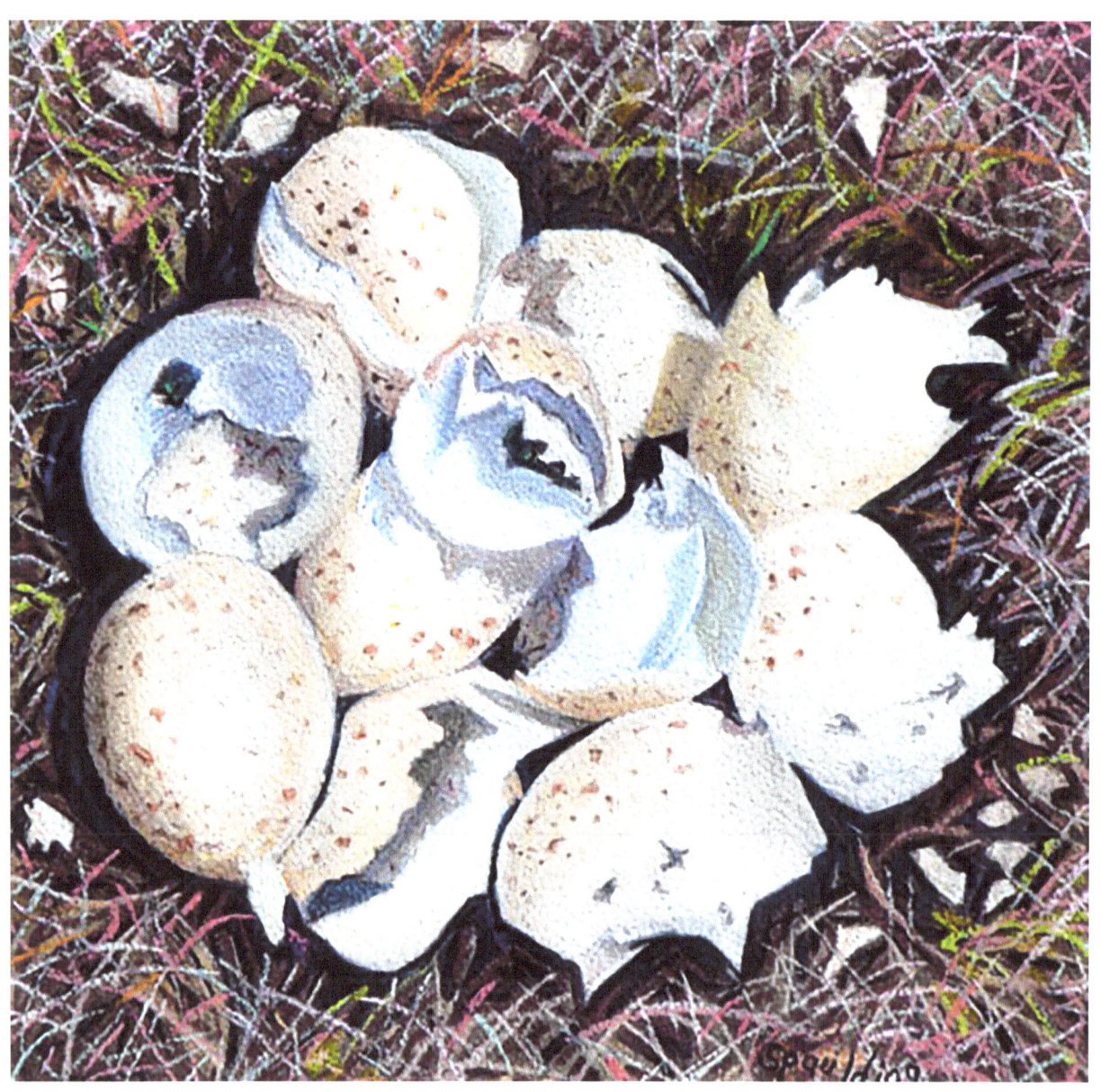

The Ragged Edges of Life

Seven

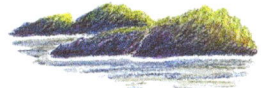

The Quail Diaries

May 2016 came with an abundance unrivaled. The garden was a full month ahead. Due to an unusually mild, wet winter, shrubs had become massive, outgrowing their spaces and laden with bloom. Lilacs were weeks ahead of schedule, and roses were covered with buds and flowers, early and profuse. Perennial and biennial flowers were ahead of schedule. Dame's Rocket, Hesperis matronalis, had self sown throughout the beds creating drifts of white, magenta and lilac, in some places over six feet tall. Annuals too. Lush California poppy plants unfurled their orange petals like prayer flags scattered amid the rockery.

I never seem to weed out enough of the volunteers to leave well behaved patches of color. I always underestimate what a seedling is capable of. Once again my garden burst forth with exuberance gone wild, this year even more exaggerated.

I parted through a patch of blooming Rocket to see if I could find the place where we had planned to plant dahlias. Several large swallowtail butterflies floated above the blossoms as though they were part of the breeze. Through the white and magenta flowers I could see the draping canes of the old Gallica rose, with deep scarlet blossoms bent all the way to the ground. The fate of the dahlias was left for the time being.

Such abundance made me nervous as though we were headed for the last hurrah. A long hot summer could be sinister. A beautiful day such as this was not to be burdened with worry, so in spite of my musings, I went out to immerse myself in its glory.

While lost in the flowers, I heard the quail calling "Ca coo couuu", "ca couuu" or just an abbreviated "couuu". Their call was clear and intended, not to be confused with the soft cooing of the Eurasian Collared Doves which emanated simultaneously from the firs just north of the vegetable beds. One quail called from across the orchard and another answered from the nearby blackberry patch.

We had been watching the quail all winter. The large covey they were then, have paired off. Two pairs remained nearby. Sometimes all four came to the feeder together, sometimes one pair at a time.

As May days went by, I often found the quail in the vegetable garden when I went out to water or weed. In a flurry of clucking they would scurry off disappearing into the raspberry rows and then over the fence. They liked the paths we had created between the raised beds where they loved to take dust baths in the loose, newly weeded soil. Little round depressions in the dirt revealed their recent activity.

It soon became apparent that I needed to put row covers over my raised beds as seeds began to germinate. The quail liked the soil in the tended beds too and could wipe out a new row of tiny beets or chard in seconds, all for the sake of a dust bath.

California Quail, the species we have here in the islands, are native to all the Pacific coast states from British Columbia to the tip of Baja, California. They can also be found in the Great Basin area of the interior. It seems they were introduced to the islands as game birds in the early 1900s and have successfully adapted to the area.

Our quail are a bluish to brownish grey bird depending on gender. Both the male and female are ornately scalloped and barred, though patterns on the male are much bolder. Adults are about ten inches long which is the same as an American Robin, though they are stouter and seem much larger in the landscape. The jaunty topknot worn by both sexes adds to their stature. The male sports a larger, blacker feathertop that often tips forward over his eyes. Their outsized feet, perfected for scratching the surface as they forage, also makes them appear larger. These large feet and stout legs enable them to cover the ground quickly. Generally, quail tend to walk or run overground, rather than fly. When moving quickly they appear quite upright, reminding me of animated bowling pins, necks elongated and heads held high. I presume the posture gives them the best line of vision over the terrain they are crossing.

Alarmed quail will fly for short distances. If you are the cause or are nearby when some danger alerts them, the sudden burst of whirring wings is as startling as a gunshot. I have been surprised more than once. Young birds, with what appear to be unsuitably stubby wings, can take to the air when necessary.

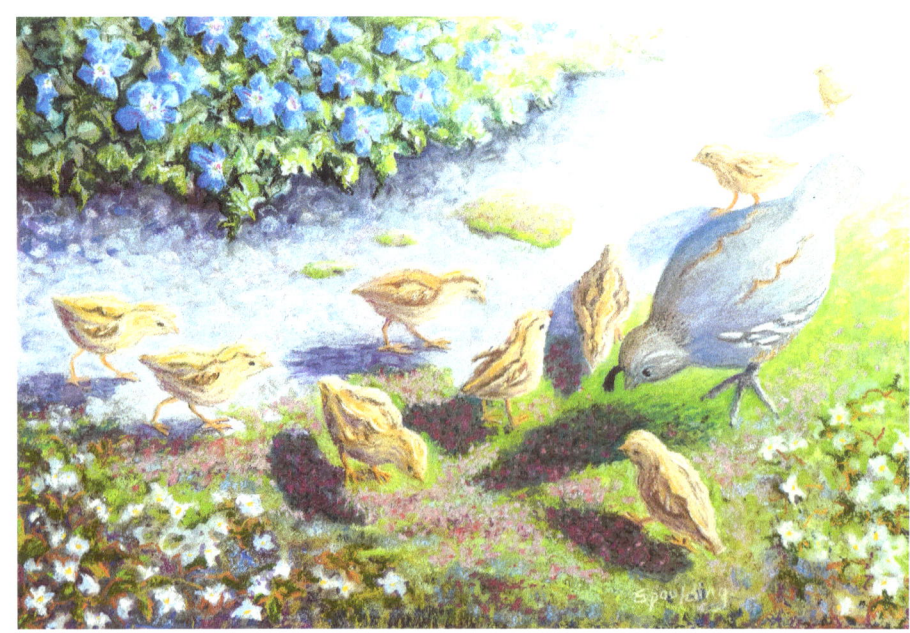

The first time I noticed a quail family in the garden was the same year our long lived cat had passed on and our beloved German Shepherd, Bridget, was in her fourteenth year, sleeping away her days.

I happened to be looking out the window at just the right moment as a quail pair worked their way up the pebble path. The male flew up to the top of the fence and watched alertly. The little hen continued on, picking at bits and pieces along the hardy geraniums that lined the walk. Then I noticed what I had missed at first. She was surrounded by little puffballs, flowing out from her sides in all directions and returning to her as though by some magnetic force. The haphazard group made its way up into the grass garden and meandered across the creeping thyme which was covered at that moment with soft pink blossoms. Up and over went the tiny legs, following their mother, scratching all the way, imitating her every move.

We saw the family several times that summer before they disappeared into nearby thickets. We wondered how they were doing as the season moved along. The survival rate for chicks is not high. What tactics for survival would this pair put to use? Might we see them again?

After several months I had doubts. Fox, hawks, and feral cats all hunted around the neighborhood. When a parade of eight adult quail showed up in the rock garden in November, I was delighted. Observing them and keeping track of what I saw became a focus of mine for several following years. We began taking inventory when they appeared. That fall there were five females and three males in a little covey. They took a leave of absence in early December and then surprised us by returning at Christmas with the addition of two more males.

We watched the little band frequently over the winter. By March their relaxed ways changed as the males became aggressive and sparred with each other for dominance. The females generally were oblivious. You could see that pairing had begun, and eventually all of them dispersed except for one male and his mate. We saw them often as they foraged, and on many afternoons we saw them perching together on our "peony gate" below the rock garden. Lewis had constructed the gate from copper pipe and recycled glass squares, luminescent in the sunlight. Throughout the spring, the two quail looked at home there and we began to hope they would nest nearby.

The Year of Proud Papa

One day in late spring as I walked across the deck from our house to the studio, I noticed a male quail crouched down among the stepping stones leading to the brick walk. He was so flattened he looked like a puddle of feathers. I gazed down at him with curious concern when it became apparent that he was protecting a jumble of very tiny chicks. Aware of my scrutiny, he made a sudden dash for the nearby hellebore. The chicks swept along with him as though part of his same motion. I assumed the female was somewhere in the understory of the flower bed.

As the days played out it became apparent that the male was on his own and in charge of the lot of them. No hen ever appeared. We kept an eye out for the group, anxious for their well being. A few weeks passed with no sign of them. I began to doubt we would see them again. Then like the brightness of summer solstice, they all appeared, a perfect celebratory note for the longest day.

Full of purpose, top knot aloft, the male came proudly across the lower lawn with his charges behind him. They moved into the border along the stone wall and then up into the rock garden, the line of chicks sliding effortlessly behind him. We counted eleven. They had grown!

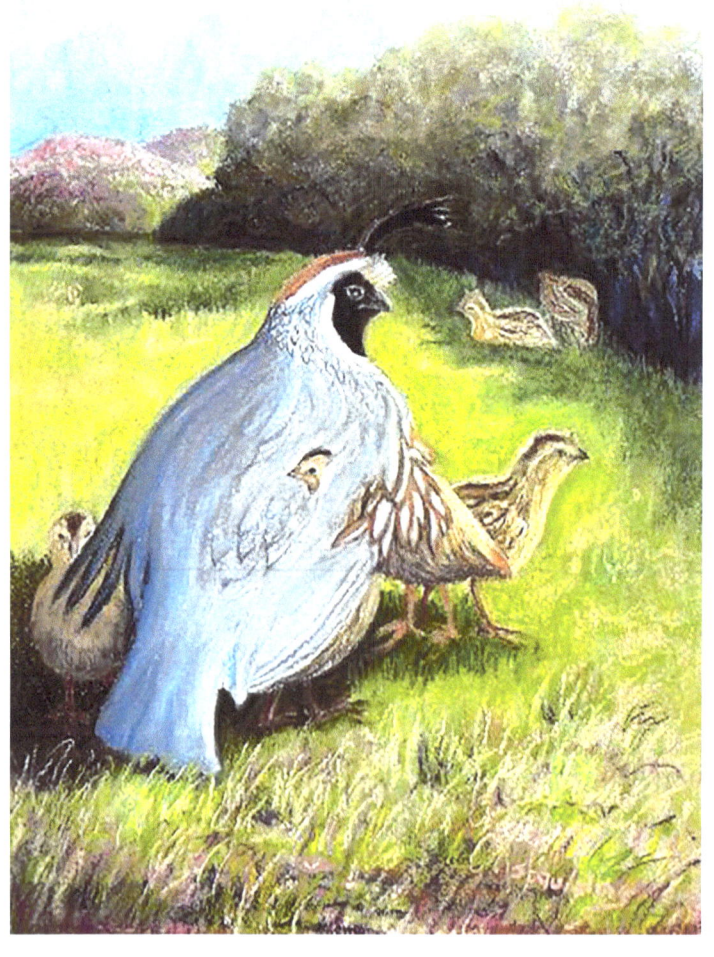

The brood stayed in the upper part of the garden for a couple of hours, following "papa", exploring nooks and crannies, and napping in the grass. After awhile they circled back down the brick walk to the potting shed and lower lawn, eventually disappearing under the rose hedge. Just by chance we saw him again in late afternoon leading all eleven down past the hop arbor and back toward the blackberry thickets. His devotion to his little crew was most apparent.

As I watched him that summer, I often wondered if this male was one of the pair that I had photographed so many times in spring as they sat on the peony gate in late light, overlapping tails, gilded in the sun. What had happened, I wondered, in the world of quail? What dramas had played out in the thickets? Life, death, and most assuredly, eggs.

In the world of a garden the mysteries are many. As life flowed on, every second, every minute, every day in the garden, I witnessed fleeting moments, and attempted to weave together the day book of quail with the snippets I collected.

A second pair of quail showed up that summer that didn't seem to have young. One day I came upon papa with his family where I was working. Startled, all the chicks dispersed through the open door of the potting shed and scattered amongst the pots, bags of garden soil, and in and out of the leaning jumble of rakes and shovels. I knew the chicks had an escape route under the siding where there was a large gap between the wall and the ground. I did back off just the same, and resumed weeding farther off behind the Damask rose, Madame Hardy.

I thought I was the cause of all the chaos but then I noticed "Papa" approached the shed door looking upward, protesting loudly with a new vocalization I hadn't heard before. "P'toooo P'tooooo" he hissed. The sound was something between a spit and a sneeze. I understood it to be a warning. On the potting shed roof was the other pair of quail. Their sturdy legs grasped the edge and topknots dangled as they peered downward.

After so much excitement things quieted down on the quail front for a number of days, but eventually the family appeared again. Some days we would see the group and count seven or eight chicks, thinking their numbers were diminishing. Later we would see them and there would be eleven again. Head counts didn't seem to tell the whole story.

The living room window seat which looked out over the rock garden was the perfect place to observe the little family. They often gathered right under the window and sought cover under the shrubs planted there. We could see a lot of activity without their knowing we were there. We marveled at how they always seemed connected in some mysterious way, leaving all at once, deciding to rest at the same time, or choosing a direction to explore all in accord. How did they communicate and keep track of each other? It did seem true that sometimes some weren't along for the outing, perhaps choosing to hang out in the deeper thickets as they were gaining independence.

Because they came so regularly we saw the transformation from tiny balls of fluff to adolescence. By the second week the little top knots appeared, tiny indications of upright feathers soon to accentuate their heads. Gradually the feathers became more pronounced, as did the pin feathers emerging, marking the growth of wings and tails and changing the patterns from their baby plumage to something more bold. Their shape changed from adorable to rather gawky and awkward. Meanwhile they hung together and Papa was as proud and attentive as ever.

Sometimes they spent time in the garden in the rain, taking shelter under the roses. They were getting more adventurous too, and sometimes appeared from the west side of the house entering the front gate and walking across the deck to reach the garden. They seemed to try out flying more, perhaps to strengthen their wings. One day when they were about two thirds the size of an adult they flew up on the roof of the dome, walked over the top and then dropped down into the garden to their usual grassy resting spot.

The male showed up with only three youngsters in late August. We wondered if these were the only ones left, but also noticed how independent they were all becoming. We didn't see any of them for awhile. They could have gone into hiding as I had been noticing more hawks and fox recently.

One morning I noticed a spot of blood where the quail and other ground loving birds liked to scratch for seed. That did not bode well. After that it was a week or more before we saw any sign of quail. We never saw proud papa again. Three of the adolescents came and checked out the feeder for awhile. The last day I saw any quail that summer, there was only one large, gawky adolescent. It sat on the roof over the window seat, lingering for awhile, and then flew off into the brush.

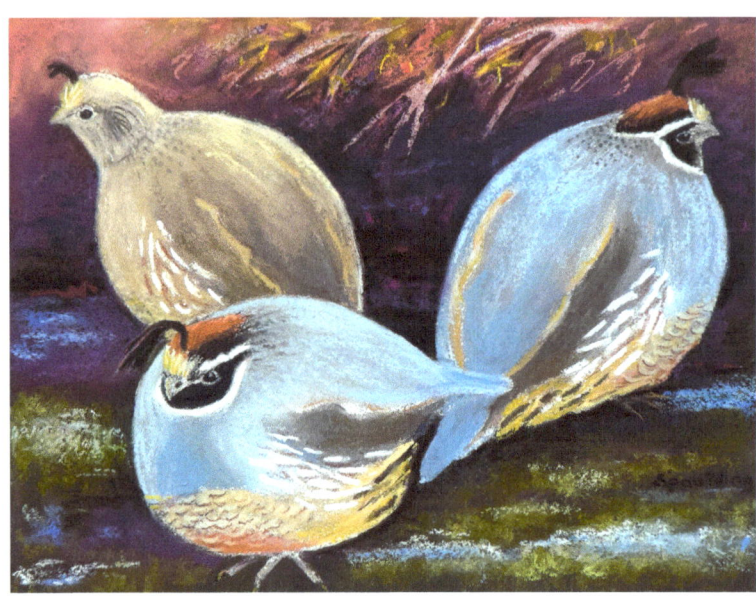

One December day the following fall I noticed what appeared to be a few extra round river rocks tucked up under the Elves' Home Spiraea. A friend had brought us rocks from a mountain stream to incorporate into the rock garden. I had never put any there. The dark, frosty shapes began to shift in the dim light. I realized they were bird forms. The quail had come back.

It seemed only obvious to me that these were "our" quail. With the possibility of living seven years in the best of circumstances, I wondered if these quail were older adults from previous years or the chicks we had seen in the summer, now mature. Whichever, by their behavior they seemed very familiar with our place and its favored nooks to hang out in.

Watching their behaviors became addictive as I became more and more aware of the subtle differences in individual behaviors as well as the overall patterns that made every year different from the one before.

Year of An Uncle and a Banished Hen

The little covey grew by several individuals over winter and as usual by February the males became competitive and aggressive. When things worked themselves out, they all integrated into the landscape once again. We didn't see them much until late spring.

In June we had visits from a pair accompanied by a tagalong male. He tried to be part of the twosome but was kept at a distance Eventually when chicks had fledged and were brought into the rock garden, the extra male was allowed to browse nearby. He often kept watch from high shrubs. They all seemed to be congenial wherever they went.

When the chicks were half grown, one of the males began to pursue the hen with a randy behavior that seemed out of place for the season. Though unusual, quail can have a second clutch in a year where conditions are promising. Quail are monogamous and mate for life. I really didn't know what was going on. The female disappeared. We didn't see her for weeks.

To my amazement, when the hen reappeared, up the stone steps she came with a line of twelve hatchlings behind her.

How had she done this all by herself? As she approached the other quail in the rock garden, both males ran at her aggressively shooing her off. I didn't expect that and it was sad to see. She made a quick retreat and as far as I know she didn't come into the garden again all summer. While walking in our lower field some time later I did run across a lone female with a few offsprings following her along the fence line. Was she the refugee banned from the garden? If so she must have found some haven among the dappled leaves and underbrush to raise her brood on her own.

The season ended once again with the knowledge that if anything, every year is different and that the relationships between individuals of a very different species than our own, seem just as complicated and unpredictable as in any human saga.

Year of Multiple Families All Around The Garden

In the winter that followed we had many quail in the garden again. It was unseasonably warm as we never had a killing frost all year. I often ran into a large covey in the vegetable garden as I took my morning walk. They seemed to like browsing on green shoots that were poking up especially in the tomato house, the little shelter with cover that we built with the hope of ripening more fruit in our mild but damp northwest maritime climate.

Then another change of season and it was that glorious spring when everything seemed to grow out of bounds. It was a happy year for the garden and the quail. We had several families in our midst. One pair nested beneath a Tall Oregon grape, Mahonia aquifolium, that had become too large and dense beside the tomato house. The nest was impossible to detect from any angle. As prickly leaves invaded the garden space one afternoon we decided to cut it back. As the pruning blades got too close for her comfort, the quail darted forth in a loud burst nearly knocking us off our feet. I felt apologetic after that and pruning was abandoned until a later time. She stayed in that spot a few days longer but then moved on, I presume, when all eggs were hatched.

One group came from the west side of the house where pines and snowberry provided cover from the county road. Another family came up from below the orchard and yet another from the blackberry patch which seemed their more usual haunt.

Often quail were on the deck poking about the planter pots, walking across the beams overhead, crossing the curvature of the dome, or lazing about in their usual spots. While in the garden working or resting I could hear them clucking just a few feet away, though

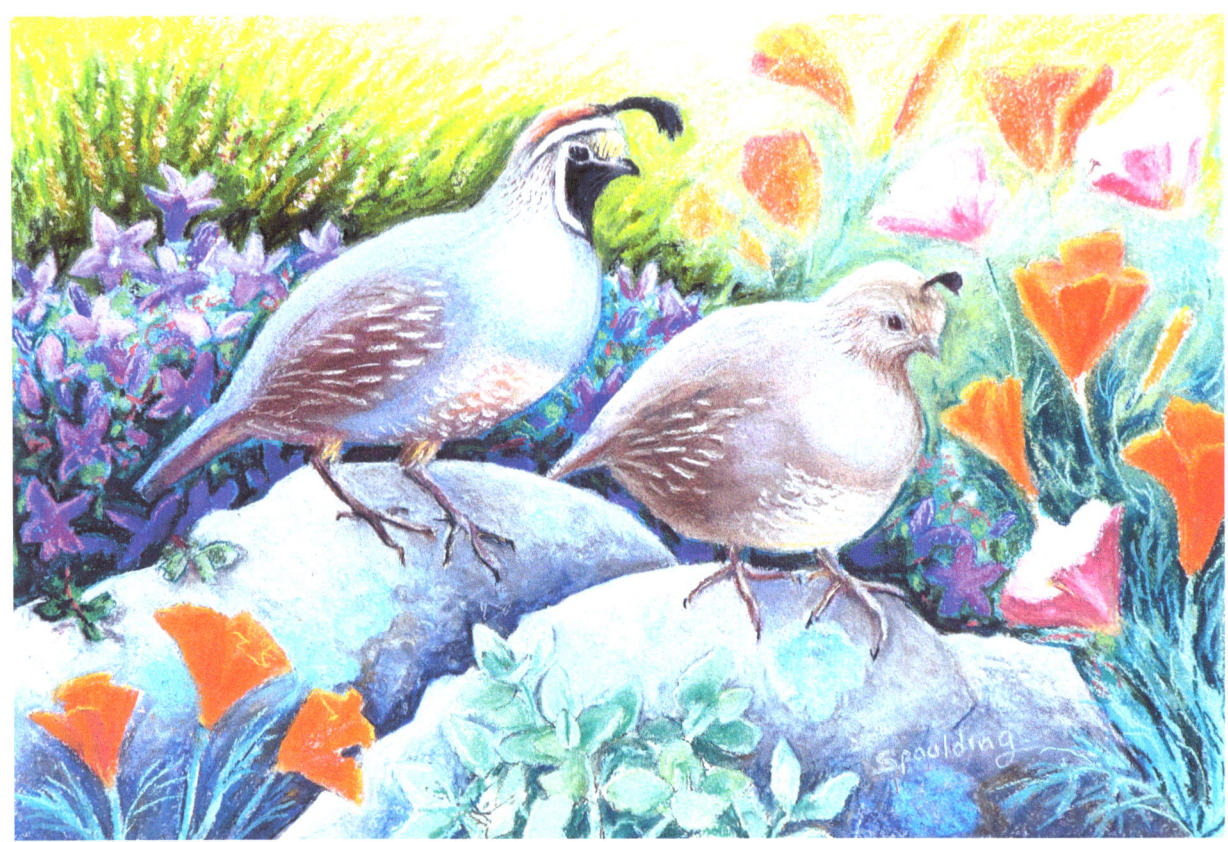

keeping out of sight. One group walked right over Lewis' shoe while he was standing on the deck in order to take a drink from a plant dish filled with water. Many were the dustbowls in the garden and the vocalizations all around. There was also a general acceptance of our comings and goings.

We watched the families with delight but only sporadically as summer went on. Pressing family matters began to dominate our lives. It became necessary for Lewis and me to be away for an extended period of time by summers end.

Year of Liberated Mama Quail

In 2017 I had thought to put my focus elsewhere, but the new season had begun with new developments. Quail were going to capture my attention after all. Breeding season started off with a bang as a pair came up the walk that May with thirteen chicks in tow. It was the largest family we had counted thus far. We were anxious to keep track of them. They disappeared though and that was that. Two weeks later a pair came with two chicks, but so young looking we decided they couldn't have been what was left of the first group we had observed. Then they seemed to evaporate into the ether as well.

In June a pair came up to the rock garden with eight little puffballs scurrying along, as though on invisible wheels, keeping pace over rock and heathers with their fast moving parents. Their visits continued on a daily basis.

Days and weeks seemed to pass and we were able to watch the eight go through all the little changes in growth as well as endearing behaviors when they rested together in the shadows, snuggled into each other's fluff or sometimes under the wings or within the feathers of their parents.

At about the time the chicks were half grown, another male showed up. This time there was no sense of rivalry and everyone got along so well it was hard to know after awhile which was the original male. All the adults pitched in to watch out for the youngsters.

Something else very interesting happened as the chicks grew larger. The female began to take on the role as chief guardian of the group. In the mornings when we came downstairs we would look out the window and there she would be on the top of the obelisk where generally a male would be on guard. Chicks and the two males browsed below. By late July the pattern continued. Sometimes we would see the female on the birdbath, sometimes with the thin spray of water from the solar fountain dripping over her back. The rest of the group foraged in the flowers below.

In July, Lewis made a discovery. He had decided to attend to the tall grass in the orchard that had been an aggravation to him. He had been unable to mow because of several piles of branches that we had never properly disposed of after pruning in early spring. As he cleaned up and carried away the heap, under the last of the pile was a circle of beautifully hatched out quail eggs clustered within a shallow indent in the grass. The chards of creamy white, speckled with copper and gold, sparkled in the sun. Inside each shell fragment the concave surfaces gleamed like white porcelain. I had passed within feet of that hidden nest every day on my morning walk, never suspecting a quail lay incubating, secretly and silently, her beautiful eggs.

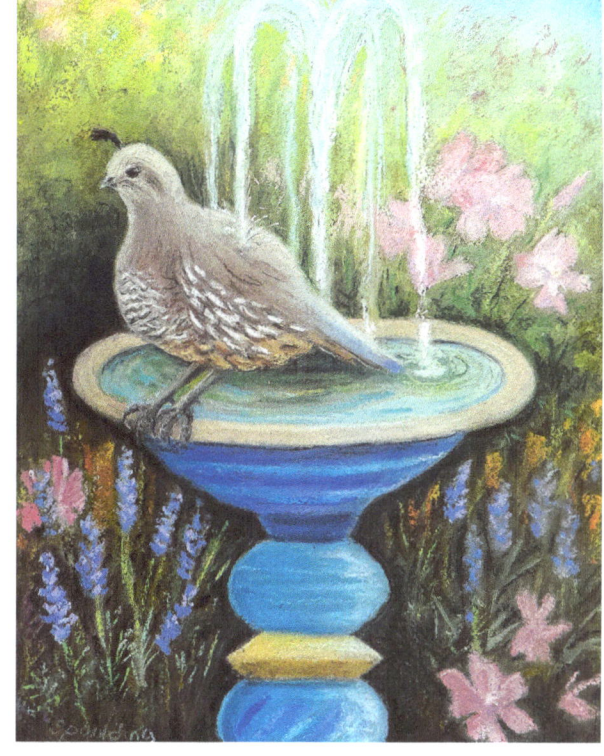

I was grateful that Lewis' urge to tidy up was delayed until after the family had moved on. It made us both realize that our habit of leaving brush piles around the edges of our property in hidden places, was in fact providing shelter for wildlife. That we had left apple tree branches lying in the orchard grass in a well trafficked area proved that if there is cover, one creature or another will use it.

In August the family came less frequently though they continued to make short visits to the rock garden. One late afternoon we quit work early and took a tray of refreshments down to the vegetable garden where the new blue wheeled bench Lewis had built lay waiting in partial shade. It was quiet and we looked out over the garden toward the east where the new moon's pearly crescent appeared in the blue. The garden smelled divine with the sweetness of ripening peaches and tomatoes. We fell into silence.

I felt Lewis tapping gently on my arm and turned to see him pointing toward the potting shed. There came the quail mama leading the band. The others were just rounding the corner behind her. She came to a stop when she saw us on the bench. For a long time she just stood there not moving as we too stayed motionless.

At length she stepped back into the cover of the Banchee Rose by the hop arbor. We waited. Several minutes later she came out again with a confident stride toward us which she kept up until reaching the aisle between the raised beds. There she turned in and was momentarily out of sight. The two males followed her and behind them paraded the line of all eight juveniles. They streamed up over the raised beds and into the raspberry canes where they all disappeared as a clucking mass, then into the blackberries beyond the fence.

I smiled. This year's pattern was enlightening with yet new perspectives into the life of quail. The little lady who became leader of her clan will always remain in my memory. I will remember her alertness and her confidence. I will wonder what it all means. It was a grand summer to be among the quail families of our neighborhood. Once again. I saw individual personalities emerge. Every year they have proven themselves to be completely unpredictable in the way they conduct their lives, within the parameters of "quailness", of course.

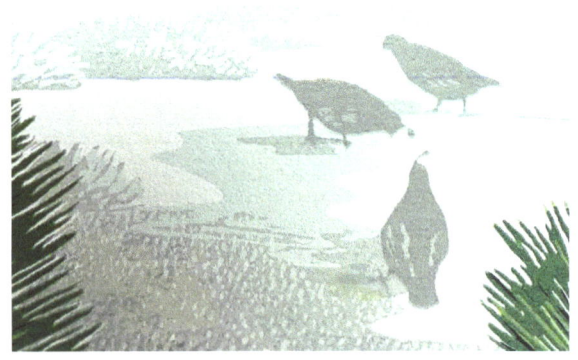

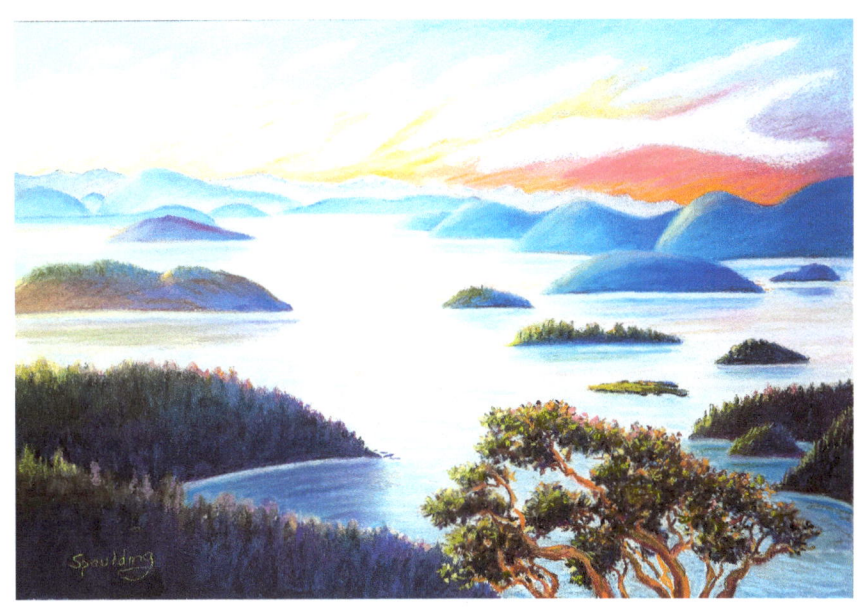

*When you have seen one ant, one bird, one tree,
you have not seen them all.*

—E.O. Wilson

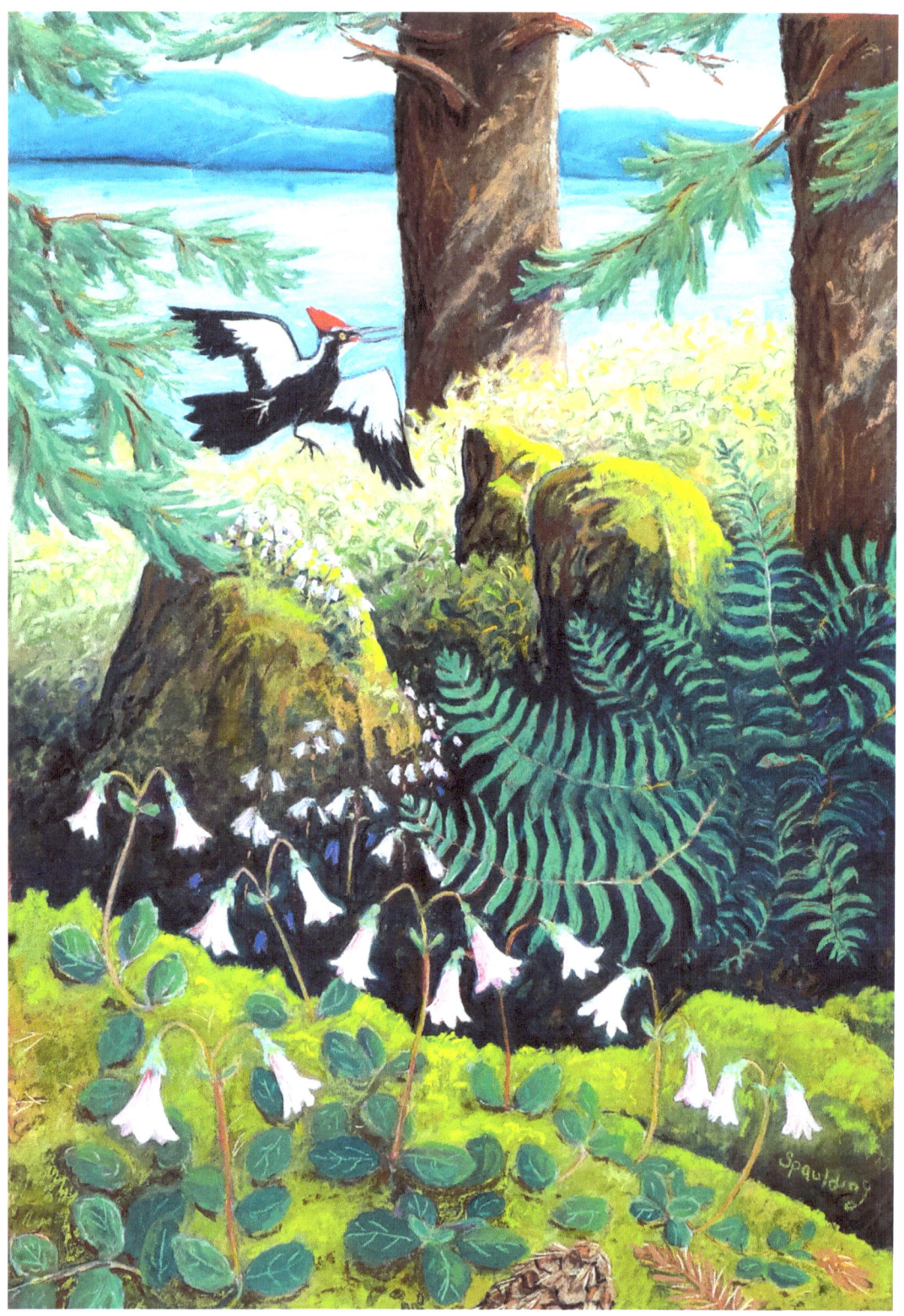

Trailing Twin Flower

Eight

A Merry-Go-Round
1983-1999

It became apparent that there was a three pronged approach to survival, if our art dream was to succeed. Foremost came research and study, which in my case meant observation observation and observation. How grand to have to make a point of looking and noticing things on a daily basis wherever I should go. I thought of Carl Linnaeus' favorite quote "Omnia Mirari, Etiam Tritissima - Find wonder in all things even the most common place."

I enjoyed a little book given me by an employer who became a life friend while I was in college. She was a palynologist from New Zealand who settled in Tucson with her paleontologist husband. Their home was called *Casa Gondwana* as she was working on ancient specimens that supported theories of continental drift. My job was to make little drawings of her specimens, tiny pollen grains, which helped her with her filing system. The book she gave me was *Carl Linnaeus Travels* which told of Linnaeus's explorations in the far north of Sweden as a young man. The little book was beautifully illustrated. I found it immensely inspirational.

The second prong in our survival approach was technique. No matter how much I had learned and practiced, a larger learning curve led me forward like a carrot I could never reach. I felt I could always do better. Technique involved sweat, sometimes tears and long hours, often into the night. When there was success, the reward washed over me, a sweet euphoria that lasted me for days on end.

The third prong was finding a home for the art once created. This involved locating shops and galleries, applying to and attending shows. Fortunately opportunities often fell into our laps when we were at art festivals and fairs. We liked being approached first as neither of us were particularly fond of knocking on doors.

We had gradually learned from other artisans what festivals we should apply to. Once a door opened it always led to another. We began to find more and more places to show our work. As we moved along, I never forgot my very first show, the one that started it all.

Before moving to the island, I had met an art teacher who was soon to retire and wanted to take up pottery when she stopped teaching. She enthusiastically suggested that we get a booth at the upcoming county fair. I readily agreed. As we set up our booth, her pottery and my assortment of drawings, paintings, and little silkscreen prints, we found that we were assigned a space between cider presses and women's custom made bras. I felt the location a strange launching place for a road to success, and as my confidence dropped, I was overcome with sudden dismay.

When the fair was over days later, we had attracted some attention in spite of all. We enjoyed meeting our booth mates and the array of people going by. Our unlikely moment in the spotlight left us buoyed up and encouraged to go forward. The next year we applied to a real art fair together. Out of the barn and at a full gallop by then, it wasn't long before Lewis got caught up in the excitement with his own creative contributions.

Our first years on the island were dependent on our travel off to shows. Even though art shows led us to the mainland, having girls in school kept us connected and tied to the community. They anchored us to our new place and to our goals.

We took delight when we first attended a graduation ceremony at our town's high school. As the seniors sat in front of us, students who had attended first grade on the island were invited to stand. Then everyone who had attended second grade was invited to stand. However, if a student was gone that year, he or she was asked to sit down. Some remained standing and some sat down. The roll call continued until twelve years were accounted for. Up and down went the students. It appeared that families left and returned, sometimes more than once and sometimes for several years. New families, like us, moved into the community each year and blended into the mix. As we sat to honor the graduates, I thought that islanders were as restless as the tides.

After living on the island for several years we began to appreciate, more and more, the community we found ourselves living in. We discovered there were many who had come to make their way by whatever means they could, just as we had, often with hardships far more extreme. We enjoyed the variety of people we met: old timers, farmers, fishermen, drifters, writers, musicians and artists, scientists, entrepreneurs or adventurers. It was a stimulating mix. As unique as the people making their homes here were, so were their reasons for coming. Unconventionality was the norm and we fit in absolutely.

Winter was our primary time to be in the studio, as well as time for maintaining and managing all our projects at home. Time was our happiness, being at home with our girls and garden, our animals. Show season was intense and often uncertain but during down time we had freedom and limited means to pursue our goals. We thought we had found the recipe to success.

One spring after living on the island just a few years, we were in for a big shock. We received a rejection notice from our very best show. After participating for six years in a row, we were taking it for granted. We depended on it for about a third of our annual income.

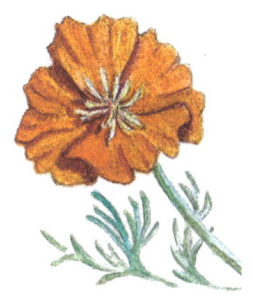

I took a long solitary walk trying to process the news. Walking and thinking, I reminded myself that nothing in life is guaranteed, that we would always need to be flexible, and that creativity was not just about making art, but about living.

As our summer went by we knew something had to change. We talked to other artists on the circuit to see what they were doing. Many were sharing a similar fate. Should we sign up for more small local shows, or travel further afield to bigger shows we wondered? The following year we decided to try every angle.

We added shows in Arizona, California and Oregon and sometimes east of the mountains, Eastern Washington, Idaho, Montana, Utah, and Colorado. Road trips were generally short and direct as we traveled with a loaded vehicle, but we made the best of our journeys. We met artists and were exposed to new arts and crafts from all around the region. Sometimes we crossed paths with artists we knew from the island or previous shows, rendezvousing in favorite eateries. We favored local pubs, pizza parlors and small cafes featuring local baked goods and produce. We shared lodging information often finding unconventional or out of the way places to spend the night. While on the road we sometimes stopped at historic or scenic landmarks, or art museums if they were along our route. It was important to pack in as many good times as possible, as gypsy like, we trundled our art over the miles.

At *Dome Home*, there always seemed to be a flowing through of family and friends from our travels, or people from our past who were curious to see what we were up to and perhaps wanted to spend a night in a pie shaped room with arching walls while sampling a bit of island life.

The best part of having company was the excuse to stop working, to show guests our favorite haunts, to share conversation around the table at night, or perhaps sitting on a log on some quiet beach.

Some people stayed. An artist we met named Skip came with his backpack tent and camped out in our garden for six weeks until he found a place to live on the island. He knew the whereabouts of the largest tree of every species in the Pacific Northwest, and told tales of hiking adventures in the high Sierra, Cascades and Alaska. He had been rolled over by a grizzly bear. He sang Donovan songs and he painted wonderful landscapes of high peaks, mastodons amid flower meadows where glaciers retreated, and looking to the stars, he painted nebulas and distant galaxies. The mysteries of the universe and life gave him a high. We felt the same.

New artists moved to the island every year. One day we had a phone call from a new arrival who was from Cornwall. She had called us with a business question for she would soon be marketing her textiles. I, who rarely talk for long on the phone, conversed for over an hour when the subject turned to roses. It turned out that she was an avid gardener and collected heirloom varieties too. We shared many favorites. She was building a garden on the island, incorporating many of her favorite English plants. When we hung up, I could hardly wait to meet her in person. When we did meet, Amanda became a rich addition to our lives and community.

So too did Melissa and Dan, she with her extraordinary metal worked insects and he with his exceptional woodworked furniture. She was a gardener also. A thread tied us all together.

As we talked with other island artists the idea of starting a studio tour on the island came up. Besides our studio featuring printmaking, that first year there were eight other studios wanting to give it a try. Melissa and Dan, Amanda, Mary a silk painter, Manya a silversmith, Thrinley a potter, Tom a sculptor, Ev a weaver and Bob a painter. Anxious to see how each other had done after the very first tour, we had an evening of sharing stories and decompressing together on a low tide beach. We discerned that we all had mostly the same guests that first year. A couple of jaunty fellows in a red Lamborghini had made it to almost every studio. We decided that in spite of our exhaustion we should keep going with the concept as it seemed to have great possibilities.

We often compared stories and shared advice and commentary with artist friends. "Why is it" we asked " that some days you would do anything but art?" avoiding like a curse that which you held as your most cherished goal. "Sometimes ideas are safer when they are kept in your mind," Rick, creator of elegant porcelain pottery declared. And yet, like gardener Mary Karen, who announced she was a digger the first time I met her, it is the process that calls us regardless of the result; shoveling dirt, throwing paint around, carving, and taking pictures, creating something no matter where it takes us. Oh to be doing things! It is a mysterious passion that drives us.

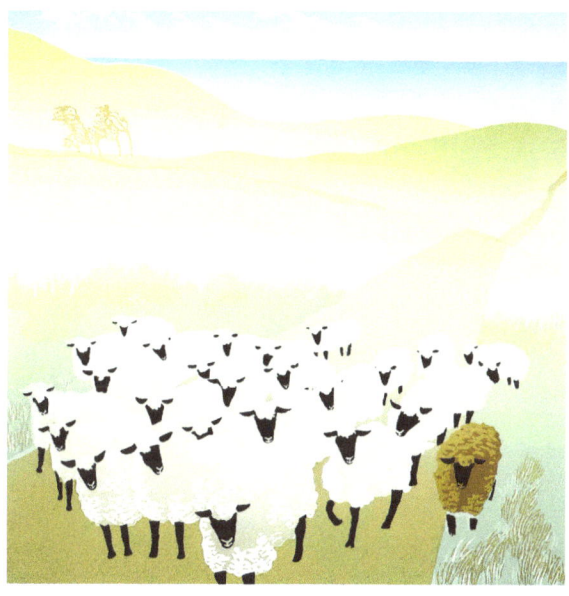

My silkscreens were becoming more and more complex. We referred to them as serigraphs, signifying that our prints were our own compositions and that we hand pulled each color separately to create limited editions. As my skill level grew and I used more color overlays to complete my work, each edition took more time.

Most of the images we created were in editions of one hundred. Since a separate screen, or stencil, was needed for each color, an image using twelve colors required hand pulling ink twelve hundred times!

Lewis and I had very different styles of working. Lewis created poetic abstracts, minimalist landscapes, seaweeds or sailboats using torn paper stencils, and commentary incorporating his droll humor. He was happy to be holed up in his creative space while he worked.

I used silkscreen more as a painting tool and I needed to get out into the landscape or garden, keeping track of what was going on, observing and looking for new visual stimulation. Every time I got out, it seemed there always was something surprising to record. I was on a continual quest for new discovery or seeing the familiar in a new light.

One spring day along False Bay a large flock of sheep appeared from nowhere and flowed down the country road with nobody in attendance. Forced to stop the car they engulfed us, we waited and watched as like one amorphous body, they baaed along their way. In those days no fences separated the road from the meadows which edged the wide shallow bay. The sheep moved along, into the spring green grass, the sea reflected the sky of blue, and little puff clouds flocked above. I pulled out my field notebook and captured the memory with a few pencil lines.

Sometimes Lewis and I combined our techniques to create images together. We created a series of clothesline images, he making torn paper clothes and I the landscape behind. We loved playing with images and titles, constantly bouncing ideas off each other.

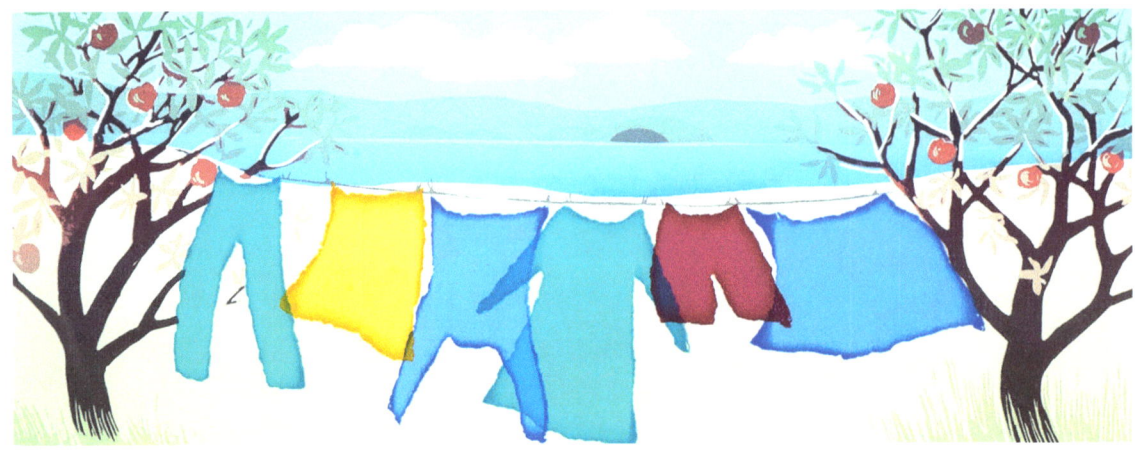

Every year when spring came the same problem arose. I would be anxious to get out into the field and ramble around with my camera and sketch book checking on wildflowers, birds recently returned, whatever was happening out there. Above all, I needed to be energized and excited to enable the creative flow of new images. And then the show season would begin. We were off and running.

Home again at the studio a voice in my head would say "Create art, you doggie dog." Then abruptly, "Heel! Get inventory ready, forget new ideas for now." Grooving along with the mindless aspect of our work, along came another command, "Pack the car. Let's get going, now. It's showtime."

Granted we were pretty good dogs. We were also our own masters. With eyes open wide, the open road was an adventure wherever we went. We understood that when we got home again it would take time to shift gears and discover where we left off. Regardless, we were soon back to work in the studio again. We had to do new work and that was that.

Deciding to apply to shows farther from home, meant yet more time on the road. Often when it was not my turn to drive, I sketched and designed pieces as we drove along. I made myself a little travel sketch book that I called *On the Road Again*, as I felt in our way we were living Willie Nelson's song.

Everywhere were intriguing sights or stories that begged to be told. One day slipping along through traffic on the I 5 corridor through northern California's oak covered hills, we passed a car pulling a small open trailer upon which was strapped down the tiniest drivable car I had ever seen, brightly painted like an iridescent beetle. An attractive hand painted sign at the rear said *The World's Tiniest Bookstore*.

Out in Idaho, alone in an empty stretch of freeway, we began the long descent to Farewell Bend. The Snake River would soon appear from out of Hells Canyon where we always looked for white pelicans that gathered on the river bend in fall. A strange vehicle appeared over a slight rise, coming in our direction, shaped like a giant hotdog on wheels rolling along in the vast, lonely landscape of barren hills. As it got closer it revealed itself as an Oscar Meyer Weiner Mobile heading somewhere farther to the west.

Driving through green farmlands of central Oregon we came up behind a 1960 Lincoln Continental with the roof down. The back seat was occupied by a large double bass, its neck pointed skyward stretching out of its bulbous body of silken wood. In the front seat sat three ladies in white, their long blue scarves streaming backward, wavelets in the wind.

We rushed along, always heading for one deadline or another. Often we left home regretfully on some early ferry. We could get to the Bay Area in a day and a half, or to Boise in nine hours, arriving in time to check in to a place to stay, have dinner and catch our breaths, then rise early the next day to set up our booth. We often left as soon as the show was over, driving off into the sunset so that the following days drive would be easier as we slipped away toward home.

Sometimes we had shows back to back which meant we would get home, unload the van, reassemble our inventory, reload, do a laundry, pet the dog, grab a few hours of sleep, and pause for dinner with Heather and Laurie. Then we were on our way again.

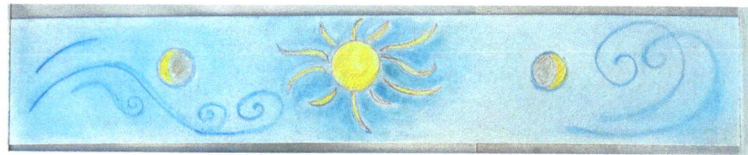

By the time the girls were in high school they had traveled to enough shows to want to stay home and they had earned our trust to manage the home front in our absence which they did very well. None the less, the split we felt between travel and home felt ever more poignant.

Our apple trees grew and we harvested fruit. Roses thrived as did poppies. We harvested sugar snap peas. The vegetable garden suffered with so many art forays through summer and fall, though we always managed to grow some fresh food.

We thought we might raise chickens and enjoy fresh eggs. It went well for awhile. We brought some laying Rhode Island Red hens home from Whidbey Island we saw on a "for free" ad during one of our off island trips. The girls named them The Mrs., Henny Penny and PJ. They gave us lovely big brown eggs. The next year we ordered Buff Orpington chicks through the mail. Peeping packages at the post office were exciting. The chicks grew into gorgeous golden chickens. With the addition of a rooster the hens hatched out chicks of their own. Eventually though, when hens stopped laying we didn't like the options before us and gave the whole lot away to some folks on the north side of the island. Nobody wanted to eat The Mrs!

Building a solar greenhouse as an addition to the dome was part of our original plan. We didn't have the means to go forward until late in the eighties. When our summer fairs were over we began to construct the simple rectangular space on the south side of the dome in the fall, putting in the glass windows as time allowed. By January it was all closed in though we had not yet cut a door through the exterior wall so that we could enter the kitchen from the new space.

Lewis was away at a show. Laurie was away for her first year in college. Heather and I were home alone tending the fires. A big winter storm came through. After a day of heavy snowfall there came a stretch of bright sunny days, as is often the case during a northeaster here. Checking on the greenhouse space which looked cheerfully bright through the kitchen windows, we tramped around through the shimmering snow and entered the side door. It was ninety-five degrees inside! We discovered our own spa. How brilliant!

Bringing pillows around from the house to set on the tile floor for seats, we read books and lounged there for as long as the sun was out, basking in its warmth as we looked out over the snow covered garden.

Eventually when the door was cut through from the kitchen, the warmth that poured up into our living space was impressive. It was a passive solar system that depended on sunny weather, but it was efficient and capable of warming our entire dome house during daylight hours in the depths of winter.

In the summer, with shades placed over the glass roof, the space remained pleasant for sitting, or sleeping, as well as a perfect home for houseplants and place to start seedlings in spring.

We readily became converts to the burgeoning solar energy age.

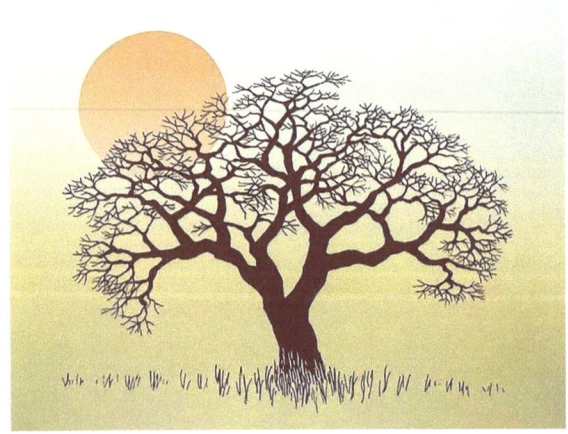

I had determined that I would create a series of large wildflower images depicting native species in their natural habitat. That meant that I would strive to explore all the nooks and crannies within our island world. Other ecosystems as the alpine areas we loved to hike drew me as well. As wild places everywhere faced increasing pressures, I felt a sense of urgency to portray the things I loved.

Woodlands near salt water were filled with carpets of Linnea borealis, Carl Linnaeus flower! On high open slopes there were wild delphinium and foxglove, the prairies covered in camas lilies: treasures everywhere. There was endless inspiration and I was a happy adventurer out in the field doing what I wanted to do.

In the late nineties still working primarily with serigraphy, I found that the new complex pieces I was creating, while exciting, were achieved by an arduous effort. Most of the pieces involved overlaying at least thirty colors. It took about a month to complete any one edition. I began to realize that I needed to find a medium where I could work more expediently, in a safer and less stressful way.

My personal life felt in disarray as I reviewed my process and all the travel we were doing. I needed to make changes but wasn't sure how. Where was it all going to lead?

We began to stay closer to home. With the cost of road trips on the rise, the advent of the prestigious *Flower and Garden Show* at the convention center in Seattle in February was perfect for us as I contemplated a transition. It proved to be a venue we enjoyed for many years. With our booth amid the show gardens it was like a trip into spring, offering all the optimism we could hope for during winter's cold. We took turns tending our art booth, attending seminars and wandering through sensational display gardens and plant booths. Many gardening notables came to speak and their talks were inspirational and educational. Octogenarian Rosemary Verey, noted garden designer from England came. Michael Pollen well known author, and Cisco Morris of local fame were some of the presenters we made sure not to miss.

Rosemary Verey's book, *The Scented Garden*, had been in my collection for years. It was a thrill to see the author in person. I will always remember her practical advice: If you become overwhelmed by your garden, just work on one small space at a time and make that beautiful. With my tendency to dart about from one project to another, the wisdom of her remark stayed with me. I could see that it applied as well to art and life.

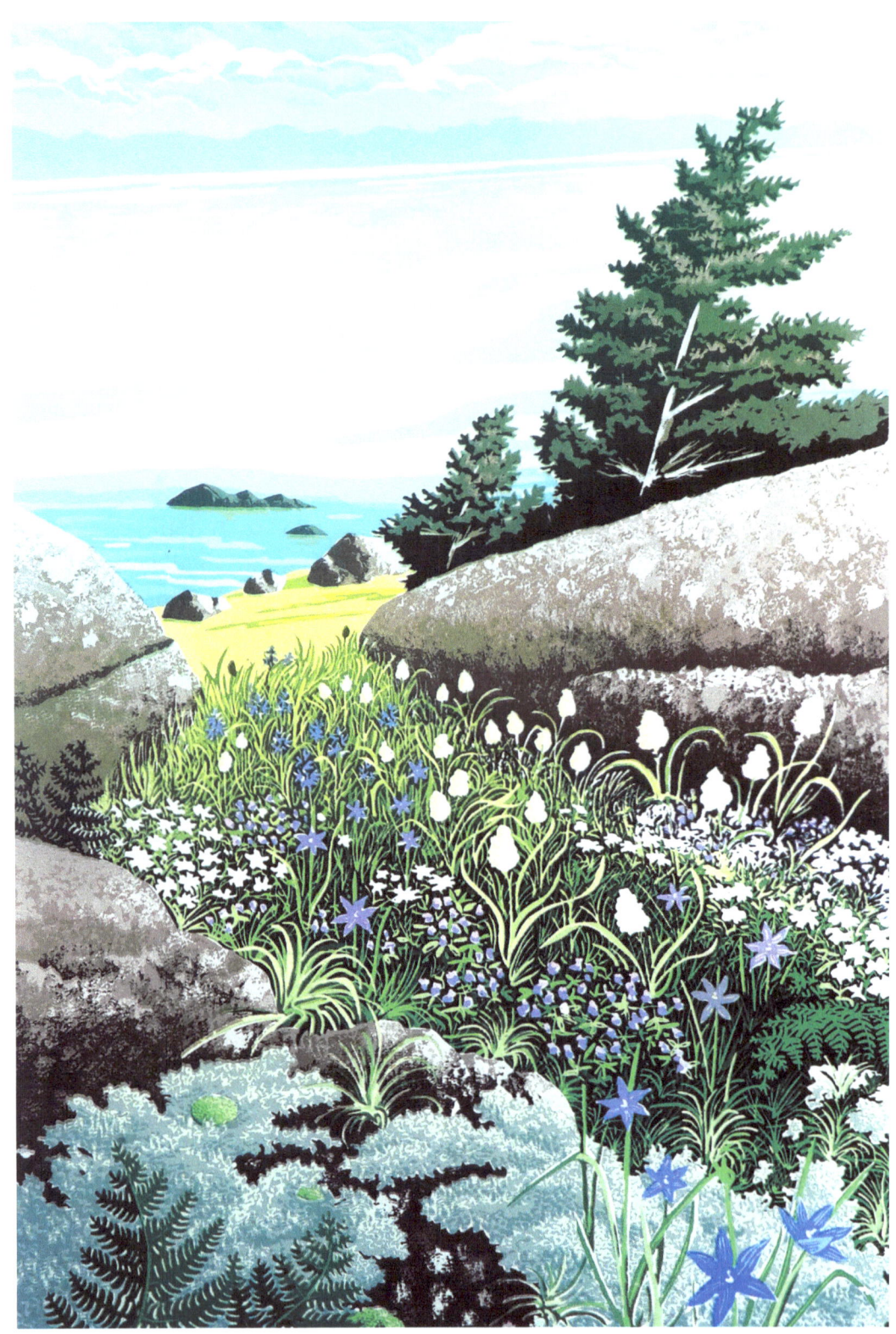

Blue Eyed Grass at Iceberg Point

I paint flowers so they will not die.

—Freida Kahlo

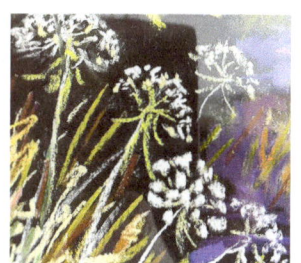

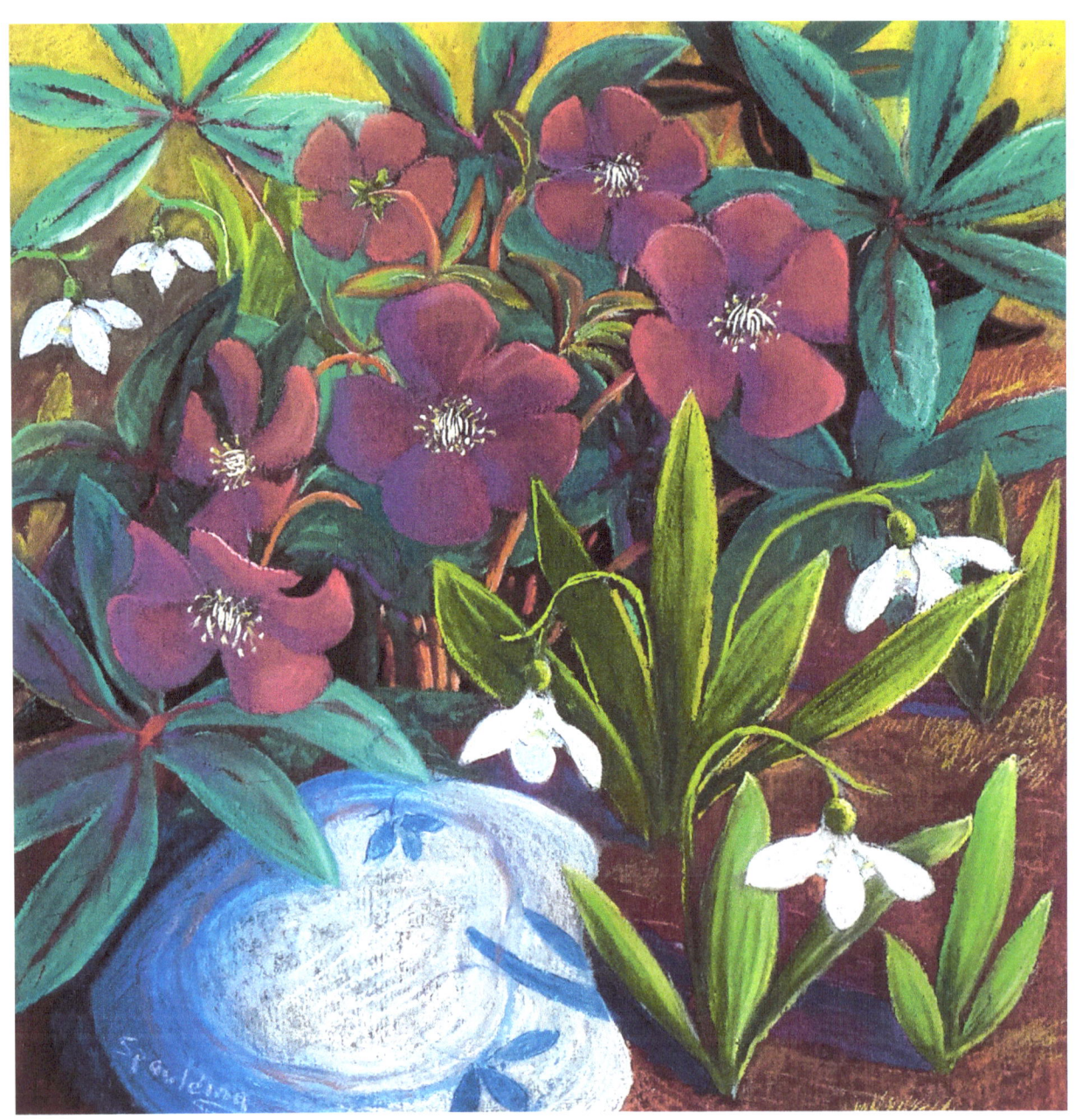

Hellebore and Snowdrops

Chapter Nine

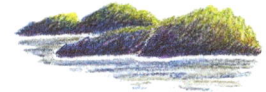

The Garden In Winter

The angle of sunlight is almost horizontal and shadows long and deep as I wander outside. Most plant life in the garden seems dormant or in quiet repose. Emerald mosses and curled brown leaves appear to glow in the deep shadows where light is dimly diffuse. Frost decorates the grass with shimmering crystals. Dancing sunlight filters through the feathery tops of the fir trees which I have let grow on our south border. Could we ever have imagined that those tiny seedlings would become grand trees, now threatening our sunlit space? Striving with their every fiber to create a forest barrier, the trees will soon capture the low arc of winter sun. Then we will be at odds.

In November, when light is seeping out of every corner, feelings of loss hover. It happens gradually at first. Weather in fall can remain mellow and sweet as the low light glows on the last of the dahlias, asters, calendulas. For a time, the roses seem willing to bloom their hearts out, as though there will be no change in season. Then the storms begin. Driving wind and rain from out of the Pacific, or a cold snap perhaps blowing down from British Columbia, bring a sudden change of attitude.

Mildew and decay become more evident. Annuals die and perennials die back. The days shorten with an alarming pace as we arrive in the month of December. Each week is noticeably darker, damper, colder. Shadows lengthen on the north side of the house and provide a haven for moss, and algal slime makes the deck hazardous. It becomes pitch black before dinner and breakfast time comes long before sunrise.

After many years here, I have grown wiser as I face fall and winter, though perhaps not always wise enough. I know that the sunrises that have been marching south along the North Cascade range will eventually find a stopping place and begin journeying north once again. Like a pendulum, it does not stop. My feelings of abandonment as it swings south will eventually find a counterbalance. To the east over the water lies the jagged horizon where peaks have become my calendar and my solace.

When the sun has moved southward past Glacier Peak, White Horse and Three Fingers, and as far as Mount Index, I have learned there is a certain mellow quality to the darker days that I should take advantage of while it lasts. Winter solstice is a thoughtful time and comfortable if you have put away enough wood and stores for the winter. Preparedness and acceptance are key to survival, both physical and mental.

It is also true, upon investigation, the garden is not as quiet as a first look suggests, even though it rests.

I fill winter days with forays outdoors, balanced with contemplative work inside. This is the time of year when the studio can be its most inviting, if I make sure it is warm and there is good light. This is important when darkness begs me to curl up somewhere with a book and a blanket. Activity and discovery in the garden also help combat a hibernation mode, the inclination toward slumber.

I look for light anywhere I can find it, a fading glow in the afternoon sky, starlight in the velvety night, or a moon when its cycle comes around. Sun makes me glad when we have clear days, even though its strength is weak. When obscured, I turn on the full spectrum lights, search through my sketchbook and photos from the last year's adventures and latch onto ideas for creation.

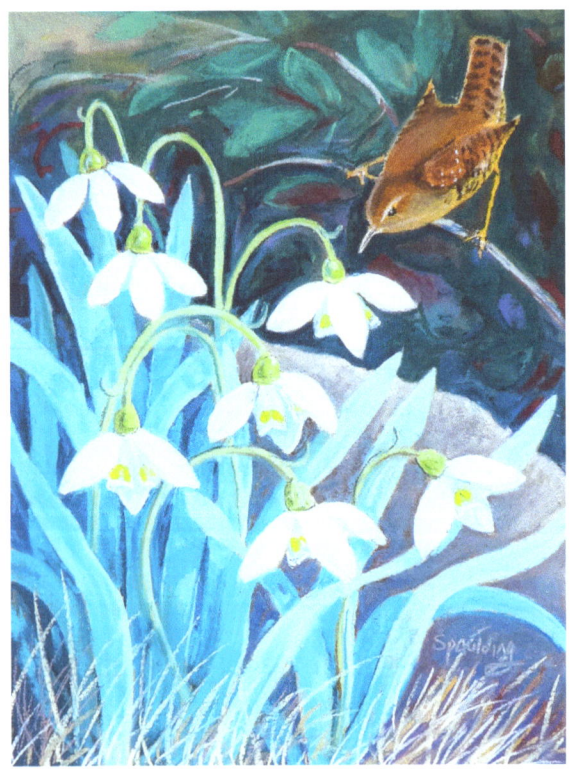

Pacific Wren with Snow Drops

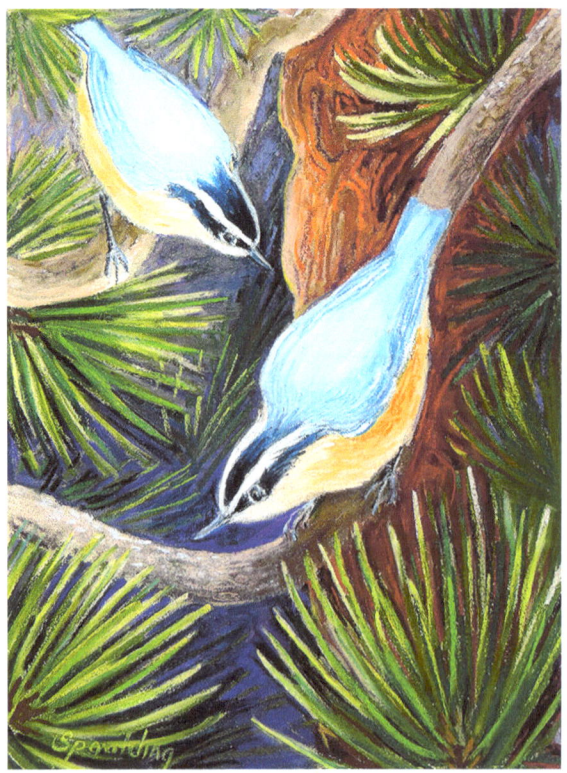

Nuthatches in the Pine

Each morning I step outdoors before sunrise. In the slow dawning I hear the soft flutter of wings. A Pacific Wren slips through a tiny square in the lattice, a motion so fluid I wonder if it was really there. Red-breasted Nuthatches are "beeping" in the driveway pines. The flock of Chestnut-backed Chickadees flutter through the buddleia calling "dee dee." A few silvery green leaves remain that provide the little birds with hiding places.

The chickadees are a spritely lot, perennially jaunty, feathered in brown suede vests and perky white scarves. Black eyes the size of coriander seeds gleam like glass dots, barely visible against the black feathers of their caps. A happy insistence seems to define their congenial personalities. "I'm here. I'm part of this day," they seem to say as they flit past through the branches.

I deliver the daily allotment of sunflower seeds to the bird feeder. Spotted Towhees slip out from under the heather plants daring to come within inches of my feet, then thinking better of it, with a flip of their long tails, they scurry off over the frosty grass. I listen to their soft "kereeee" call. Hiding out under the hardy geraniums and other leafy cover, the towhees prefer to forage on the ground.

Towhees are large, colorful members of the sparrow family. The female, mostly chocolate brown with rusty flanks and a white bib, is a muted version male whose dark black back and wings contrast sharply with his robin red sides and his white breast. White spots punctuate their wings and tip of their tails. A pair peer at me cautiously with their striking red eyes.

I notice that the bright white spots can vary from bird to bird. One male is easy to identify with spots much larger and plentiful. Will his unique flashiness make him more desirable to the ladies, or will he be more of a target for predators? I keep an eye on him, happy to observe his frequent visits.

In the early dawn, I can just make out a cascade of yellow blossoms covering the winter jasmine which drapes over the rockery wall. In a mild winter the plants may start blooming as early as November but in colder years wait until February. The golden blaze is a cheerful sight in the muted morning landscape. Nearby the jasmine is a sprawling shrub, a winter blooming honeysuckle which blossoms in early February. The blossoms, though diminutive, provide a sweetness both visual and aromatic. The dainty white flowers attract the Anna's Hummingbirds who hang out in the spreading branches.

Clumps of hellebore fill the rock garden with colorful blooms. At the center of each cluster of large, palmate evergreen leaves, multiple stems push upwards producing buds for flowers that will bloom in winter for weeks on end. Unlike the first hellebores I acquired years ago with mysterious papery green flowers and silvery foliage, the Lenten Roses and Christmas Roses produce large colorful blooms. The large petal-like sepals make up the color while the actual petals at the center have evolved to become a ring of small green circular cups that produce nectar. With a color palette that ranges from white, pink, mauve, burgundy to nearly black, it is not surprising that hellebores are referred to roses. Of course they are not, but rather members of the buttercup family, Ranunculaceae.

Some fifteen species of hellebore exist in nature, hardy perennials originating in the Middle East and Eurasia. In recent years hellebores have been crossed to create arresting double blossoms, enchanting speckles and further variations in their color pallet. An endless array seems to be available these days for the gardener who delights in unexpected blooms throughout winter and early spring.

Looking through the early morning light toward a mound of double pink hellebore flowers, I notice the first of the bulbs have appeared. Snowdrops are poking up through the hellebore leaves, and a first dainty white blossom has opened. The year's bulb sequence has begun!

As I turn from the bird feeder to go back inside, a Song Sparrow and a Fox Sparrow appear at the edge of the Elves' Home Spiraea, where they wait in the shadows. The less shy Golden-crowned Sparrows have also flown in. All these birds inhabit the winter garden where they will come to the bird feeder but they prefer to scratch on the ground.

The Golden-crowned Sparrows live in our midst from late September until early May when they take a short migration trip to their breeding grounds in British Columbia. Their plaintive song "Oh Dear Me" fills the air with a sense of longing and puts me in a pensive mood.

In most sparrows, the difference in plumage is not sex determined, but age defining. Adult plumage is not achieved until their second year. First year birds show no yellow on their heads but as they complete their first winter, the black stripes on their heads outline burgeoning yellow crowns. Second year birds sport a bright yellow crown with the approach of breeding season.

I enjoy these stocky, handsome foraging birds in winter as they poke about in the grass or hang out in the shrubbery, eating seeds and bits of greenery, buds and shoots. I didn't expect them to have a taste for yellow sedum, though. They can remove all the fat colorful leaves, leaving me nothing but the wandering stems, if I don't remember to cover the plants with an overturned slotted potting tray.

I also have noted that they are fond of peas, so that any early plantings must be covered by row cover cloths, a valuable gardener's helper for early crops. The floating covers create a space out of the wind that rain can still penetrate, raising the soil several degrees, and speeding up the germination process. Keeping out the marauding birds has been an added benefit.

A few White-crowned Sparrows often frequent the rock garden this time of year. I have learned to identify their juveniles too. Only brown stripes appear on their heads, but in the pattern that eventually will become bright white. Like the towhees, when spring comes these pretty birds will find some secretive spot on the ground for their nests. We won't hear their song until spring when we hear them sing sweetly "Oh me, pretty, pretty me. Tweet tweet tweet!"

We are often visited by hawks during winter. Cooper's and Sharp-shinned Hawks are hunters supreme, with streamlined wings and piercing eyes. They are hard to tell apart as size, not plumage is the most defining feature. They descend out of nowhere with incredible speed. Their boldly patterned feathers are a thing of beauty as they perch along the fence line or on garden stakes or lattice. They are hungry and song birds are their prey.

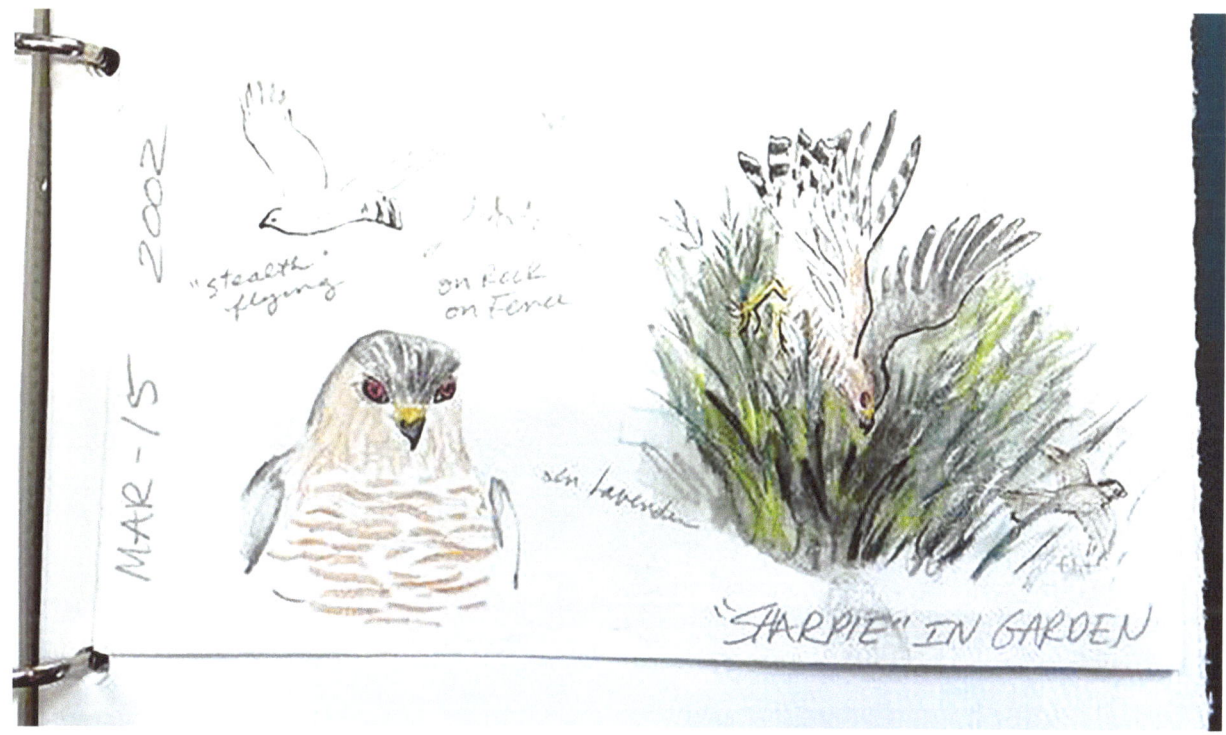

Birds at the feeder know the difference between a hawk overhead or a crow or raven. Those they will ignore. Nor do they pay attention to an eagle or heron flying past. When they see the silhouette of a Coopers or a Sharpie, they are gone in an instant.

There are plenty of hiding places in the garden. The spiraea is densely branched and allows the little birds to hide within its tangle. The low growing heathers provide cover impossible to penetrate, and the rose Petite Pink Scotch never loses its leaves in winter. It is a mass of thorn covered, entwining canes of a daunting nature. Once within, small birds cannot be reached.

Rarely do we see a hawk catch a bird, but of course they do. One day in the living room I approached the window and realized that a young Sharp-shinned was sitting on the obelisk just below the window, putting the bird at my eye level. It looked directly at me through the window with eyes that seemed all knowing, piercing through me. Bright yellow legs fiercely clasped its perch, and its breast feathers, scalloped in gold and white, riffled in the breeze. Its long tail, barred in charcoal and cream, twitched ever so slightly from side to side. As I moved closer to the pane, the hawk, just a few feet away, was gone with no apparent motion.

In seconds, already below the orchard, swift, sharply angled wings propelled the agile flier away into the distance and in moments it became one with the sky.

I was left to contemplate the braveries, the songs, the sheer exuberance with which the denizens of the garden seem to meet each day. On any given day, a life will be taken, a meal will be eaten, energy will move from one form to another. Though death is a daily ritual, we are all absorbed in living. I am filled with gratitude. Today I am lucky. The hawk of my destiny as yet flies somewhere far away.

Sunrises in winter are spectacular when the eastern horizon is clear. Regimented by the clock, we arise in the dark and watch the dawning light unfold before us. I will collect sunrises. I say to myself.

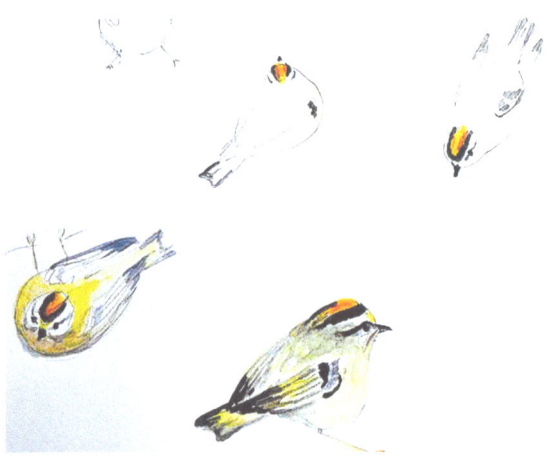

Many days there is no sunrise at all, just a slow infusion of light through water droplets in our highly humid atmosphere. On those days, I have to push myself out the door for a walk. On such a morning, as I rounded the corner of the north side of the studio, my eyes caught the fluttery motion of tiny little birds dropping all around me from the fir boughs above. I had come upon a flock of Golden-crowned Kinglets. Always on the move and constantly in motion, they flicked their tiny wings and tails as they hunted for small insects in the grass. "As small as some hummingbirds, four or five birds to the ounce" I read in my *Sibley Guide to Birdlife and Behavior*. We only see kinglets here in fall and winter. These tiny birds of the north find ways to survive in extreme cold. After their daytime foraging, the flock crams together in some secretive thicket, the birds warming each other through the night. I will think of that next time I am sleepless in the dark. Somewhere close by, kinglets may be cuddled in a ball.

Our first winters on this piece of land were stark. Cloudless days brought distant views and sharp starry nights. Cloudy winter days brought a bleakness that seemed to leach color out of every object. If it snowed, whiteness stretched out over the fields and little pocket ponds became silvery with ice. Wet rainy days brought a shadowy glistening to the monotone panorama. In this world filled predominantly with bleached and graying grasses, I ached for greenness.

On our many winter walks, however, I discovered a world of greens around the island, thriving in winter. Varieties of mosses and lichens practically glowed on rocky outcrops and under the deep green boughs of fir, hemlock and cedar. The understory of the forest was filled with a wealth of green ferns, salal, and high and low bush mahonia. These native plants have long been valued by landscapers and I became inspired to plant them around us, in our once farmer's field. As it turns out many of them have begun to plant themselves!

We constructed the rock garden next to the house visible from both the house and my studio windows. To create this section of the garden, we backfilled below the house using all the dirt piles left from our construction site, carting it by hand with a wheelbarrow. The result was a space that seemed a perfect replication of a mountain scree, on a small scale of course. It would have been nice to have some impressive boulders for a bold statement. As it was, we carried, pulled, and rolled the biggest stones we could handle into place.

The completed terrain has made a perfect environment for alpine plants. The drainage is excellent, the soil porous, and the rocks mimic the outcrops we loved so, as hikers.

I began to collect heathers and heaths which tucked beautifully into the rocks. My penchant for collecting was again satisfied by the challenge of so many available selections. With so many differing growth habits, bloom times, varied coloration of the scales or needle leaves plus differing colors of the dainty bell flowers, I realized that with some thought, the rockery could have one variety or another in bloom throughout the entire year.

Every year the surprise of willow catkins in January is a delight. By the end of January and early February they begin to attract honeybees in the neighborhood for by then the catkins have passed their pretty silver stage, and are yellow with pollen. With a range of several miles some of these bees could be coming from friends over the ridge in the valley to our west. It's fun to think we are feeding their bees.

Another encouraging surprise early in the season is the hardy cyclamen covered with deep fuchsia flowers. It blazes with color in the shadow of the Elve's Home spiraea. The copper colored flowers of the winter hazel make a nice gleam as low light hits them and a pink winter blooming viburnum opens its few offerings behind in the hedgerow. Each little flower shines like a beacon.

I round the corner one winter day to find that the sarcococca in its large pot on the shady portion of the deck has suddenly come into bloom. The tiny filament like blossoms are spread sparsely throughout the shiny evergreen leaves. Though the flowers are small, the intensity of their aroma comes as a surprise every year. This demure shade lover, a winter blooming member of the box family, offers its sweet gift at a time of year when there are no other perfumes in the garden. Some may find the scent cloying. I find it a pleasant mix of gardenia, orange blossom, and vanilla. "Sarcococca! Sarcococca!" I say in admiration for its ability to perform so outlandishly from its cold, dark vantage point. My visiting granddaughter looks back at me from the brick walk and laughs.

Rosemary, the big Tuscan Blue, is covered in sky-blue buds. It won't be long before it opens. This statuesque herb makes a fine landscape plant as it grows six feet tall and blooms for weeks on end. All the while it provides the gardener with culinary offerings as the pine needle leaves can always use pruning. *Rosemary For Remembrance* I say as I pick some sprigs to bring inside. Several thymes and winter savory have all survived the cold as well. Fresh herbs in the winter are good for the spirits as well as our health!

In February, when light is more assertive, crocus begin to show up along the paths. We are halfway between winter solstice and spring equinox by the middle of the month. A frog croaks somewhere down in the shady dampness near the deck. Another long drawn out "creeeeee" alerts me toward its hideaway. One night before long, from all along the nearby ditches, a tree frog chorus will fill the nights and signal the coming of spring.

As I ponder the lengthening days, I stop to admire the many ground covers that are also showing signs of growth. The heuchera plants are emerging as little clumps of gold, lime, amber and purple. These coral bells are all lovely foliage plants which will shoot up sprays of airy blooms on tall stocks when spring arrives. Clumps of primulas and polyanthus, many of which need dividing, are filling spaces with their crinkly rosettes of leaves, little flower buds and stems in the center are just beginning to form. Lychnis, campion and dianthus all appear to be waiting to leap as soon as the days are warmer.

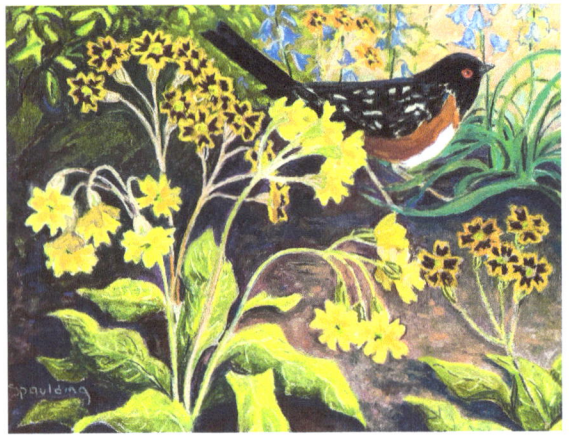

I am awakened from my thoughts by the Anna's Hummingbirds. A male is performing his loops for a female that must be perched somewhere nearby. It almost seems he is performing for me and I allow myself this bit of flattery. For just a second I think how lovely to be courted. The tiny flash of jade ascends straight up effortlessly until he disappears from sight. There is a hesitating moment. Suddenly he cascades downward in a rush. As he nears the bottom of his loop just a few feet from the ground, I hear a sharp whistling squeak as the rapid flow of air passes through his tail feathers. It startles me even though I expected it. Another flash, this time watermelon pink from his head and throat, and he is up in the air again, seeming to hang, motionless, before showing off on his next descent.

I head back inside, happy to have surrounded myself with so much life. Each plant and shoot contains energy and determination, each creature seems equally filled with purpose. There are so many patterns, shapes and colors and so much moving and shifting toward new beginnings.

By late February and March I notice perennials and biennials that are mounding up here and there with new growth, whether newly started from seeds or from roots ready to come back to life. Among these are hearty clumps of hesperis, feverfew, mullein and foxglove.

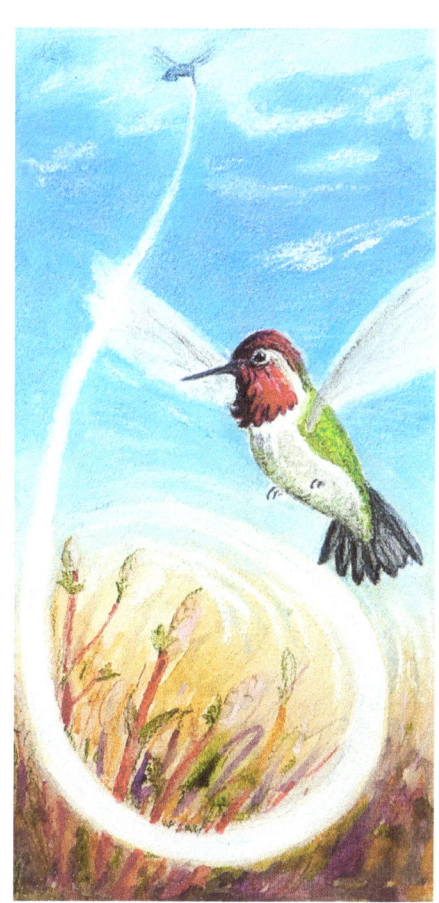

Now as they are getting larger I plan what to do about the ones that have volunteered. I have made the mistake of letting volunteers take over in the past, smothering out bulbs and perennials that I had thoughtfully planted. After losing some choice plants to such folly, I now realize I must move these enthusiastic interlopers to some other spot, give them away, or resort to the compost. Colleen, a garden friend who tends a meticulous landscape of unusual plants, says "Be tough!"

Winter is not over, yet in addition to all the other hopeful signs, Siberian Iris in blue are poking up in the rockery. We must beware. We could still have a snowfall or deep freeze. I can hear my mother saying "The days grow longer, the cold grows stronger." For the moment though, life is bursting forth, taking a risk, making the best of every day. I take a deep breath, head back to the studio, and promise myself the same.

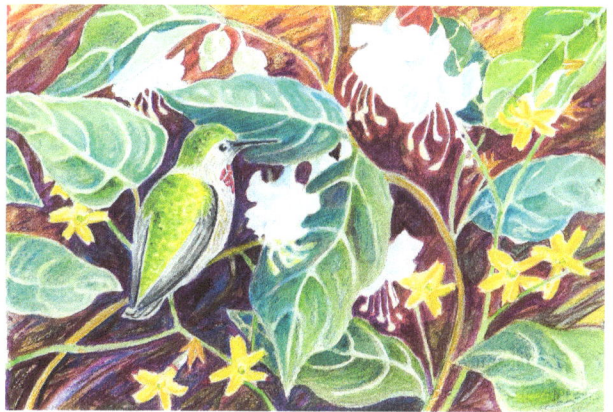

"And when the wind and winter darken
All the loveless land, it will whisper
of the garden. You will understand."

—Oscar Wilde

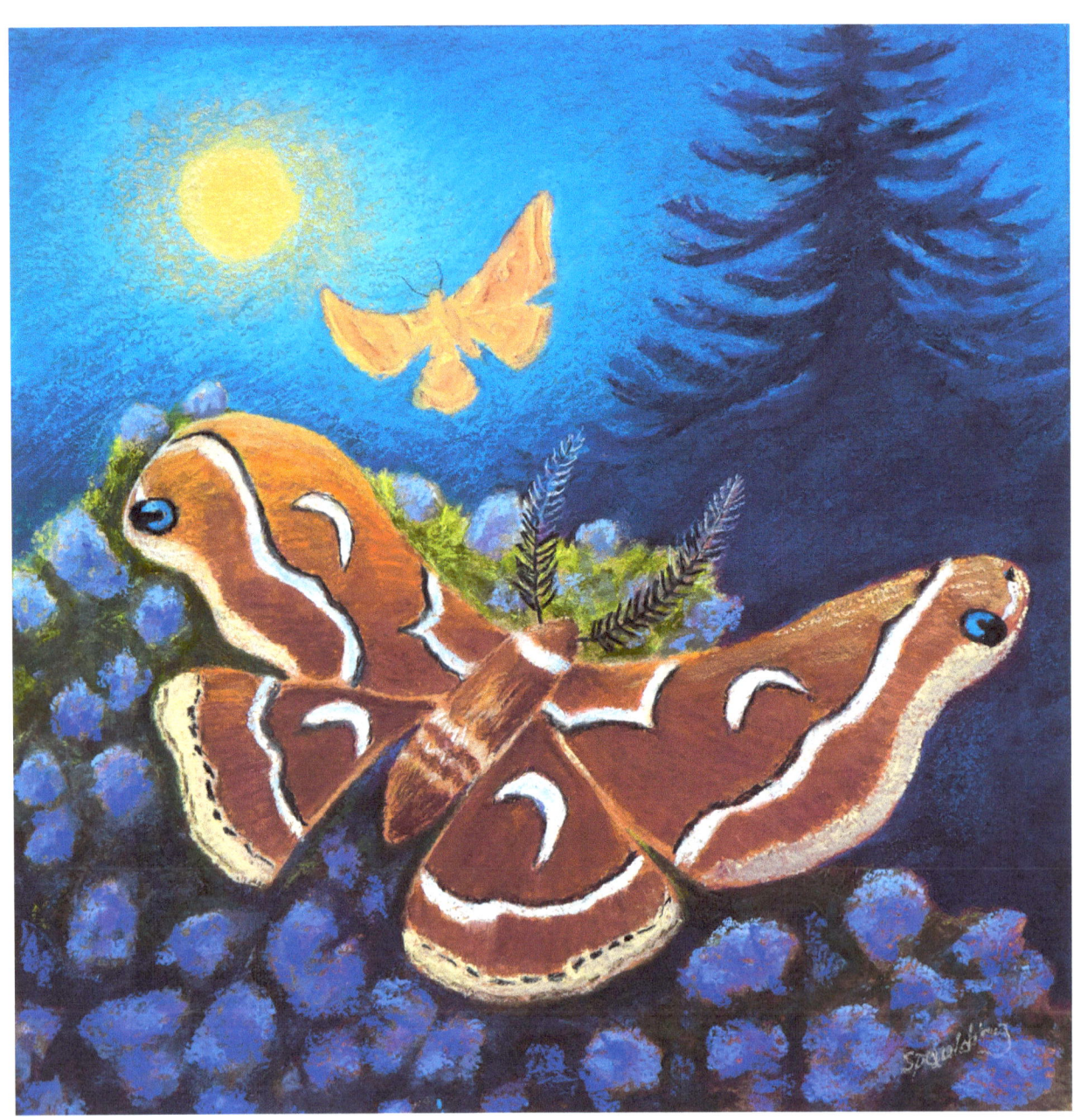

Ceanothus Silk Moth

Chapter Ten

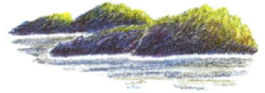

The Exuberant Season

By the time the equinox has arrived and the length of day has grown to equal the span of night, hope revives. In spite of the unsettled nature of spring, mild weather followed by wind, rain, and flip flopping temperatures, some form of advancement seems to mark each day.

Crocus line the walk in pools of purple. Cupped petals, that embrace the stigma and stamens within, attract the waking bees who tumble in. Their shadowed forms are barely discernible through the translucent petals that bulge and quiver as the bees dance their harvest dance. Like the fading snowdrops, the crocus flowers and the pollen they have to offer last but a few weeks. They are all the more cherished for their brevity.

As the crocus fade away, little grape hyacinths fill out the edges of the borders with pencil high stems topped with rounded caps of tiny sky-blue bell flowers. The larger hyacinth follow in shades of purple, blue and peach which fill the air with a glorious sweetness.

Along the driveway the native currant comes into bloom. With cheerful patches of color unexpected in a far north spring, currants bloom in cerise, sometimes redder, sometimes more pale, but always cheerful in the woodland edges or dappled understory of the forest. Currants make delightful additions to any northern garden.

Rufous Hummingbirds return from their grand tour. How can small birds just shy of three and a half grams fly away from here in a previous summer, migrate south along the rocky mountains into Mexico and then return north up the California coast in a following spring? It is mind boggling.

By early March as I work in the neglected garden, I ponder that in the moment somewhere miles from where I am, certain Rufous are heading our way with purpose. Then one day it happens. They have been spotted on the island. Several turn up at our place, bombing about like little copper rockets, as though it is no big deal.

The Rufous make themselves at home perching in the roses, the barberry, lilac and all around. They frequent the feeders with the Anna's hummingbirds who reside here now all year round. When the Anna's range moved northward to include the islands a few years ago, they relinquished their territory as soon as the Rufous arrived. As time has gone by, Anna's seem more confident, keeping a hold of their home ground. Both species seem willing to share the garden these days.

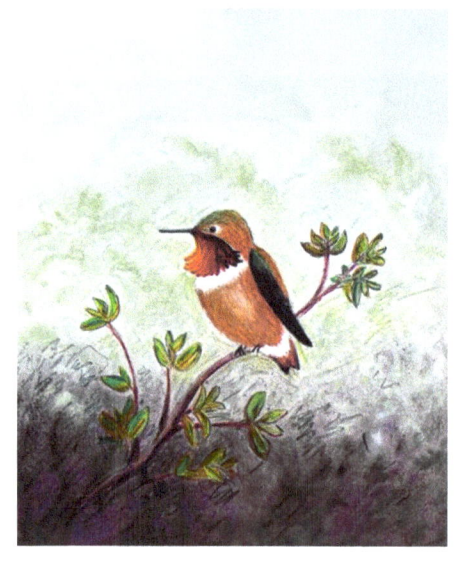

A metallic red/orange, dime sized flash, sweeping back and forth has captured my eye. A Rufous male is showing off for a demure female within the tangle of the Petite Pink Scotch rose. She appears not to notice. The Anna's come and go at the nearby feeder. When the male flies off, the little female comes out to perch on a ragged stem of fuchsia that is just showing signs of new leaf buds. Her little body of green and gray washed with a rusty blush, and a bit of white collar, help me differentiate her from the green and gray Anna's females. Both wear a little jewel of iridescent feathers at the center of their throat. I watch the Rufous as she perches. Her tongue, a silk thread, slips in and out of her beak, catching the light.

The male performs his J dives, looping from above and dropping fast, much like the Anna's that I have been watching earlier in the year. The sound his feathers make, unlike the Anna's sharp whistle, is a humming sort of sound, a mini whining siren, stuttering past the shrubbery.

April comes and the world is still wet and soggy. I launch forth on a morning walk across the meadow. As I am about to enter the grove of fir and pine, I hear the distant chortle of a raven, coming ever closer. I stop and turn back westerly to see what the raven is up to. By the time it crosses the road, heading toward our field, its scolding is louder. As it comes into view over the hedge I hear the "kakakakaka" of a Cooper's Hawk barely staying ahead. This sky train is brought up in the rear by a crow, adding its "caw". It seems the corvids are giving our resident hawk a lesson in boundaries. They all slip off over the firs and out of sight, leaving me to ponder the outcome.

By the time I cross the lower field, my jeans are freckled well above my knees with mud cast up by my footsteps as I trod along. My old *wellie* boots keep my feet dry but not the rest of me. It is hard to believe that this ground will be rock hard by the end of July, for now it is a sweet earthy soup, supporting green shoots that will become swaying grasses and summer flowers.

As I head back to the house I stop to admire the azaleas and rhododendron that I have planted in shady places. They are showing off with opulent, brilliant blooms that make spring here a storybook season.

In the midst of this world of enchantment, like the animals and plants around me, I am feeling an intense sense of urgency every day. Time lines are looming. Mine are self imposed, but none the less critical. Nature herself is imposing others.

I feel better once vegetable seeds have been planted in the raised beds outside and the seed trays inside. Art deadlines are unforgiving as summer approaches and I spend hours working on new pieces and designing others. Either new work is ready or it is not. No middle ground. Sometimes pressure is good for creativity and sometimes it is not. Weeds are looming in the garden and in my mind.

Lewis feels pressure too and I am thankful for all he does in the office, as well as general upkeep and repair of things around the place that are continually clambering for attention, all while working to fit in his own creative endeavors. We both feel gratitude for longer days and energy that comes with increased activity.

It is no wonder that I feel the planet is tipped in our favor as we find ourselves in late spring. May is perfection. A wander out into the twilight garden is like floating through a Maxfield Parish painting. Sweet Rocket casts its scent throughout the evening landscape, now awash in translucent blues, greens and golds that speak of infinitesimal distance and mystery.

One such evening I found myself weeding until dusk, kneeling down and yanking out unwanted plants until my ungloved hand wrapped around a large slug. The four inch long slimy mass in my hand brought me back to reality. The sticky goo simply would not wash off until I remembered to cover my hand in salt, the antidote for slug mucus.

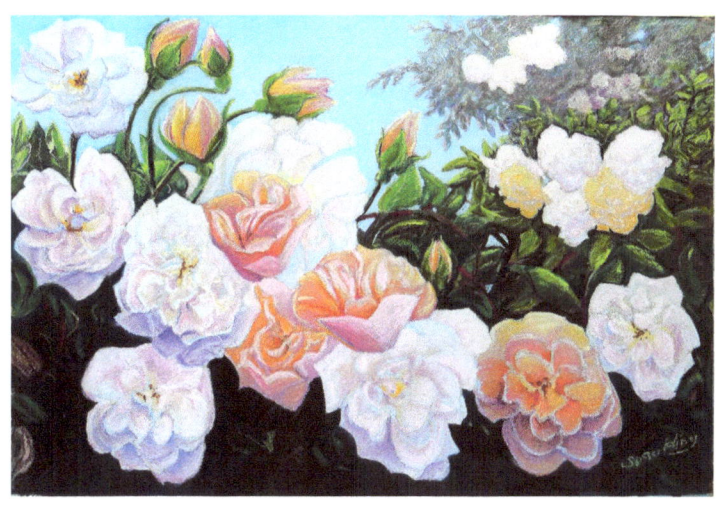

Another lovely night I stepped into the secret garden. This small square compound is contained by the back wall of our studio building, the woodshed, the driftwood log constructed barn, and bordered on the north side by a fence supporting a massive Himalayan rose, Climbing Treasure Trove. The climber produces an abundance of peachy pink roses, born in clusters, which for a short length of time are interwoven with purple clematis flowers.

Through the rose canes I could see bits of sky which still held onto the light, though the sun had set a while ago. Gazing at the soft glow beyond the silhouetted stand of oaks on the rise to our north, I imagined how the last reflections of light would be coloring the Straits of Georgia and the Canadian Gulf Islands on the island's west side. Somewhere far beyond, over the rim of our magical earth lies the land of midnight sun. This time of year we see its light seeping over the rim on either side of night.

The secret garden suffers from neglect because it is so hidden away. I had intended it to be a neat, formal, little garden, echoing the geometry of the overall space, a meditative place with a bench to sit quietly. But the beds rapidly became ridiculously over planted and I find myself wondering every year what to do about it. The place is a constant jungle. Roses, Twinberry, Salmonberry, Heavenly Bamboo, Ornamental Cherry, Corkscrew Willow, Ceanothus, Japanese Maple, heathers, and honeysuckle abound. Perennials underneath battle for space and light. Because of the shady moisture Hellebore, Primrose, Ladies Bedstraw, Jupiter's Beard, and Lithodora Blue merrily survive the chaos.

Still remembering the slug, I gingerly yanked a few errant hawkweeds from the row of boxwood that never became a knot garden as visualized. They rarely ever were clipped. Never mind. It was fun to dream of such perfection and order. Their evergreen leaves have been a welcome addition, even untrained. It was pleasant to walk around with my hands busy as my mind drifted.

Hovering motion in the Graham Stuart Honeysuckle caught my eye. Little airborne creatures were moving about amid the vines. In the magic of late light, I could discern iridescent, hummingbird shapes, but very tiny. "Baby hummingbirds?" I whispered to myself mystified. "What is going on here?" my awakening rational mind asked itself. Recently fledged hummingbirds are not half the size of their parents, nor would they be so numerous, I reminded myself. What were these endearing creatures?

I stayed and watched the whispering flyers move from flower to flower, long narrow tongues unfurled as the mystery beings neared the blooms. From their tiny emerald, velveteen bodies dangled little insect legs, and their antennae curved outward giving them an inquisitive look. Finally when I could no longer see, I retreated to the house to do some research.

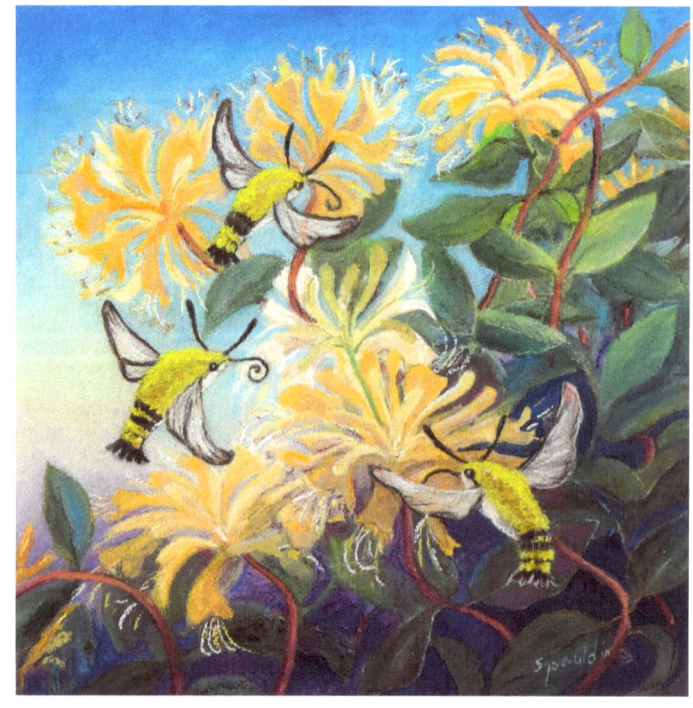

Hummingbird Moths seemed to be everywhere on the island that year. I compared notes with gardening friends. Laura, Melissa and Mary Karen had all seen them. We all wondered just who they were, and we all hoped for a chance to see them again. Laura sent me wonderful images she found online. We contemplated with curiosity.

I did run across a single hummingbird moth in the field months later, as it coursed along the hedgerow, passing right in front of me at eye level. I was again struck by how the moth's posture and wingbeats mimicked its namesake, even to the slight arching of its tail.

To have been able to witness so many of the moths at once had been thrilling. Sadly, I have never experienced a repeat performance. In spite of conditions seeming right, I have come to realize that I had participated in a unique and elegant moment that night, one of the great moments in my gardening experience. It remains to this day like a vision etched in my memory. Nature can be so lush and unexpectedly exorbitant. At such times one can only hope to be there.

Years later I have seen clearwing moths in the hesperis. In several successive springs, just one at a time, but a lovely secretive discovery; a reminder that there are always new things to ponder.

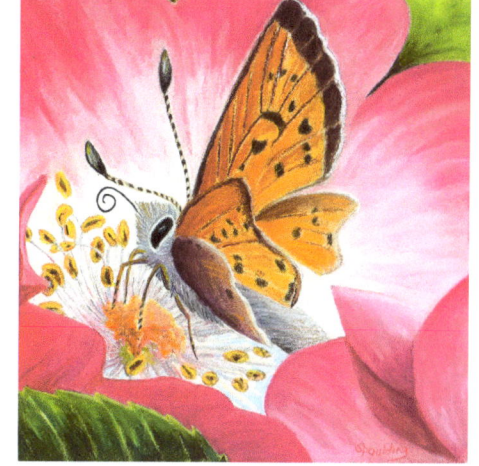

Butterfly gardening is popular and I felt attracting butterflies to my garden an appealing endeavor. More to the point, I like creating a safe haven for these lovely animals. I attempt to select plants that both the larva and adult butterflies use as food sources. Encouraging native plants that I know they depend on is a logical first step. Some of these are not always plants that people like to surround themselves with, yet many of these "weeds" are critical to their survival. Encouraging native plants and wildflowers outside the fence have given us the pleasure of seeing many species over time

I remember: Swallowtails need many flowers including blackberry blossom, hawkweed, helianthemums, hesperis, yarrows, columbines, Sweet William. Their larvae like willows, birches and alders. Red Admirables nectar on oxeye daisy, buddleia, fireweed, bull thistle, chrysanthemums. Their larvae depend exclusively on Stinging Nettle. Mourning Cloaks adults nectar on currants, and asters, various fruits and sap. The larvae need willows, alders, hackberry or apple birches or maple. There is so much to remember.

For every species of butterfly, a variety of plants are necessary for their survival. It is not enough just to provide pretty flowers.

Many years we miss seeing some species altogether, but hopefully they are thriving somewhere on the island. Survival is dependent on climate and habitat as well as food sources. It's about weather too. Perhaps a cold wet spring has reduced their numbers. Perhaps the caterpillars were destroyed somewhere along their complicated life cycle. Predators, poisons, plant loss, all play a role in neighborhood populations.

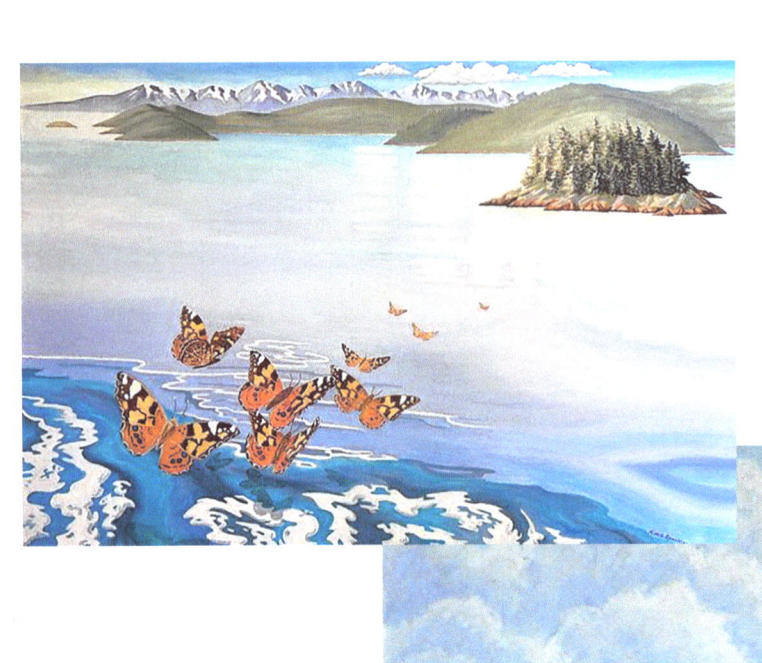

Painted Ladies Cross the Channel

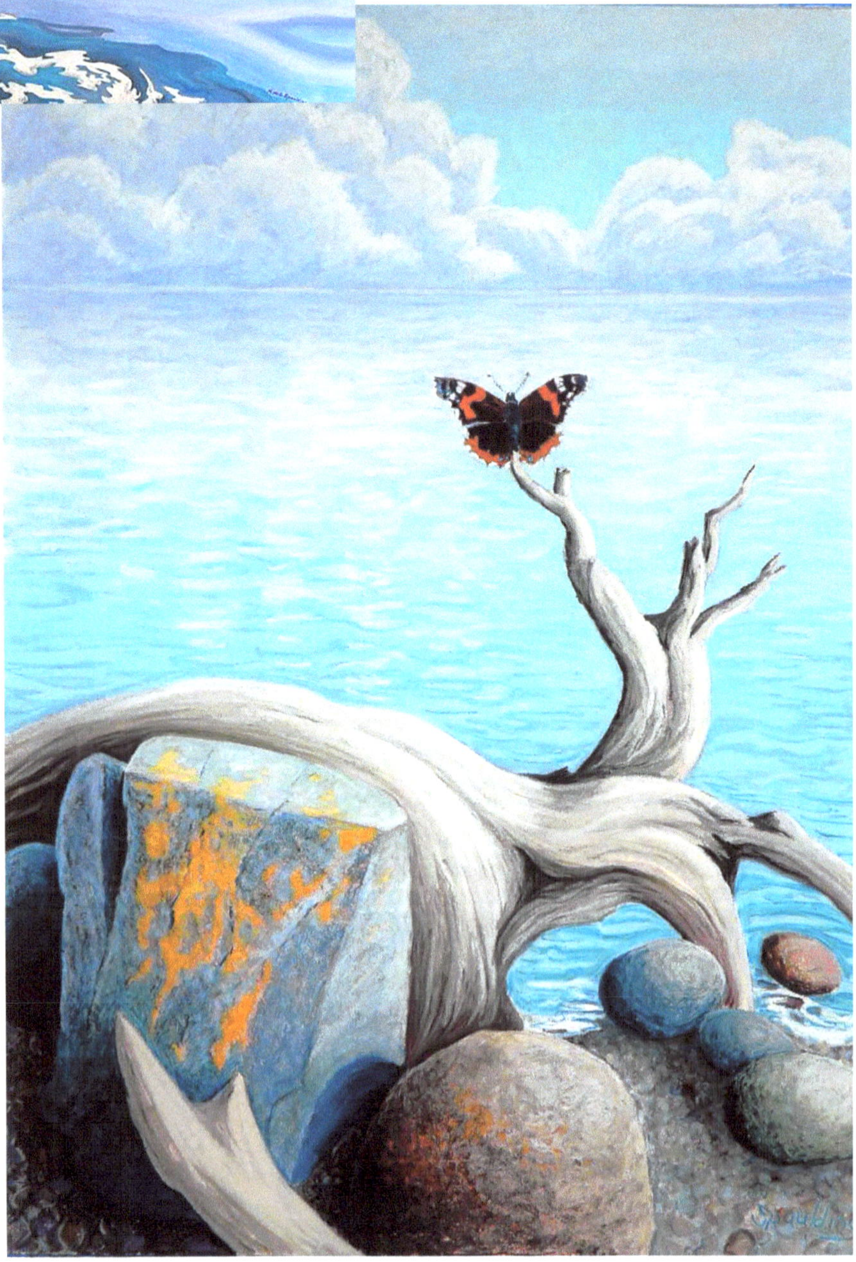

Contemplating the Void

In addition to butterflies and the delightful hummingbird moths, I have discovered many other appealing moths as our garden developed. One such moth found me. I was in my studio working late one spring night. From my brightly lit upstairs studio it seemed completely dark outside. I was deeply engaged in my work. A soft incessant tapping against my window pane gradually awoke me to the moment. I moved to the pane to see. Who was this voyeur?

Beating against the glass was a huge moth with a wingspan of at least five inches. Like a miniature Persian carpet being shaken in the breeze, the wings gently slapped the window. Through the glass I could see its fur covered abdomen, colored brick red with white stripes. Searching eyes in a dark red face were topped with fantastic black ladder-like antennae. The outstretched wings were velvety, the same brick red with lapis blue eye spots near the outer tips. A deep brown edge defined the wings. The overall design was accented with two pairs of white crescents.

I had met this unusual species once before. In the previous year we had found one that had perished near our front door. I had kept it in a box and admired it from time to time. I drew and painted it. I had looked it up: A Ceanothus Silk Moth whose range stretched from Baja California to British Columbia.

As one of the largest moth species of North America and uncommon to see, I became curious. The larva feed on Ceanothus or California Lilac, madrona, birch, alder and Douglas Fir. All of these species are nearby. The chrysalis overwinters in branches of the chosen host tree. The metamorphosis in spring results in a gorgeous creature whose lifespan is only a few days. The amazing moth has no mouth parts or digestive system. It is not here to eat. Its purpose is only to find a mate.

I regarded the moth at my window and its urgent quest with wonder. Perhaps it was time to turn out my light and retire for the night. It seemed only fair to remove the studio's distraction. I wished it well in its urgent quest and hoped for a successful next generation.

Was the Silk Moth occurrence a blip? Was it far out of its normal range, an explorer expanding its territory, or does this species live in the islands nearby, secretly amongst us? I check for sightings, and notice that occasionally someone reports seeing a silk moth on our island. That gives me hope that I shall see one again.

We have seen other beautiful moths, including the Eyed Sphinx. One spring a mating pair perched on a flower stem near our front door for over twenty four hours. The Elegant Day Moth with its peachy, yellow wings occasionally passes by. One white moth I found in our ornamental pear seemed to be wearing a mantle of soft ermine and all six legs were striped black and white, like GoGo boots. Where is the party, I thought?

Life goes tumbling forward. Seedlings stretch upward, producing flowers which transform into seed pods, seemingly overnight. Nests recently filled with eggs empty as fledglings take flight. Fruit trees blossom and once pollinated, begin to form fruits. The rapid succession of events seems relentless. Oh, to be everywhere all at once and soak it all in. I take frequent breaks from the studio. Every moment in the garden this time of year feels like the moment I have been waiting for.

Along the brick walk the sunlight streams toward me like a river. Leaves of the Virginia Creeper vine drape down around me, freshly green like emerald stained glass chips, backlit with the sun. Peach-leaf Campanula shimmers blue violet at the head of the walk. Lavender plants, Provence and Grosso, have filled out and doubled in size as their flower spikes shoot upwards. They sway in the breeze, grasslike. Already the burgeoning buds are highly scented. With the long hours of daylight they will soon be perfect for cutting.

I will harvest some lavender. Most though, I will let stand to provide lovely mounds of color which the bees love. As the flowers reach the end of their blooming season there is usually an emergence of little skipper butterflies. Where one day there

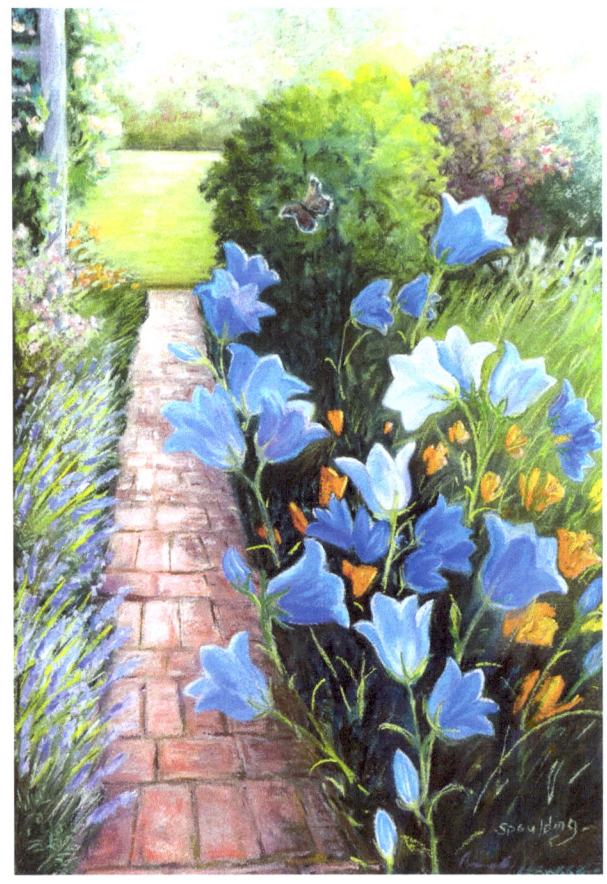

were none, all at once there will be some, then several, and then a cloud. I love to sit on the brick walk in their midst, as some will inadvertently light on me. What bliss. In their closeness I can observe their furry faces, bright black eyes, curling tongues and little nob tipped antennae. There is a fascination in their wings which are uniquely positioned, one atop the other, making them appear like folded paper airplanes.

Lilies appear in July with their sensuous smell and form. Gold, white and burgundy trumpets create an understory for the blue butterfly bush which arches over them. I bring out my drawing pad to draw their sinuous petals, all in excuse to stand amid the scent. Then I create a drawing that demands to become a finished piece.

The intense orange of California poppies vibrates in the sun. Nigella, or Love In A Mist, provide a delicate ground cover of annual flowers, soft blue in a fernlike mass of foliage. Mounds of Campion in cerise and white fill in other areas with their soft gray green foliage.

Everyday is filled with expectation and surprise. Many flowers open as planned. Others have been forgotten and reappear with familiarity. Some were gifts from friends. Some came on the wind or from birds, or perhaps I had scattered seed on the ground with a blessing and they survived. Still others have been nurtured in little pots in late winter, potted up larger and finally set out with care and anticipation.

As June becomes July the garden transforms to include yellows of evening primrose, santolina and sedum accompanied by the whites of mock orange, mallow and lily. Where the brick walk ends, the pebble path begins. It forms a gradual curve defining beds below the stone wall and functions as a barrier to the lawn. As I walk along the path to inspect what is happening there, my feet make a crunching sound punctuated here and there by the snap of a ripe poppy pod releasing its seeds. I cross over to the rose walk where the Beauty Bush still hangs onto its flowers.

Beauty Bush is one of my favorite shrubs. I ordered a plant years ago from a catalog that had no pictures. The verbal description wowed me on a dark winter night and the gamble was well worth it. This shrub bears showers of delicate salmon pink bell flowers freckled with orange spots within. Tall and graceful, it makes a lovely accompaniment to the climbing roses at the entrance of the walk.

A series of posts with cross beams provide the structure for Madame Alfred Carrière, City of York, Ash Wednesday, and Baffin Bay creating a corridor between the roses and the ornamental pear tree. The tall shrubs provide gentle shade for hellebore, primrose, Jacob's ladder, ferns, and Solomon's seal.

I follow the corridor out and find myself facing the orchard. I watch as the barn swallow pair slip past silently on their way to the barn. They have already had one clutch and taken them away mysteriously. Absent for over a week, they are now back and starting a second family.

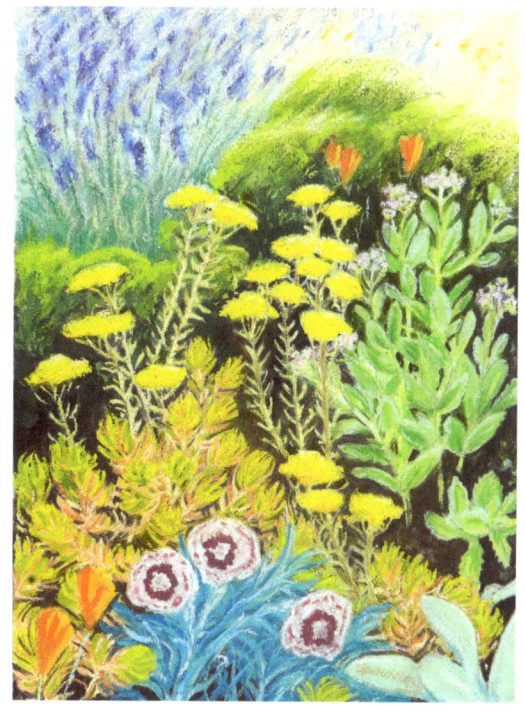

An undulating wave of sound and flight crests toward me as goldfinches head for the garden and bird bath. They are cheerful, a twittering passage in black, yellow, olive green and white.

Heat days begin, followed by cooling fog and incoming mares tails, mackerel skies, or sweeps of pearlescent white and darkly shadowed cumulus clouds. Dragonflies come up from the ponds below us, White Tails, Red Cardinal Hawks and big Blue Darners. The smaller damselflies come to the garden as well.

Though the Rufous males have disappeared, heading for the mountains, it alway seems too soon. At least the females and juveniles will stay a bit longer. One young fellow practices his sweeping maneuvers for a large male Anna's at the feeder. The Anna's looks over his shoulder unperturbed as if to say "You doofus." A doofus Rufous!

My time is spent watering vegetables. Plants need shearing and deadheading. I work a little. Then I take a notebook to the shady arbor, under the pretense of accomplishing something useful.

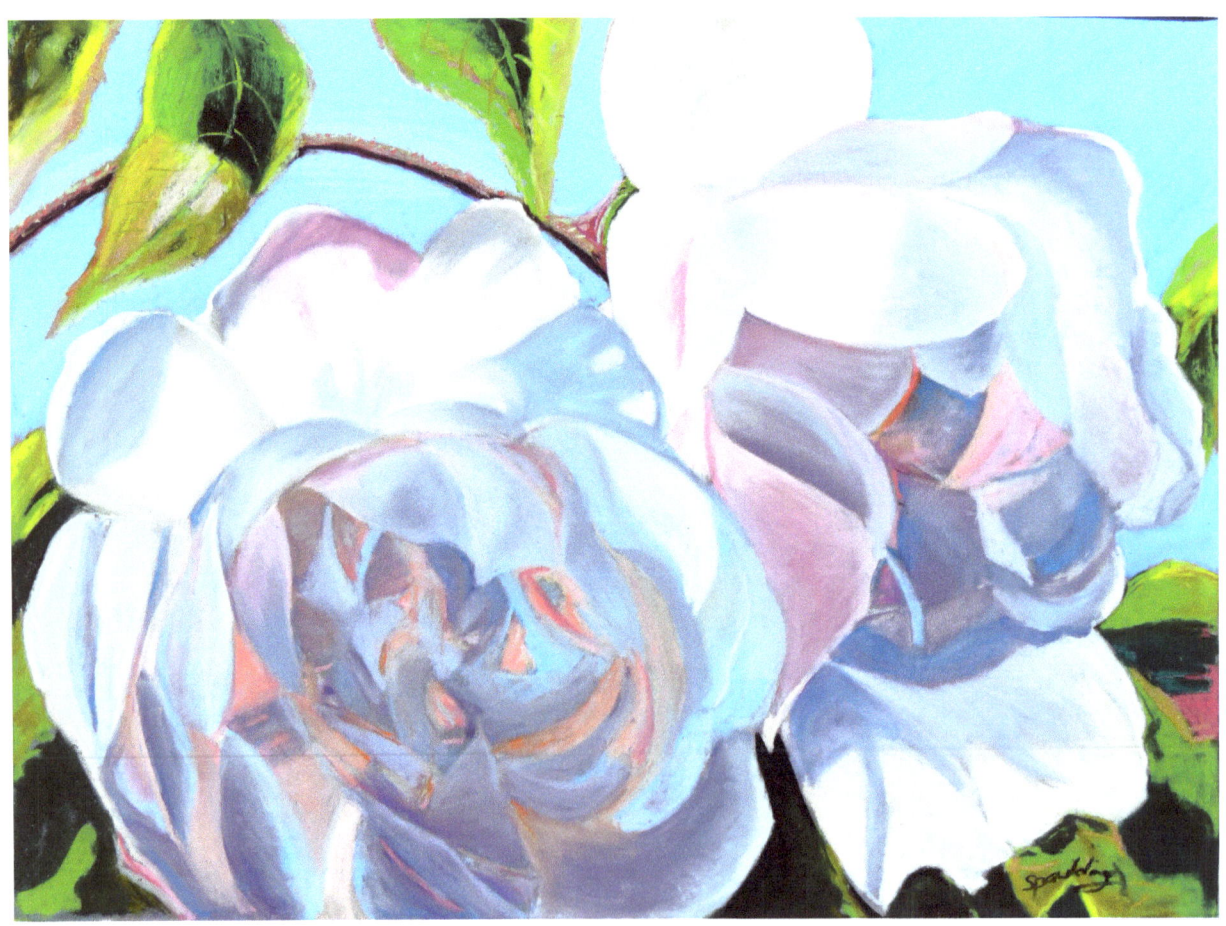

Madame Alfred Carrière

Spring is when life is alive in everything.
—Christina Rossetti

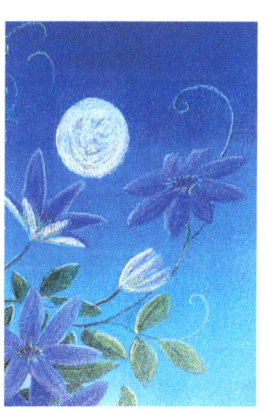

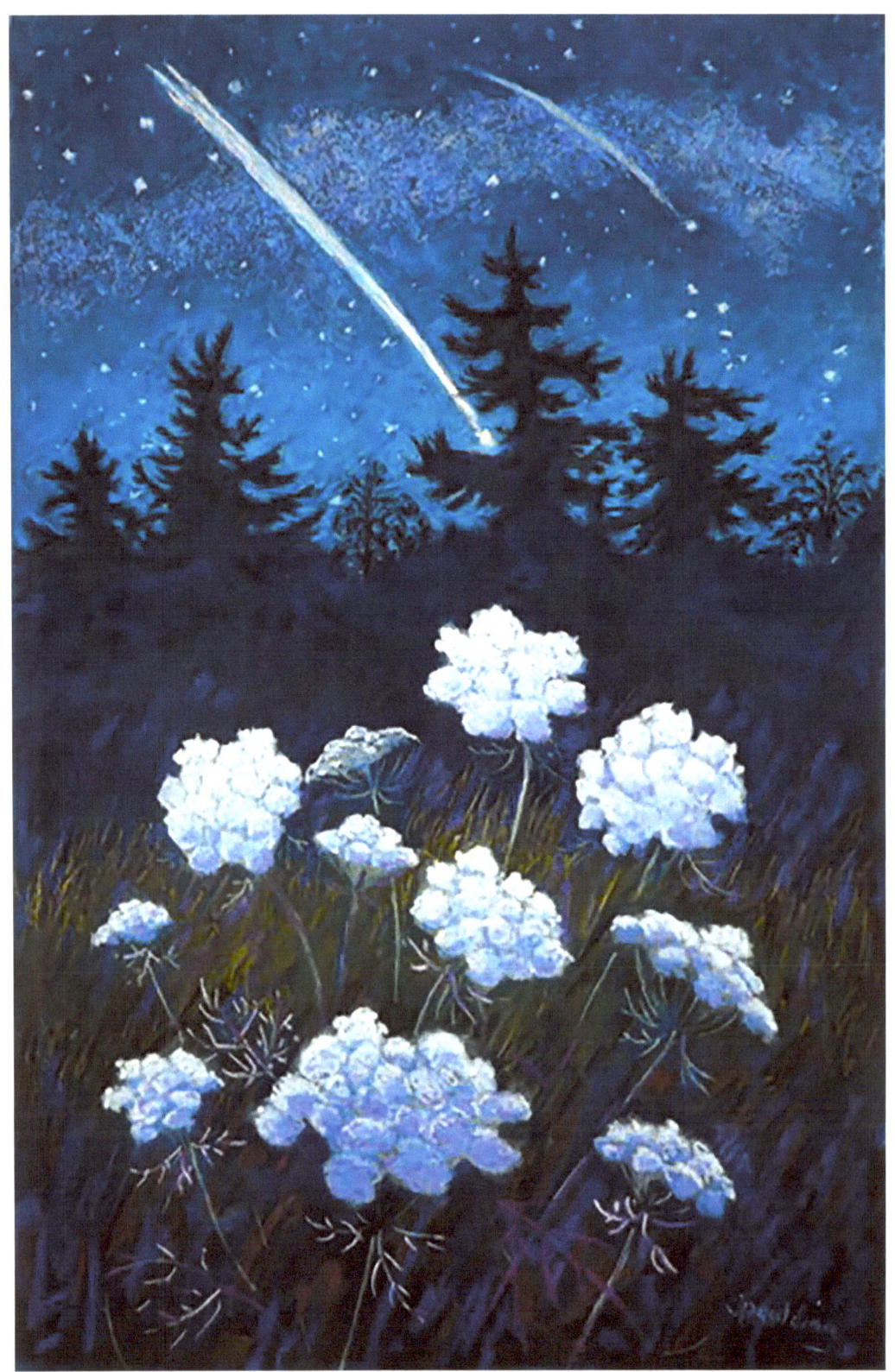

Stargazers

Chapter Eleven

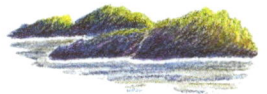

The Glories of Summer and Fall

As July slips into August, a pervasive laziness dominates the days. The garden is dominated by dried grasses, toasted in the sun. Golden light filters through leaves and flowers that are left standing. The palpable energy of growth has dissipated as plants respond to heat and lack of water. Sunlight is still intense, though lower in the sky. What energy the plants have left has shifted to the production of seeds and fruits.

The garden I tend relies on natural rhythms. I water where I can. However most of my plants have to brace for survival when the typically hot and dry days of late summer arrive. In order to help them, my planting strategy has been to pack them closely together into beds where they shade each other and the earth. The importance of mulching during the summer season was a lesson I seemed slow to learn but I am catching on. Mulch keeps the soil shaded so that it can retain what moisture comes its way. Compost, grass clippings, pine needles, and dried leaves of bracken fern are useful allies.

I move slowly on hot days. It is an easy choice to leave the weeds standing and leave the deadheading until later. I am conserving my own energy while letting the garden rest too. Exceptional to the shrubs and perennials, are the vegetable beds which I tend and water each morning. Tomato, squash and pepper plants are finally growing mature, filled with blossoms and setting fruit. Zinnias, Crocosmia, and Sunflowers contribute their snappy primary colors to the parched landscape. Vegetables demand water if they are to be productive. I put mulch around them to at least make the moisture last longer.

The enervating heat in some ways is strangely stimulating. My laziness becomes dreamlike. I feel I have shifted to some exotic place somewhere on our planet that I would otherwise be unlikely to visit. The evenings are mild and we leave the windows open, delighting in soft breezes flowing across us as we sleep. I go out to watch the night sky without wearing shoes. I think about images as my studio and trips to nearby coves beckon. I tiptoe to the studio in the morning, across a deck dappled with early sunlight. I remember that it is a luxury to sit at my desk without turning on heat, or starting a fire, or switching on lights.

Large drawing papers cover my work tables and I begin to draw up several compositions. I keep my sketch pads handy and a travel bag of watercolor and colored pencils. When I have had enough of being indoors I take a break. I am off to harvest images and peas.

I gather raspberries in the sun. My fingers become stained with juice. There will be enough to freeze. I sneak several into my mouth where I let them dissolve on my tongue where they release the perfect blend of sweet and tart. Hoping not to stain my clothes with telltale blotches of red, I reach under the jungle of leaves for berries hiding underneath.

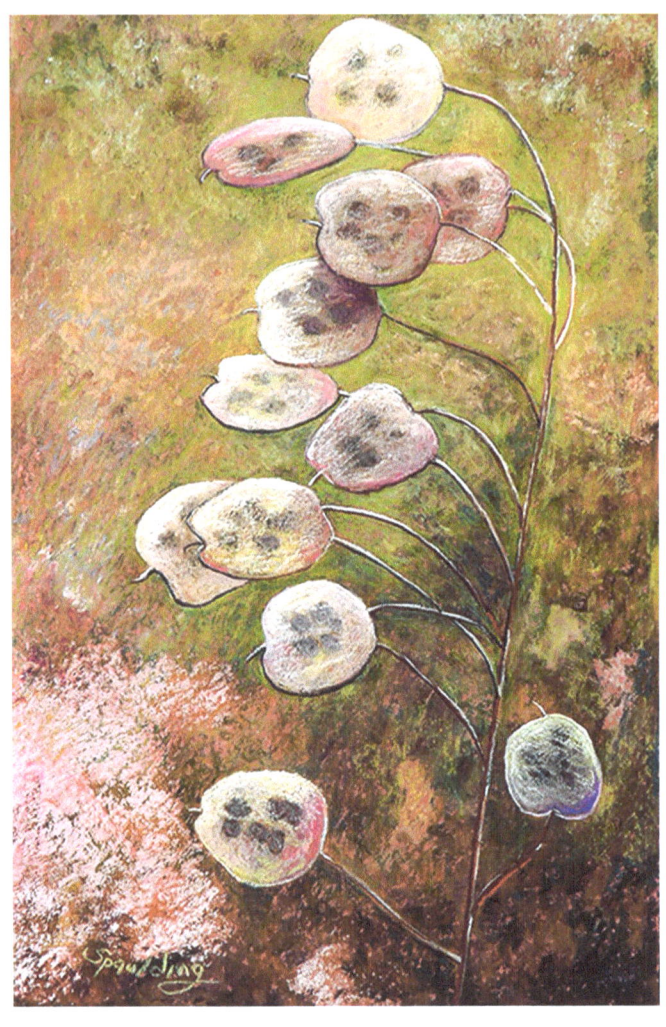

The canes are hopelessly entwined. A quail flies out from the shadows, surprising us both.

For months we have been confused by hawks. Now they are revealing themselves and I realize we have been oblivious to what has transpired. We have had occasional visits from the smaller Sharp Shinned Hawk throughout the year. Then in early spring we noticed a very large version of "sharpie", as a Cooper's Hawk landed on one of the garden gates. It seemed twice as large with similar markings. Since then, the Cooper's Hawk has crossed over the property frequently. While I attempt to key in on small differences such as shape of head and length of the tail, I feel much more confident in identifying the hawks by their calls.

In a previous year, a pair of Cooper's had built a nest in our grove of Douglas Firs which the female defended with bravado, causing me to wear an old fedora while taking my morning walks, as well as using my walking stick. She had swooped down over me several times as I walked past her nest tree and if she didn't leave her nest, I could hear her objecting "KAKAKA" from above as I went by. Nothing seemed to have come of her nesting attempts that season and the nest was abandoned a few weeks later. Barred Owls frequent the woods and could have discouraged the hawks. I often find owl pellets on the ground along my path though rarely see the owls.

One day in mid July we were startled to see two Cooper's Hawks in the fir trees. The next day I was astonished to find that three hawks had landed in the field between the trees and the house. The day after that there were four hawks in the firs. It was clear that there was a family this year and the young had just fledged. Because their presence had been so secretive we had not even the slightest premonition that there was a nest nearby. We wondered curiously what would happen.

As I walked each day, I often spotted the youngsters perching on limbs where their white, vertically streaked breasts caught morning sun. I was often struck for a moment that I was seeing small owls as they stared back at me with forward facing eyes. That they were hawks was obvious though. Their heads were small and squarish rather than large and round; their beaks more predominant.

The youngsters were awkward, and constantly crying out with a sharp downturned whistle. They seemed to be calling out for attention, but the parents were seldom seen. They called out to each other, answering each other's whistles as they moved from bough to bough. Their size was impressive for young birds and I had to wonder what was the source of nutrition that had sustained all this growth. A lot of birds and small rodents, I surmised.

With the hawk family near, all the birds we loved in the garden could be easy prey. Newly fledged chickadees, looking very smart in crisp new feathers, were everywhere. They still begged to be fed. Their devoted but tattered looking parents going through their summer molt kept working hard to keep up. Fluttering their wings and forever peeping seemed unwise behavior for the chicks with hawks nearby. The young raptors began to frequent the garden. One day three of them perched closely together on top of a trellis. They looked hugely out of scale compared to our many song birds. Hunting skills needed refining, however. I saw a hopeful hawk chase a juvenile Purple Finch into the brush. The hawk, its large wings outstretched, barred tail fanned out, legs and talons ominously ready to grasp, while keeping up its constant keening whistle didn't prove to be a good tactic. Its siblings watched from close by as though taking a lesson.

The Barn Swallows had their third clutch of babies. I had spotted a row of beaks yawning out from the edge of the mud nest in the barn. When the hawks came anywhere near the barn, the pair were out in pursuit. Calls of alarm alerted other swallows, that appeared out of nowhere, as though conjured up. They all pursued, bombed and dived at the young Coops, through the air and into openings in the firs where they perched. The acrobatics and possibility of physical contact from the swallows' onslaught must have been unsettling to the bigger, but still clumsy hawks for they disappeared deeper into the thick boughs where we could hear their mournful whistles.

One day as I looked upward to wispy clouds in a mackerel sky, I saw that the hawks were out together, flying higher and higher, riding the thermals. It was a beautiful sight and I think the first time they had taken to the skies. They seemed to glide effortlessly in wider and wider circles until slipping out of sight. Would they be leaving soon to establish their own territories? Would they remain nearby? We had gotten used to watching these hunters and seeing them support each other as a family. The piercing gaze from those sharp eyes remains haunting: All knowing, accusatory, menacing or simply observing?

By early August the woods quieted and the hawk family seemed to have moved farther away. I noticed robins calling from the hedgerows, nuthatches rustle though the pine limbs, toes grasping flaking bark, up and upside down the trunks they go. Even the quail family made an appearance after weeks of stealthy quiet in the blackberry thickets.

I finally found this year's hawk nest. It was high atop a broken off fir trunk where it was enclosed by other firs. There was only one spot on my path where I could see it. A bit of cottonwood down stuck in amongst the sticks gave it away, other wise I would have never found it.

Hawks or not, birdsongs have decreased dramatically by August. Call notes fill the trees and meadows, but the melodic songs of so many species no longer serenade in the garden as we move past the breeding season. A clipped clean whistle gives away a Swainson's Thrush and I listen for the fluting trill to follow, just in case. I am not likely to hear that beautiful lilting rhapsody again this season. No more twilight forays to enjoy their concerts. I was glad for the whistle call note though, as it let me know the thrushes were near for awhile longer.

The rambunctious singing of the Black-headed Grosbeaks has ended too. A few lingered in the garden until the end of July. We heard them calling to one another, the youngsters very vocal. Quite suddenly they have set out upon their migrations south. Do they leave at night in silence? One day in the garden I notice the emptiness that they and their songs used to fill.

The Rufous Hummingbirds are all gone too. The males left in early July and in weeks that followed the females and juveniles also departed. An occasional loner briefly appears, curiously approaching flowers, our faces if we were wearing bright colors, or the hose spray, until they too disappear and it has become the Anna's garden again.

Finches fill the void in August. Flocks of goldfinches, in particular, have doubled in number as they bring their families to the garden. The juveniles, a lovely tawny olive color with caramel colored wing bars, are asking to be fed by their ragtag parents. The adults have begun to molt from summer to winter plumage. The bright yellow males show motley patches of olive brown and will soon blend inconspicuously with the females and but for the adult's white wing bars they look much like their offspring. We will see them through October and then they too will find a winter range, a seedy place, somewhere near, but not here.

In spite of plant growth slowing down there is one noticeable exception. Himalayan blackberries are in the midst of blooming and forming fruit but in spite of how dry we are, they are producing huge whopping canes that lurch forth from the base of each plant. They stretch over the tomato house, out over the eight foot high rugosa hedge and over the towering blackberry bushes themselves, in what may be their attempt to camouflage and protect their ripening fruit. Where the firs have outgrown them the berries still reach for the sun sending canes upward through branches twenty-five or thirty feet high.

Thick thorns are piercing and positioned on the cane to capture bare skin and slash as they puncture. The canes themselves are sometimes an inch in diameter, solid and woody, able to snap back with a smack, anyone moving through their space. They are dangerous weapons and I wonder why I have let them grow until berry season arrives. Then, laden with pounds of large juicy berries we are grateful for their gifts. Berries, an inch in circumference, warmed in the sun, taste like a pie already baked.

When my grandson Robert was four years old he picked blackberries with precision. His tiny fingers grasped and teased the fruits from the menacing vines as he took his time filling the bowl. His head covered with a straw hat, light freckling his tanned cheeks, he was a picture of summer.

The golden hops struggle as the weather gets dry. They cover the arbor by the vegetable beds with walls of chartreuse-golden leaves. By June they reach the tops of the eight foot posts and even higher up the pole where the wren's bird house sits. The vines creep up over the house providing a new unexpected front door garden for the wren family living there. By the time the young leave the nest, the entrance is curtained by draping verdure. The vines make a canopy over the top of the arbor where they meet and entwine the Banshee Rose. Their roots have dug under the pebble path beneath the arbor where they absorb what moisture is left in the earth. As I look upward, I see vines that have braided around each other to build stability as they climb optimistically into the air, seeking a new repose. Their quest is a graceful sinuous reach.

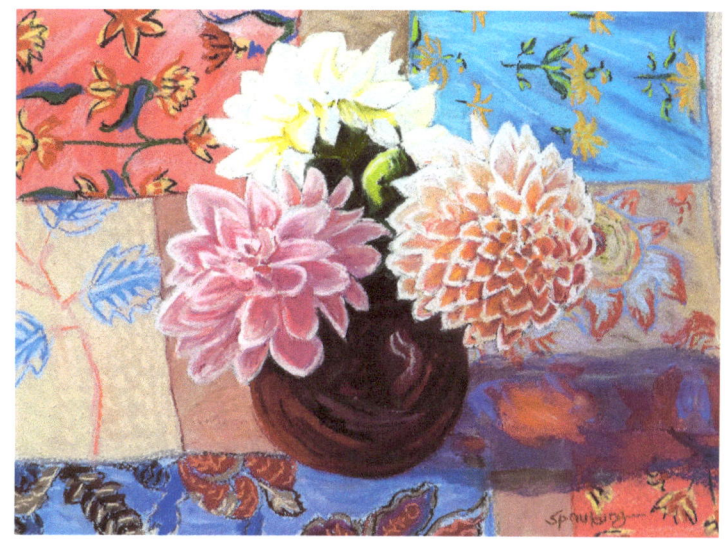

Plums, peaches, pears and apples come in succession. Tomatoes and basil, and this year two tiny eggplants about the perfect size for a doll's house. It was worth the try.

One could spend a lot of time putting up food. One could share and we do. We feel gratitude for so much bounty. There is a sublime happiness to nurturing things. It is a joy to watch things grow. Deeply mysterious, it is a downright wonder to see a tree create a fruit.

Bees and paper wasps are at the height of their populations in the heat of summer. Like the bumble and honey bees, the paper wasps are busy and keep mostly to themselves. They create little paper discs for nests, with exposed larva cells which a few individuals tend. The nests appear in odd places, just inside the door of the potting shed, in an empty plastic pot, between the studio wall and a downspout, under our wooden bench and under the sun umbrella. They remain mostly oblivious to our presence as we go about our affairs.

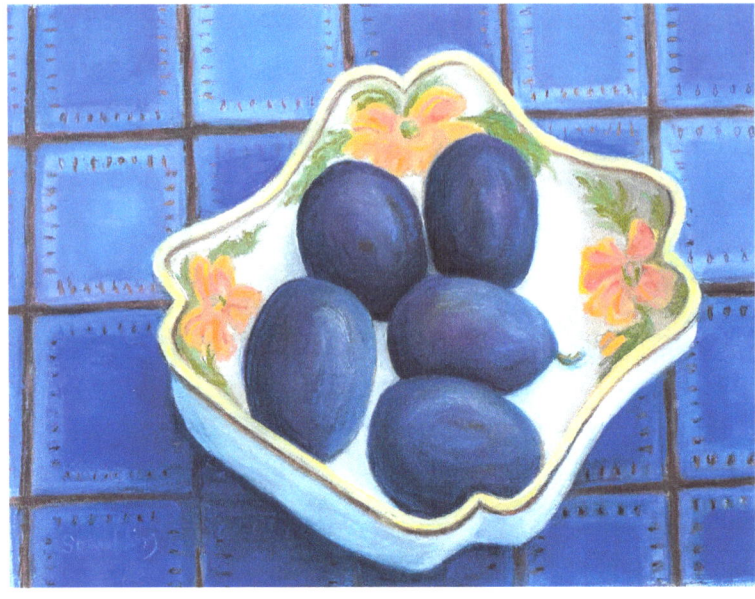

It is the burgeoning populations of menacing yellow jackets and aggressive Bald Faced hornets that give pause. Twice this summer raccoons have visited in the night and ripped apart the large balloon like nests that we had been watching and avoiding as they grew ominously bigger and bigger. Raccoons forage on the larvae and seem to know just when they are big enough to be a perfect meal. I can't imagine attacking a hive of vicious, stinging and biting insects, but over and over we have seen raccoons wipe out large colonies, redeeming themselves in our eyes for their otherwise mischievous and undesirable behaviors.

When raccoons climb in the fruit trees and break branches and steal the fruit, especially Italian prunes which they particularly love, it is annoying. It is worse than maddening when they raid a birdhouse, perhaps stealing eggs or killing the nesting parents, or hatchlings. In my book, it is unforgivable. We look out for ways to foil them from such ravaging behaviors. Even with these frustrations, they remain my favorite tactic for eliminating wasps.

Inside the fenced garden ungainly flower and weed stocks dominate in late summer. Foxglove spikes six and seven feet tall are laden with seed pods. I hope they will succeed in scattering their seeds here and there. The wild evening primroses are also ungainly and spread more seeds than the garden has room for. The seed pods, like green herringbones adorn the stems which birds enjoy foraging upon. Mallows have become scraggly and unwieldy. With flowers turning to fattened seed pods, they topple into the paths. Queen Anne's Lace that once proffered up its starburst blossoms to the skies, have turned their umbel flowers into baskets of upturned pedicels, curving inward, nestlike, embracing many sculpted seeds.

Who but me would raise so many weeds? Yet, I know I am not the only gardener who has enjoyed a touch of wild. I often think of Edna St Vincent Millay's poem "Portrait of a

Neighbor" : "Her lawn looks like a meadow, And if she weeds the place, She leaves the clover standing, And the Queen Anne's Lace." Perhaps I see myself as that absent minded person who "walks up the walk, like a woman in a dream" and "weeds her lazy lettuce by the light of the moon."

This beloved weedy place is welcoming to itinerant travelers too: White -throated Sparrows, Townsend Warblers, Evening Grosbeaks, Red Crossbills, Indigo Buntings, along with other seldom seen sightings, birds blown off course or who have drifted out of their usual range. We wonder about their wanderings. There are other passersby. Seeds of Salsify, Storksbill, Self Heal, Scarlet Pimpernel or Watson's Willowherb have traveled on the wind, hitched a ride on fur or feather, or traveled through some creature's digestive tract to fall upon this land and grasp a life. The land awaits. Life flows through, as do our errant thoughts and dreams.

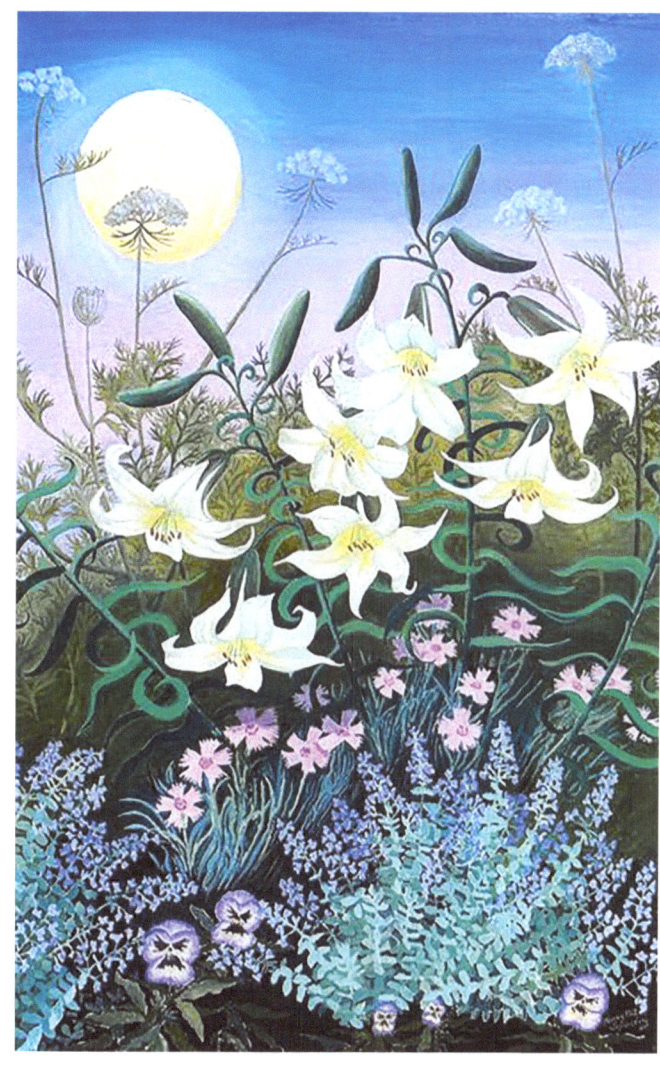

As summer nears its end I find myself spending more time in the studio as I feel too lazy to work outside. I look out over the garden and then lose myself in artwork. It can be difficult at times as my upstairs room becomes sweltering in hot weather, even with the windows wide open. Lewis brought me a fan. During a succession of such hot days I stood in front of my easel as the fan blew wildly, carrying away the heat, the sweat on my brow, and blowing hair away from my face. I worked for hours laying down color, windswept.

So much heat and we beg for rain. Sometimes it comes at the end of summer, though it never soaks deeply enough into the ground. It will take weeks of wet weather to make a difference. Fog comes with comforting moisture droplets hanging in the air causing mysterious disappearances of hedgerows, garden fences and neighbors, of sea and islands and sky. Colors mute, and sounds exaggerate as fog horns echo in the distance.

In recent summers we have also been covered in smoke from distant forest fires, turning the sun and moon red, obscuring distances with an ominous murkiness and feel of pending destruction.

Then the days cool. Somewhere between the Perseid Meteor Showers of mid-August and the coming of September I find myself stunned by the shrinking of daylight. It seems almost a personal affront as sunset closes in on suppertime. Evenings outdoors after our supper have become a habit, but that time will soon disappear. The equinox arrives. Equal day and night! Then nights slowly grow longer than days. The time has arrived when I tell myself that I must adapt and seek comfort in the rhythm of the spheres.

By October losing three minutes of light a day does grab my attention. However I adjust and find that I am enjoying each new angle of the sun with its ever changing light. Leaves and flower petals take on a golden translucence, peaceful and serene. Cooler temperatures add a new liveliness, a spark of excitement. There is the satisfaction of fruits put up, a garden readied for winter and the knowing that I have a new season of collected memories to muse upon.

As I am working in the studio one fall day, there is a rapping on the metal roof that grows louder and more incessant. I am trying to concentrate and ignore the raucous interruption. It quiets, but later when I go downstairs for a break, I hear fluttering within our little wood stove. Even though the glass needs cleaning, I can see enough to make out a flicker inside in the shadows of the firebox. It is staring out at me. Its long chiseled beak and wary, dark eyes question my intent as I look in to ponder how a bird of its size could have made it down the narrow chimney.

Just this very morning over a cup of coffee, my daughter Laurie had told me she had been observing two flickers fighting over a small cranny in the overhang of the cabin where she is staying.

I grab an old tee shirt and open the door of the stove carefully in hopes of capturing the bird before it escapes from the burn box. I want to avoid it crashing into the window in a panic. Holding my breath as the flicker begins fluttering up and down anxiously, I throw the shirt over it and grasp it firmly in both hands. I find that this woodpecker is a lot of bird to hold. Unlike the little wrens we usually rescue, this bird has the weight of a duck! I am able to rub most of the soot off its feathers and carry it to the door where the flicker immediately recognizes its freedom. As I release it, it flies off fast and far.

The very next day we heard BirdNote on NPR airing a segment about woodpeckers that stay north in the winter. This is the time of year they hollow out a hole in a tree to winter over in or look for solitary cavities that will serve that purpose, the program tells us. Our Red-shafted Flickers are right on schedule!

The most beautiful gift of nature is that it gives one pleasure to look around and try to comprehend what we see.

—Albert Einstein

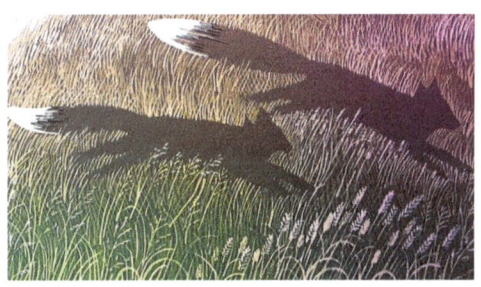

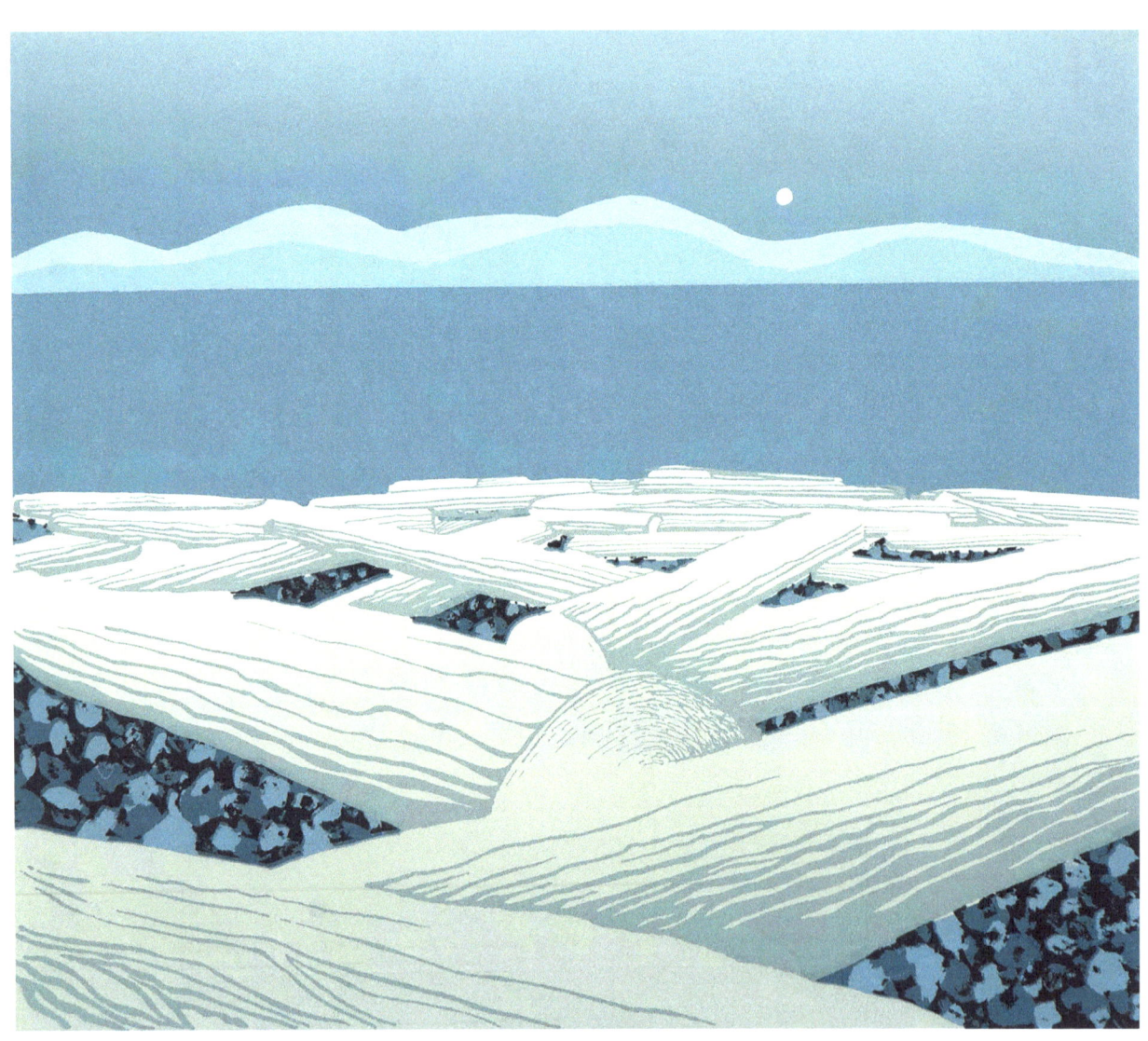

Beach Logs

Chapter Twelve

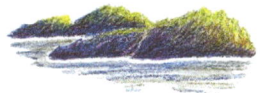

Transformations
2000 -2008

We sat on the beach in the cold dark, warming ourselves by the only visible light, the curling flames of our crackling bonfire. Sparks from the driftwood logs drifted off, spitting into oblivion as we looked out into an infinitesimal emptiness. We could see neither our island world nor its encompassing night sky. Damp sea air brushed our cheeks as water lapped ever closer, its motion rocked the cobbles at our feet making little hollow claps and clinks. The rest of the visual world had been erased by the night.

With the dawning of a new century we had a lot on our minds. Good friends, Cal and Mary Karen, lived down on Griffin Bay and decided to have a midnight beach party to celebrate the New Year. It was such a big deal to cross over into the 21st century. We had all been listening to the pending disaster stories for weeks with the Y2K prognosis of possible computer failures around the world. What unknowns might that trigger? We decided marking the moment together would be memorable and if disaster struck we would stand together.

We talked while kids and dogs ran up and down the beach in the nearby safety zone of half light from the flaming fire. We talked of provisions laid by as suggested on the news. No problem, we always had our pantries full, just by the fact that we were islanders. We wondered what would happen with no electricity or delivery of fuel. Most of us were used to falling back on kerosene lanterns, candles, and wood stoves with the many power outages we experienced here. We were fine for short term disasters. Beyond that, well, who could say?

Darkness predominated New Year's Eve as the old year faded away. At midnight the grand fireworks display across the channel began. Lights sparkled up like fountains, pinwheels, and rockets, reflecting their metallic rainbows of color in the black water below. There was a world beyond the beach after all and there appeared to be no signs of it crashing or coming to an end. We had made it safely over the threshold.

I kept some thoughts to myself that night as we sat and soaked in the cold beauty. It wasn't only the uncertainty of a new century. It was also the uncertainty within myself. My breaking point had come. I just didn't have it in me to make another silk screen print.

We had been resourceful all these years. I had to keep telling myself, that would not change.

A few days later I told Lewis I couldn't face the rigors of silkscreen printing any longer and to my surprise he told me that he felt the same way. The big hurdle was to find something else that we could become competent at, quickly, and something we each found rewarding.

Our new path was going to be a gamble. Would there be an audience for our new work? With an inventory of already created serigraphs we could float along for a short while, but without the excitement of new prints we would not say afloat for long.

Within a few months Lewis had returned to photography, exploring with a new digital camera. I painted, returned to drawing with colored pencils and back to painting again. My progress was slow.

Finding a direction took me much longer than I hoped. I had a sense that staying connected with those things that gave me inspiration would be the most helpful. I tried to be patient and confident that a natural transition would unfold eventually.

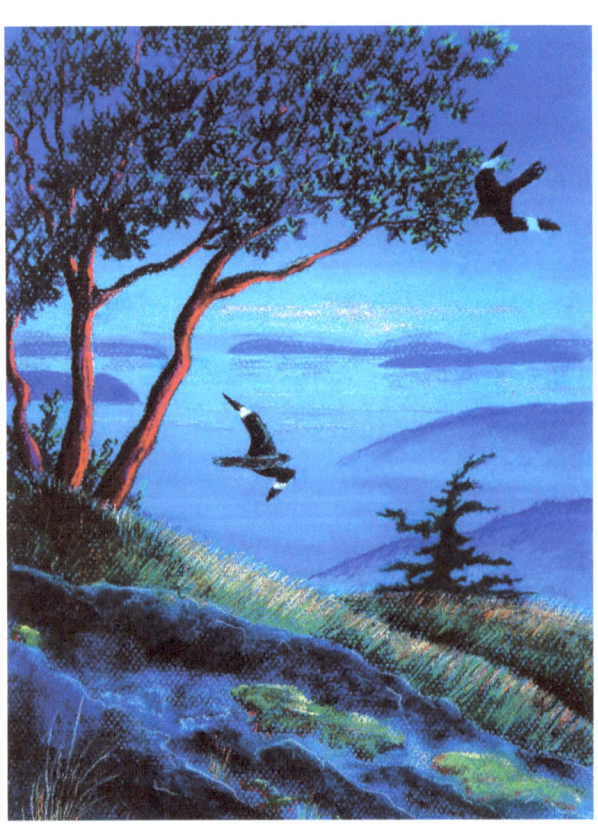

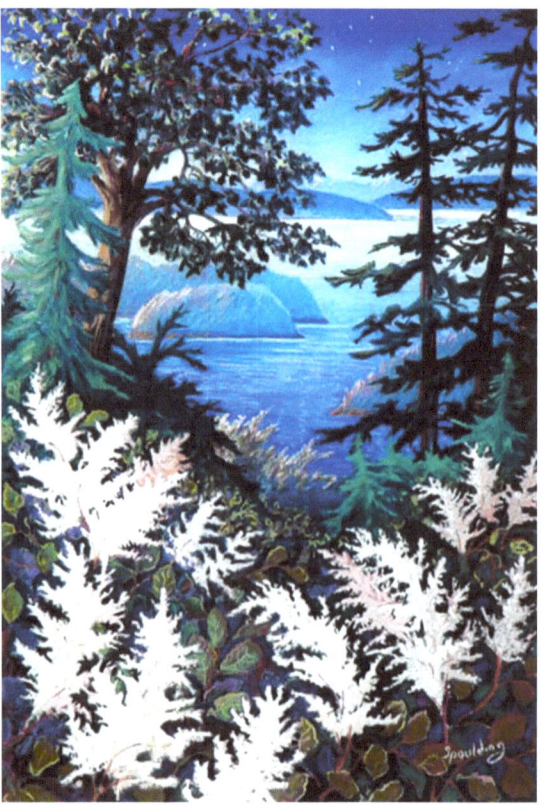

As I searched during the following summer, I kept active outdoors. I celebrated the solstice by getting out of bed to greet the earliest of glint daylight. At day's end I stayed awake until the latest twilight disappeared. Bathing myself in long light, I hoped would work magic. Throughout June, I hiked on beaches and hillsides and gardened in the rain. I carried my notebook and sketch pad wherever I went. I thought about the artists I admired. I practiced and made odd starts with different materials as ideas flourished but were unsatisfactorily expressed, incubating.

Taking a complete break after our only art show in June freed up the rest of the month. One June day Lewis made focaccia bread and a cake and I made arrangements to pick up our art buddies, Rick and Paula, who lived up the hill in a yurt they had built. We were off to celebrate a west side sunset together.

We circled around the island toward the county park. Red and yellow columbine reached up through salal and dry Madrona covered banks alongside the roadway ditches. We stopped to walk along poppy paths by the shore making our way to the lighthouse before heading up Young Hill. The mountain was peaceful and quiet as we picnicked on bald rocks facing a view of Vancouver Island. The evening stretched out before us as though time was caught in a vacuum. Hours with amiable chatter and good food sent us into a meditative mode while taking in a show of endless shifting colors and light dappling the islands, waterways and clouds that surrounded us.

Some quail rustled in the underbrush close by. We hoped to see nighthawks. They seemed to have moved off toward the quarries or northern shoreline, but we kept a look out just the same. These whippoorwill related birds are an integral part of our longest of days, gliding above in the twilight. As they drop rapidly to catch swarming insects they make a memorable "poink or pzeent" sound. I keep a mental checklist each year. If I am fortunate enough to see them, I mark off their presence and feel that all's right with the world.

When the sun set above the horizon into a cumulus bank of clouds, foaming upwards on the horizon, we headed down through the shadowed woods, creamy light still beckoning through the tree trunks. Lacy Ocean Spray that bloomed in the understory captured the last luminescence as darkness fell. Dancing white blooms guided our way.

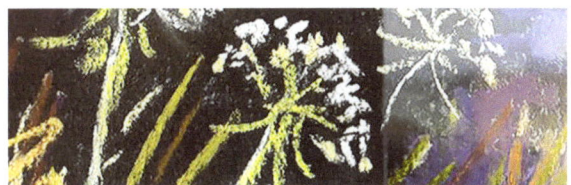

Shortly thereafter I made a discovery.

On one of her many solo drives north over the years, my mother had brought me art supplies she thought I might enjoy. Amongst them was a dusty wooden box of used Gerault pastels, made in France, that had been her uncle's. The rediscovery of my Great Uncle

Sidney's pastels buried and forgotten on my studio shelves sent me off at last in a new and wonderful direction.

Sidney had been head of the French department at the University of Arizona for many years, long before I was a student there. He had also taught French at the university in Montpelier, France before World War II. I remember him as a most genteel man who possessed a mischievous smile. He loved to play the piano and paint southwest landscapes in a plein air style. After he died, the little house he lived in near the campus in Tucson became a student meeting place and poetry center where friends and I used to go sometimes. That his pastels had somehow made their way into my possession was a comfort and delight. Using the materials he had painted with felt like a physical link to a bygone era, the fin de siecle, the cultural milieu at the turn of a previous century, a time that fascinated me.

I created many messes at first but I quickly came to understand what artists meant when they talked of finding medium that felt like a match. I found pastels were expedient, forgiving, and capable of beautiful color transitions. There was excitement with each discovery and the vibrancy of pure pigments was joy to work with. I often started a piece and left it as another piece called. I then worked on that for awhile. Pastel can always be set aside to wait. It is a freeing and malleable medium. It allowed me to contemplate as I worked. An image could always be altered, eradicated and begun all over. Best of all I had found the perfect medium to create the complex pieces that had been haunting me. I was now back on my way, playing with new subjects and continuing the wildflower series.

It was refreshing to work in new ways. Our shows on the mainland and the growing island studio tour were always a big incentive to get new pieces done. I had learned long ago that deadlines were my friends. Slowly and steadily we progressed.

In just a dozen years, the number of main studios on our island studio tour doubled. With the addition of many guest artists participating at most studios during the big weekend, the tour had grown to represent a wide range of disciplines.

After many years being on the tour, artists Yvonne, Darleen, Paula, Mary and I forged a sort of sisterhood, united in our commitment to the tour and combining our diverse areas of expertise, working together year after year to insure the community event would go on.

Preparing the studio for the tour was a never ending affair. Hosts, myself included, always envisioned perfection. For us that included art and garden. In striving toward that goal it soon became apparent that expectations easily become too grand. Finally, with a freeing sense of relief, I would begin to remove things off my "to do" list. Such was the timing when Mary Karen came with gloves and clippers to help us get the garden in shape. Before getting to work we sat on the steps of the deck in the sun talking of favorite plants, relishing time just to be part of the scene.

How lovely the blues are, we agreed. What was the name of that lapis colored flower on tall stems? We laughed as we tried to remember. Not the mounding Lithodora Blue that creates indigo pools around the edges of beds and paths early in the season, but its tall relative.

At last it was recalled and we laughed again, relieved to have recovered its name. Anchusa! We must plant Anchusa again in our gardens, we said.

Summers became luxuriant as the garden grew. Roses towered over the beds, the grape vine and honeysuckle draped over arbors and walls like curtains. Creatures moved in and around; a deer reaching its head over the fence to eat tendrils, raccoons, an occasional fox or rabbit, and once in a long while, a roaming river otter. Little birds of summer rustled out bugs as they secreted through twigs and branches: Orange-crowned Warblers, Yellow and Audubon's Warblers, natty House Wrens, once a Western Bluebird family.

Naturalist Susan Vernon often came to stroll on sunny afternoons through the garden and across the rest of our transitioning field. We checked on butterflies and we spotted many species over the years: Tiny coppers and blues, Ochre Ringlets, Painted Ladies, Red Admirables, Lorquin's Admirals, Mourning Cloaks, once a Sarah's Orange Tip. Sometimes Sheep's Moths, Cabbage White butterflies, often angle wings, three species of swallowtails, fritillaries, tortoiseshells and teams of skippers!

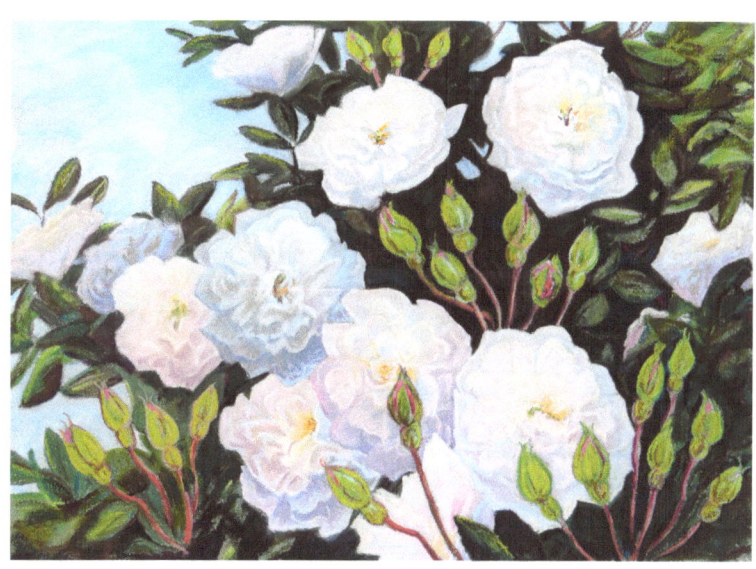

Félicité et Perpétue

Susan became a good friend as we shared forays and explorations of the outdoor world. We liked to keep track of things. Besides butterflies, Susan made notations of returning birds in spring, where dragonflies migrated, where skunk cabbage bloomed. As we shared excitement and discovery, we made everything a celebration. The sun setting on winter solstice, the first Indian Plum to bloom each February, or the first currant to appear, the appearance of Satin Flower in late winter. One March day was so cold on the bluffs, the wind blinded our eyes with so many tears we could barely see to admire unfurling purple petals blown out like windsocks where bedrock edged the sea. Everything had a place in our calendar of the extraordinary.

Getting out on hikes was part of my work and we explored every chance we got. We had become acquainted with Ellis Ridgway, a professor of physiology from the University of Virginia, who had been coming to the marine labs for research since the early sixties. He suggested one summer that we hike everywhere we could where there were no "no trespassing" signs. He anticipated pending development. Getting out to see special nooks and crannies around the islands became an urgent goal. I was ecstatic to sketch and photograph the terrain wherever we went. New perspectives were always refreshing. Happily, since that summer, several of our favorite hikes have come into the public trust after being purchased by our local land bank and preservation trust.

We often went to the mountains with Ridg when the opportunity arose. One year we went specifically to hike to an alpine lake where we planned to sleep out under a late summer full moon. Crammed into the front seat of his pickup truck we talked about our upcoming hike as we sped along the freeway. Out the passenger window I noticed something flapping in the wind. A bulbous amber shape patterned in bars of white, held on by a thread of its own making, its spider form battling the wind until she heroically pulled herself into the corner of the rear view mirror. The large garden spider must have made a web there where she had probably prospered for days while Ridg's truck remained parked. Now as we hurtled down the highway headed toward Mount Baker the amazing spider, whose domestic attempts were now enduring a hurricane, hung on fiercely for hours with her pretty banded legs. I named her Aerial. When we got to the trailhead, Aerial was still on the mirror.

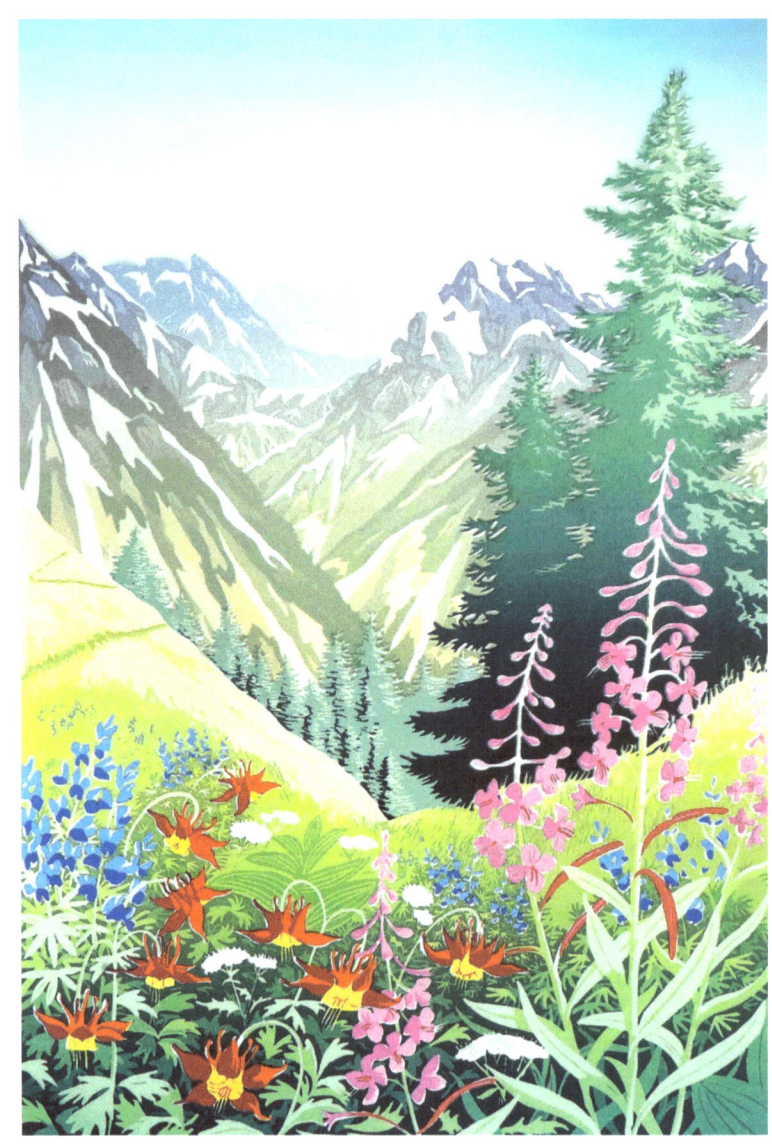

Off we went down the trail. Heading into the lake we passed through several miles of lush forest. We had been walking over an hour when Ridg called up from behind, "Did you know we have met twelve people and seven dogs heading out!" Amazing I thought. Who was counting? We were all keeping track of different sorts of data, that became apparent.

When we got to the lake we set up camp and explored the area until supper when it began to grow dark. A glow in the sky above revealed the moon had risen but remained hidden by the peak behind us. On the opposite side of the lake we could see its light casting a gold glow on the crest of a slope of rock and scree. Spontaneously, we decided unanimously to scramble up to the top and catch the moon where the light fell. Once we made it up through a cascade of boulders and rock parked by eons of glaciers, rocks with their own stories to tell, we sat observing the distant ranges and mountains around us. Range upon range were both illuminated and shadowed by the moon, a feast of space and mystery. Eventually we began to slowly descend going just far enough down into shadow that we could watch the moon rising again moments later. We repeated this game again and again until we reached the lake and our tents, at last shimmering in light.

In the morning I took a quick dip into the crystal ice water of the lake. Behind us on a sheer rock face were mountain goats impossibly balanced high above us. Our hike out brought us back to the truck where the spider was still hanging out in her web on the mirror, determined. She made the trip all the way back to the island and was able to bide her time a while longer at the labs. If she were Charlotte, she would probably have had interesting things to say about travel.

Shifting seasons all had their moments of beauty and reflection. One cold winter morning, pal Melissa stopped in to say hello and we talked by the fire while sipping coffee. How were her artistic endeavors in her studio going along, and how was her garden faring in the cold? Then we went out for a walk and a survey of what was happening in ours. I showed her the winter blooming honeysuckle, now forming flower buds. Some delicate white petals had already opened to offer subtle sweetness in the air, oblivious to the freezing temperatures and attracting the Anna's Hummingbirds.

Over time Melissa and I shared many gardening enthusiasms, and also plants. We walk past some of my "Melissa" plants as well those of other mutual friends, "Amanda" plants, "Colleen" plants, "Manya" plants, "Koz" plants, "MK" plants. We commented on how different plants respond in different locations. The Keria she gave me takes on a much different character where I have planted it than ones at her place. She grows a lush garden on rocky outcrop, mine is situated in an old field once farmed, where I struggle to create interesting landscape settings. She grows many of the same plants I do, as well as many I am not familiar with. The uniqueness of our locations and new varieties we share, make tours of each other's gardens are all the more interesting.

Down in the lower garden on that winter day we found the wheelbarrow frozen over with a plate of ice about a half inch thick formed from water collected during recent rains. Feeling frisky and silly we pulled the ice out together in one piece and carried the entire sheet across the lawn where we artfully placed it in the branches of a currant bush. It made a sparkling window pane with the morning's low light luminous through it. We laughed in our shared "Andy Goldworthy" moment, hoping our temporary sculpture might survive for at least a couple of days during the cold spell. If we had thought ahead and had laid out many containers overnight, we might have produced a dozen or more frozen sheets to play with and what might that have been like?

Months had gone by, perhaps years, without a building project, so in 2008 when Lewis was offered a whole truckload of firebrick from a printer we knew in Seattle, he jumped on it. The bricks were being torn out of a back yard where they had been used as edging and were headed for repurposing. Lewis offered half to our potter friend, Rick, to use for his kiln and the two of them drove down to the city in Rick's truck to pick up the load.

After taking up bread baking in the mid nineties, Lewis had dreamt about building a wood fired oven. He had been pouring over designs, and now with the bricks he had material and impetus to begin.

He built the oven in the middle of our vegetable garden area, a rectangular shape with an arched roof. The oven section stood waist level above a storage area where he could keep wood handy and dry. The fire bricks were stacked until the structure was about four feet high and at the point they were made to curve inward to make a dome. He used a plywood form for support. Would it work, this mini bread cathedral, Lewis wondered? But once the mortar dried it held fast. Once cured he applied washes of cement over the exterior to seal the oven from the rain. Our granddaughter Ashleigh helped at this point, climbing with agility over the top, to complete the seal where it was hard for us to reach.

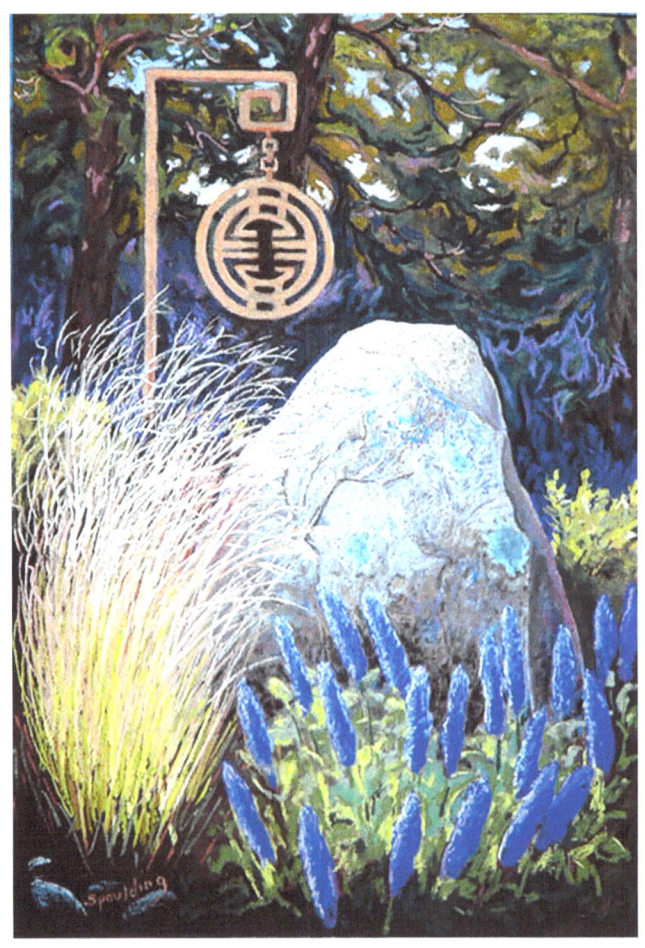

Ashleigh swam in the Salish Sea no matter the time of year, she could hardly bear to wear shoes and was a force of energy that left us breathless with admiration.

The oven was finished with a red brick chimney constructed on the front end over the oven door. A couple of pearly oyster shells from the beach were added on either side for decor.

The first time we built a fire, Lewis got the oven up to eight-hundred degrees and was able to cook a series of pizzas in a matter of minutes. Being able to bake bread with a golden crisp crust, without relying on conventional energy was very satisfying. As in places around the world where villages have big ovens fired up for friends and neighbors to share, we could always offer to have community baking days should the need ever arise.

Our "field" has become overgrown in many sections with small trees that needed thinning every year. They are a perfect source for firewood. How comforting to have these resources. When we find the time, we cut and stack wood for pizza, bread, and warmth. It is a mindful activity, like gardening, that keeps us grounded.

One late night toward the end of summer we sat on the small platform Lewis built over the woodshed and arbor. We climbed up the four runged ladder connecting to our deck. It is an ideal place to watch the sky and survey the garden. Heather came to join us as we looked at stars, enveloped by the dark velvet dome of sky, sprinkled with light from distant universes. Now and then a shooting star shot across the sky and fell downward toward the garden. Dreamily, we contemplated the mysteries above and around us.

Meanwhile back on our "rock", the place we all home, somewhere not too far away there was a party with a live band playing, notes wafting about in the mild night air. We heard the late ferry come into the harbor, three miles away, the horn blasting, announcing the last trip of the day.

It was fortunate indeed that we had been young and foolish enough to come here when we did. We raised a family, devoted ourselves to our art, and lived a homemade life in which we created our own rules most of the time. If time was worth money, there were times when our lives were rich indeed, as we jogged down a road both demanding and relentless. We had just enough failures to keep us humble and just enough success to keep running with our dreams.

Optimism is the faith that leads to achievement.

—Helen Keller

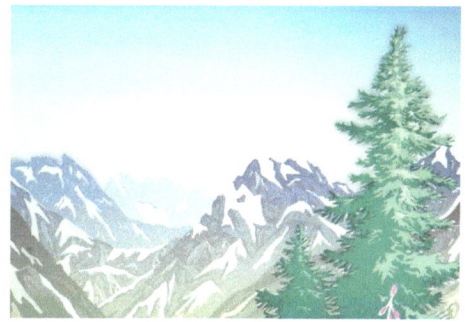

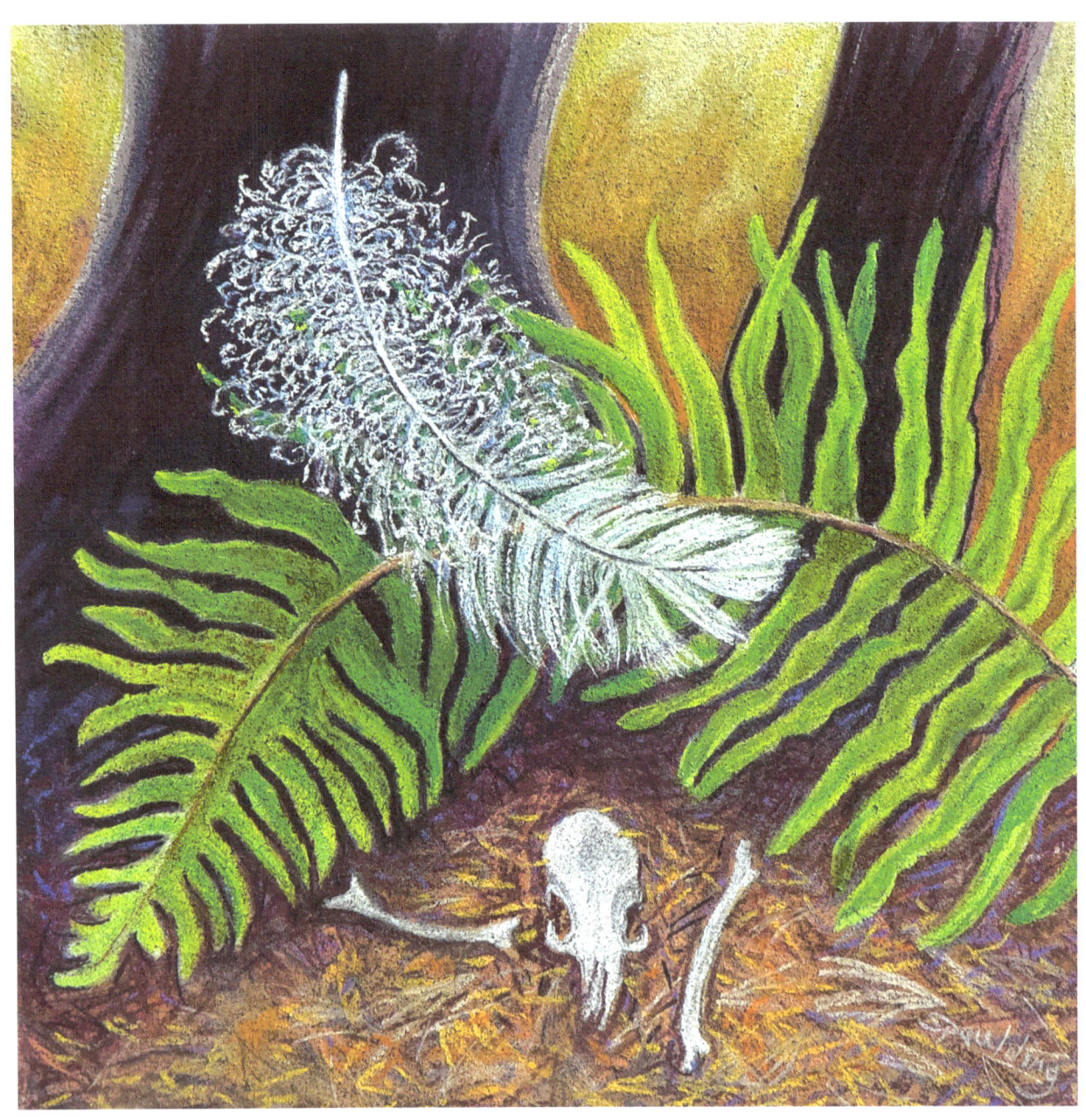

The Cycle of Life

Chapter Thirteen

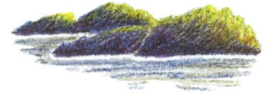

Riding the Wild Wave of Time

Living forty or more years in one spot was never our intention. We fancied ourselves as adventurers and travelers. "New experience" was Lewis' mantra. Instead we put down roots. It is not to say we haven't traveled, for we have, but we certainly settled in. I have watched five acres slowly evolve after several decades.

Changes that occur over time in one location became my fascination. We weren't on the move, but nature was. I have known a seedling, a simple whorl of tender evergreen needles shyly poking out of the grass in its first year, vulnerable, awaiting its fate, striving for success. I have watched its progress until it has become a formidable forty foot pine. The tree and I have seen a lot together.

Similarly, I have watched groves of firs shoot up before my eyes, becoming solid and tall, ring by ring, until they have altered my view, changed the course of the wind, and provided habitat for birds and deer. There is a comfort in bearing witness to these transformations as there is wonder at the forces we don't see or hear.

During our first years, while the land was yet an open field, Belgian Hares that so overpopulated the island, lived all around us. The children captured baby bunnies and kept some as pets. Our cats hunted baby bunnies, as well as overly abundant field mice on a daily basis. Eagles and Red Tailed Hawks caught rodents regularly too. At night we often heard owls nearby. It was a world out of balance seeking to find its equilibrium.

One magical winter evening we attended a concert at the Grange in town. A family of Celtic musicians from "down sound" was performing to a full house of islanders eager for live entertainment. Our younger daughter, age six and under their spell, slipped out of her seat and moved forward to the first row where she climbed on the lap of an absolute stranger. There, enraptured, she watched the harpist playing just a few feet away. When we came home on that frosty night, still under the spell of the music, we stepped out of our car to a night sky lighted by iridescence, pulsing curtains of green, purple, and turquoise. The beautiful display of Northern Lights continued with mesmerizing changes and shifts as we looked upward to see a Great Horned Owl perched on the roof of the studio, also silently gazing into the night.

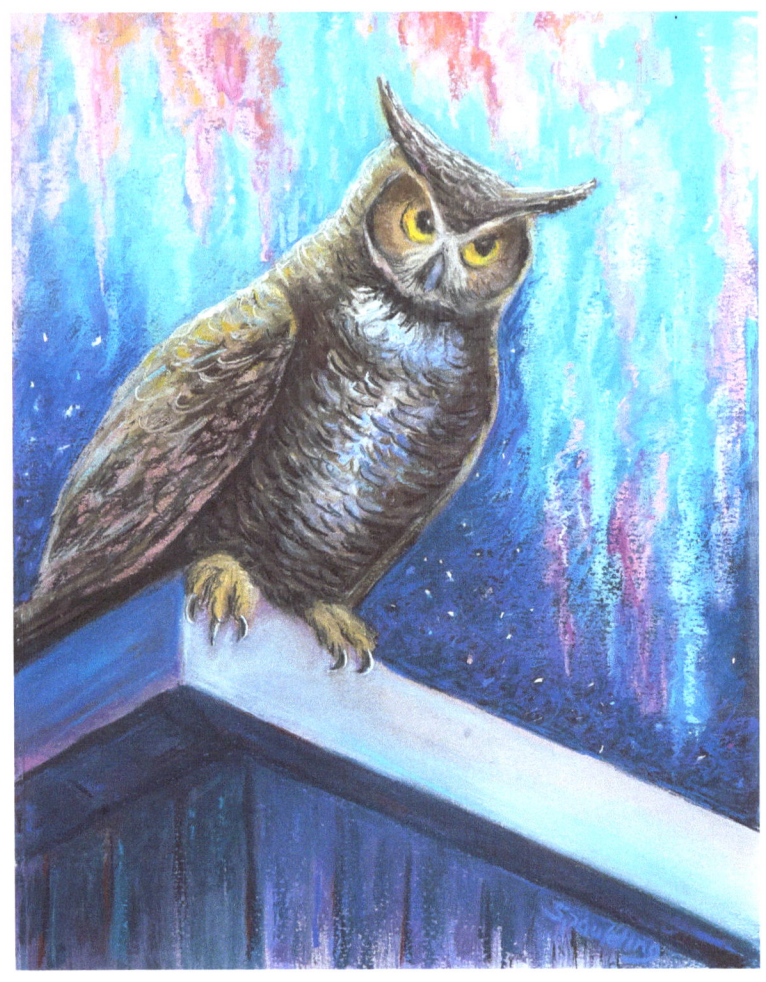

In those days of wonder and wide open spaces, we almost never saw songbirds on our property or that of our neighbors. We did however have several breeding pairs of Killdeer in the open fields. We would often see them in spring, feigning injury, most likely a broken wing, to distract us should we inadvertently come close to their nests. We often heard their piping calls that sounded out their name, "ki deea, ki deea". Nesting in the open was a strategy they preferred, laying eggs in small indents in the grass or dirt. There they incubated their eggs, hidden in plain sight, and once the eggs hatched, their precocial chicks could run like the wind.

The pretty little Savannah Sparrow, another lover of grasslands, was the first of the songbirds to arrive. As the rabbits went into decline the grasses grew healthier, other plants survived as well, providing hidden spots for the sparrows to nest. We enjoyed their songs in early summer, a gentle trilling preceded by repeated soft notes. We began to see Rufous Hummingbirds that were attracted to an occasional thistle or wild cinquefoil with its pale yellow blossoms. A few robins and goldfinches appeared as more flower seeds became available. Raptors and owls were still the predominant species.

As grasses thrived, we hired an old time islander to come and mow our field every summer. He spun us yarns when he came by, about his garden, his chickens, his children growing up on the island, and making do off the land. We enjoyed his visits and appreciated his work. Eventually when Lewis got a small tractor and did the mowing himself we became more self-reliant but we missed our conversations with Lyle.

We began to choose areas to mow and areas to leave wild. In a year or two uncut sections seemed to spontaneously sprout bracken ferns. The spores could have drifted in from miles away. The bracken shaded the ground and visually hid and shaded other species that began to show up underneath their protective umbrella like fronds. Within just a few more years our open field had transformed itself to verdant chaparral while I was preoccupied with studio work and tending the garden within our fence.

There appeared a plethora of English Hawthorn, Himalayan blackberry, the native blackberry, native spiraea, and native crabapple. Not as numerous, but also in evidence were young starts of Saskatoon berry, Soopalalie, Snowberry, Pacific Red Elderberry, Tall Oregon Grape, Low Bush Mahonia and sword fern. Red Alder, native Black Hawthorne and several species of willow also thrived as they reached our land. The willows, such graceful friends, lined the lower border and ditches where there was more water. We found Sitka Willow, Piper Willow, Scouler's, and Pacific Willow. To these species we planted several other natives: Red Osier Dogwood, Mock Orange, Vine Maple, Evergreen Huckleberry, Oregon Ash, Big Leaf Maple, Salmonberry, Salal, Red Cedar, Pacific Ninebark, Indian Plum and several species of birch. Where there was none, there was now increasing diversity, exploding exponentially.

Nonnatives, Mountain Ash, Cotoneaster and a mysterious bearer of white blossoms and red berries, also appeared: plants on the move. As years slipped past, several curious rose crosses seeded themselves successfully and flourished. A wild pear gained my notice when it bore a crop of yellow but tough little puckery fruits. Until that time I hadn't noticed its existence. Two distinctly different wild apples of unknown origin matured enough to bear fruit, though they weren't going to take any prizes for taste.

Birds were no doubt responsible for spreading plants around as they dined on the fruits and berries. What is mouth dropping is that these plants have reached maturity as we have passed by, oblivious, apparently for years.

With the alteration of the meadow to chaparral and young forest, wildlife we had not seen before began to be regulars in our little realm.

One day in early summer I had to fetch Lewis from the lower part of our field. He had received an important phone call and as one who seldom carried cell phone, I needed to find him. As I unlatched the lower garden gate I noticed a healthy looking fox in the middle of the orchard with its nose buried in the grass. As I passed by a few feet away he remained preoccupied. On our way back to the house the fox was still there. A little while later, I decided to return to the orchard to see what the attraction had been. To my surprise, the lovely blond fox with long tail draping tail was still in the same spot. I very soon figured out what was keeping him there. Using his incisors and tongue he was delicately extracting wild strawberries hidden in the grass, enjoying their goodness. Fruits had been plentiful that year and the plants had spread to become a thick ground cover between the apple trees. I have found harvesting the tiny wild berries tedious, but the fox had a knack!

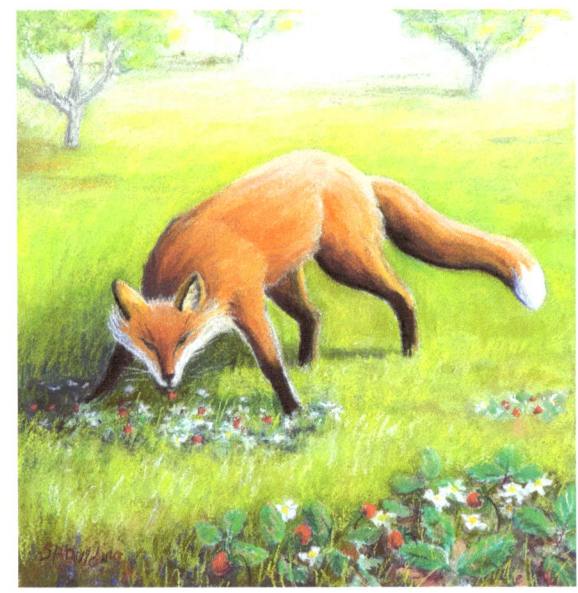

Deer have a way of materializing out of the thickets; not there and then there. A doe with twins came regularly to the apple orchard in September when the apples began to drop. Her teeth gently snapped apples in half for her fawns who could not yet bite through the skins. If I stepped out of the gate and saw them there, I often said "Hello." The doe then faced me with big ears like oven mitts, spread out to catch my words. When spoken to, the deer stare and seem unperturbed. The fawns lie down in the shade, dropping to their knees and then lowering their bodies, front end first, to the warm grass. One rests its head on the other's back. Later when I walk through the orchard again, they slip effortlessly into motion, melting into the tangled blackberry hedge that edges the grass. How did that happen? Raccoons and fox, and the occasional otter are just as stealthy. We see them sometimes if we happen to glance in the right direction at just the right moment.

One mammal that has always been in our neighborhood seems much more numerous now. Bats! I walk at twilight and in the fading light see them fluttering over the meadow. From the house, should we glance at the right moment, we see them flying past a window as dusk falls. One little bat liked to spend the day in our folded up deck umbrella until warm weather came and we kept it open.

When we had to replace the cedar roof on the studio, several bats were displaced. I watched sadly as they flew off into the woods when the old roof was torn off their hiding place. When the construction was over we put a bat house up on the studio near the eaves close to where they had been discovered. It was hard at first to tell if any bats were using the house. We didn't think they were until we began to see them flying out at dusk. As many as twelve have slipped out of the tiny eight by ten inch bat house, dropping downward in a free fall before spreading their leathery wings to glide silently away. Since then, we think it likely females roost and raise young there.

More recently we have noticed bats dropping out from another tiny crevice where a metal trim strip protects the siding from roof drips. It is such a narrow space that the bats must have to hang in a row, politely waiting their turn to exit.

One early dawn Lewis caught sight of bats returning to their roost, one after the other, swooping into their daytime hideaways, thus fixing a time for bedtime for bats.

There are ten species of bats in the islands. We are not sure what lives on our studio but we are happy they abound and are out at night on insect patrol.

Where we left the meadow to naturalize, wildflowers profited by not being mowed: Asters, Goldenrod, Self Heal, Rose Campion, Field Chickweed, Centaury, Eyebright, Butter and Eggs, and an array of "roadside weeds". Bees, both honey and bumbles began to appear in much greater numbers. Sensational native flowers came too, the lily Blue Camas and the native orchid Ladies Tresses, *Spiranthes romanzoffiana*.

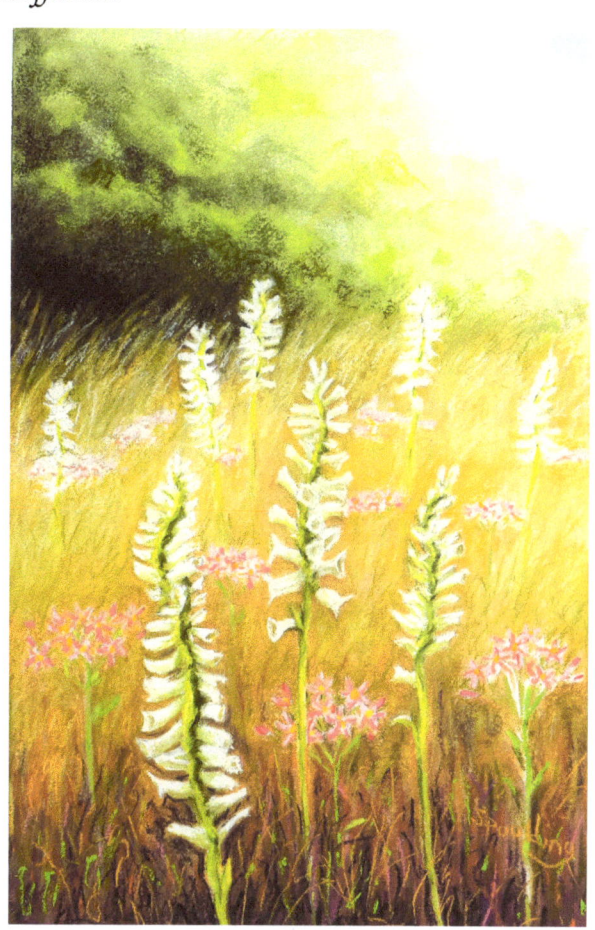

Spiranthes Orchids in the Meadow

During July, counting Spiranthes becomes my daily ritual. They have been waiting underground where it was wet and mucky all winter, waiting throughout spring when grasses and field flowers all raced for the sun and claimed the turf. Then with the arrival of summer's drought, when other plants die back, the orchid stems discreetly poke out into the browning grasses. Basal leaves are barely noticeable as the single unadorned stock grows taller, bearing several rows of minute white blooms that spiral to its top. When they are fully open the seductive twist becomes a fanciful braid of white.

When family members are available I enlist them in the count. Two or three are discovered each day until finally at their peak we might find seventy or eighty in our wildflower plot. The peak in their annual display tends to coincide with Perseid Meteor Showers early in August. Shooting stars arc overhead to punctuate our white orchid meadow, each stem an elfin staircase to the stars.

I draw to record. I paint to say "see it!", just as my toddler daughter used to say as she cupped my face in her little hands and pointed my head toward some recent discovery she had made. I need to keep my childlike sense of excitement and discovery. With so much to keep track of, so much to learn, so much to love, we can never experience it all, but what we can, needs celebrating.

Forces are at play all around us, bombarding us with their singular beauty. It is important to notice, and to remember.

As larger plant species began to create a sea of thorny shrubs, we spend time every winter clearing areas by hand. Its good exercise and fresh air we say. We intended for shrubs and small trees to stay as little copses along the edges of grassy areas, providing bees with blossoms, birds and animals with shelter, and fruits and berries for browsing.

Like the problematic Himalayan blackberries, the English Hawthorns have also sprouted in every corner. In spring their blossoms, born in sweet corymbs, enchant from a distance. The lacy white and pink blossoms produce abundant red berries that provide winter forage for birds, but all year their thorns are a menace. Sharp needle spines upon every twig and branch pierce easily through leather gloves The wily, serpentine branches reach out menacingly, just waiting to drive their thorns through tough denim jeans. They could easily put out an eye. We arm ourselves.

Keeping land open where we want to keep meadowland has become an overwhelming task. I laugh at our attempts to be groundskeepers year after year, yet we continue, steadfast.

Inside the garden, nature is gaining hold as well. To keep harmony between plants that grow out of hand and invading interlopers, my loppers and clippers are in constant use.

As I garden, I watch the Barn Swallows that live in the beach log barn we built years ago. Now it sits at the edge of our vegetative beds where a paddock used to be. Generations have nested there, using the mud nest just within the door. If another summer can provide several clutches of new baby swallows, it is a gift for the planet, I figure. So I go to the barn where I turn on the water for the garden hose. The swallows slip past me through the open door as they go to and from the nest. We have an understanding. They sit 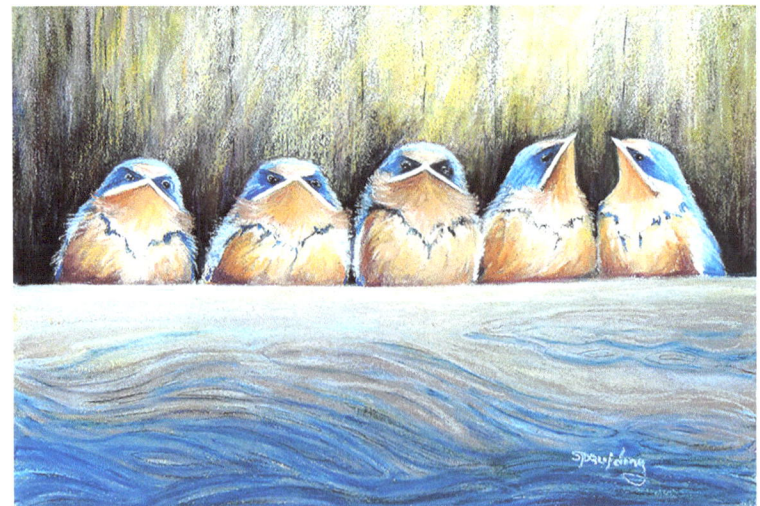 on the trellis by the Banshee Rose keeping an eye on the barn. I go about my work.

Barn Swallows sing, glide through the sky and swoop in carrying a massive amount of bugs, until one day the youngsters fledge. They fly around above me strengthening their new wings, in what appears a gleeful show of prowess. They line up along the eaves of the studio when they need to rest, forming a line of fluffy balls with yawning mouths chirping out for food. Every year the pattern is very much the same. When they are able to feed themselves, the parents take them away to some secret place and then they return to lay another clutch of eggs. When the second group hatches out, swallows appear from all around. A celebration, a legion of protectors, a family connected. We all but join in.

One day on the path beside the little lily pond, a garter snake lay in limbo, attempting to consume a large slug. The slug had a girth as large as the snake's. Writhing, the snake could not make its sticky prey progress either in or out. It was hard to tell if it wanted to rid itself of an undesired meal or whether the snake was working to force the mollusk down its serpentine gullet before going off to digest in peace.

Riveted by this drama, we checked periodically. Eventually the snake disappeared and we never knew the outcome. Mucous from a slug is hard to remove, it is a hydroscopic gel, a lubricant and an adhesive. Eating one would be unpleasant I should think, but snakes feast on worms, snails, amphibians. leaches and slugs in addition to small mammals. They are helpful, controlling many garden pests.

Once I picked up a potting tray to find a dozen or more baby snakes, not much bigger than earthworms, coiled together in a cluster. Snakes in our garden appeared mostly amber colored but sometimes with a band of orange or green.

One summer we had such a large snake frequenting the rock garden, I wondered if it was some invasive species that I should perhaps be wary of. It slept in a coil atop the rocks between some heather plants. I began to imagine rattles at the end of its tail as I walked by at a safe distance. It, however, just lay in repose. One day I saw the snake was gone but had left its skin in the spot where it had been sleeping. A tissue paper tube of translucent parchment, etched with ghostlike scales was all that remained. Upon measuring this artifact, we discovered the length was a whopping 37 inches.

I decided to call Eugene Kozloff, noted biologist and fellow islander, at that time still working throughout his retirement years at the University of Washington Marine Labs. He was delighted to talk about the snake and assured me it was a native garter, that they could indeed grow that large if times were in their favor. He added that if the snake had shed its skin it was because it was growing. Our snake would already be longer and perhaps a bit thicker in girth. He talked of snakes that he had seen at the tideline where they sometimes attained a similar impressive size. Before he hung up the phone he suddenly remarked, "You aren't going to hurt it are you?" His kindness warmed my heart. I assured him that we were glad to have the snake in the garden where it no doubt was eating a large number of voles.

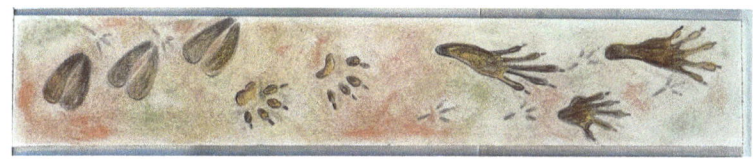

We didn't see the big snake after that but I kept the skin on the windowsill in the studio for a couple of years.

Contemplating the changing world, I look for patterns to appear. In spite of nature's constant state of flux most occurrences occur with regularity, giving us a sense that all is as it should be. We orbit the sun, we tilt with the seasons, we spin with each day. In spring tulips come up, in the fall the leaves turn and drop.

In the midst of the quotidian many sporadic events catch us by surprise. Sometimes we are unruffled by interruptions in our busy lives, at other times we are abruptly awaked in a shower of ice water.

My pleasant afternoon walk of sweet grass and summer breeze is sharply altered by a heavy animal oder, a smell I remembered driving past crowded stockyards. Warily I enter the opening into the trees. In the path lies a fallen deer. Its nose still moist and coat still velveteen, its legs are still positioned in a run. Eyes that no longer see seem to question the

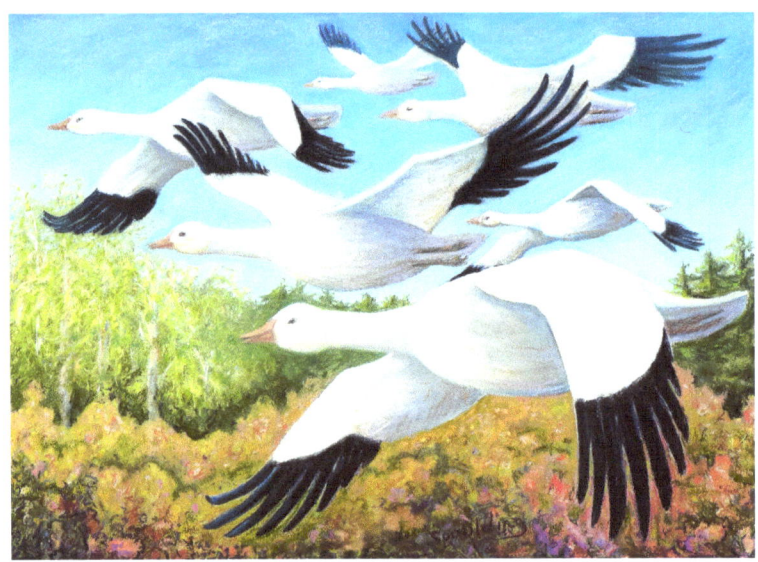

universe or me. It had run as far as its waning strength could carry it after colliding with a car, then it sank into a carpet of deep pine needles.

We leave the deer where it fell. In days eagles and vultures have found it. Finally in two weeks time a fox comes, cleaning up what remains and scattering the elegant bones throughout the trees. The deer is in its final resting place, slowly becoming the forest. I feel aware of its transcendence as I pass on my daily walk.

Early one October morning I step outside just at the very moment a flock of Snow Geese fly eastward directly over our dome house. They are low to the ground. I imagine my arms reaching upwards to touch them as they approach. If I had been standing on my roof I surely could have. Their honking voices become one continual babbling sound tossed from bird to bird. Their bright bodies look like the patches of pure white paper left in a painting that is otherwise colored in muted greens, rusty reds and deep blues of an autumn sky. Their wing tips black and elegantly curved are like fingers of a satin opera glove.

I have seen geese fly across the island before but never just here, never so close. They head east with about thirty miles left to go before they will reach the Skagit Flats, their winter home. Do they call out so wildly in anticipation? I watch until they become dots that mysteriously evaporate over Griffin Bay.

One day in late winter, Lewis and I sat on our window seat sipping tea, chatting, contemplating the day. Outside, an ordinary pale sky spontaneously poured forth flashes of falling color, white, grey, yellow, amber and black. When they reached the garden the colors transformed into a flock of big, bright songbirds we had never seen here before. Eight Evening Grosbeaks with thick, seed cracking beaks had arrived at our feeder. They came erratically for several years after, always surprising us in the same way. As suddenly as they came, we stopped seeing them. The bird book calls them a highly irruptive species, apt to appear with irregularity, perhaps following available sources of food. Like the colorful Red Crossbills that only visit the garden periodically, they enchanted us for awhile.

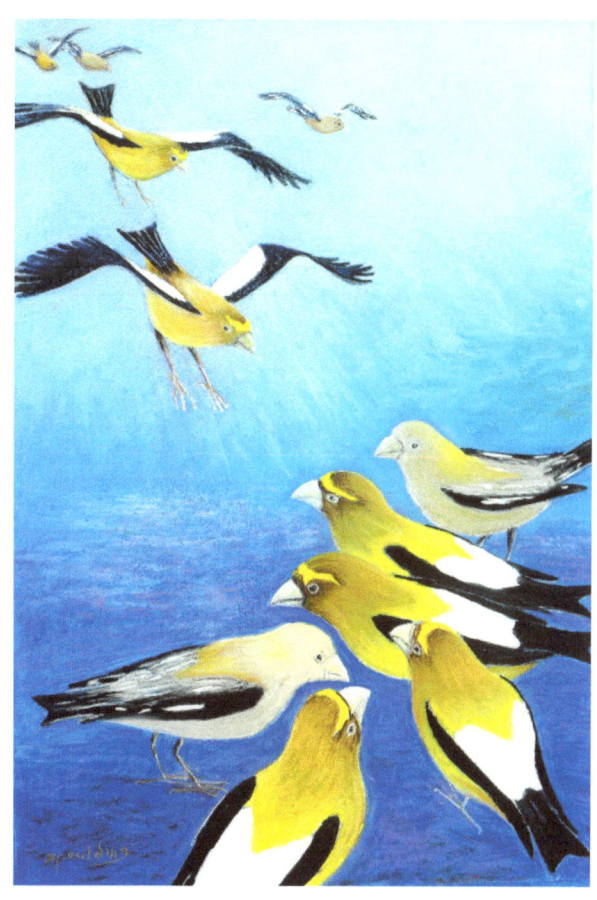

Some events move beyond sporadic, they become the new normal. As the climate warms, already we have seen some changes. Anna's Hummingbirds moved north several years ago and are now resident in the islands year round. Eurasian Collared Doves arrived here and keep forging ever northwesterly up the coast toward Alaska. The presence of Praying Mantis here in the last couple of years was strange. The disappearing of starfish along our shorelines and the starvation of Orca whales in our sea have been unsettling events. Forest fires that have raged the west every summer in recent years are sobering. Reliability in the world is a concept cracking.

Another kind of vulnerability looms. My body, like the trees I have watched grow, is changing. On my morning walk the thought strikes me as a branch falls, even if granted a very long life, the clock is unstoppable. The trees and I will someday be gone and no doubt it is I who will be gone first. Optimistically, I keep planting things. Whether I am here or not, I take joy there will be flowers for another season.

I think of my mother at age 101 still living alone in her home where a hand written quotation from Alfred Lord Tennyson's *Ulysses* was tacked above her desk and underscored, "Some work of noble note may yet be done".

I realize how fortunate I have been to have a piece of the earth to call home, to have been able to stay in a place that has nurtured our spirits, where we have felt contentment and could do the work we felt called to do. It has been more than fortuitous, it has been the greatest of life's gifts. This place has become a refuge for our family, our friends, and for wildlife. My garden—chaotic as it is—has been above all a habitat garden.

Overwhelmed with gratitude, deep in the recesses of mind I hear my father's kind and encouraging voice resonating as though he were here beside me. Blank papers await. The studio awaits. The garden awaits. I step forth, riding the wild wave of time.

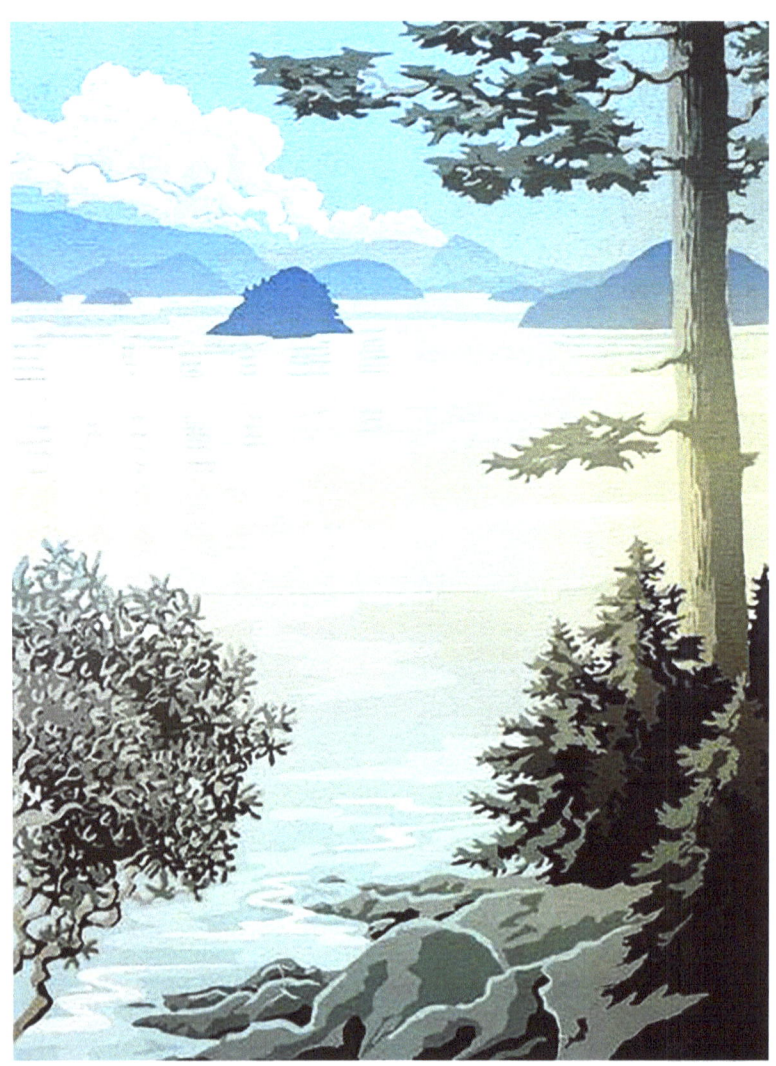

Let your life lightly dance on the edges of time like dew on the tip of a leaf.

—Rabindranath Tagore

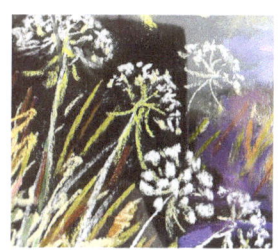

List of Nancy's Artwork
Page, Title and Medium

6	*Islands of the Mind*	pastel
9	*Bicycle Picnic*	serigraph
21	*Down at Cattle Point*	water color sketch
24	*Violet-green Swallows Return to the Island*	oil Painting
27	*Violet-green Swallows*	pastel on silk screened paper
29	*Changing Places*	pastel
34	*Moonlight Rambler*	pastel
36	*New Dawn*	water color sketch
	Tuscany Rose	water color sketch
39	*Rugosa*	pastel and water color
40	*The Alchymist*	pastel
41	*Red Rose of Lancaster*	pastel
42	*Madame Hardy*	pastel
43	*Summer Dreams with Isphahan*	pastel
45	*Buff Beauty Rose*	pastel
53	*Sunrise Through Fog*	pastel
54	*Bumblebees and Dames Rocket*	pastel
58	*Drone on Marjoram*	pastel and watercolor
60	Bumblebee Notebook	studies
61	*Little Bumble on Columbine*	pastel and watercolor
62	*Bee With Dewdrop*	pastel and watercolor
64	*Ravens with Sundog*	pastel
69	*Gentle Islands*	pastel
72	*Wildflowers of the San Juans-Paintbrush and Stonecrop*	serigraph
74	*The Ragged Edges of Life*	pastel
76	*Quail Family on the Thyme Walk*	pastel
78	*A Quail with his Chicks*	pastel
80	*Winter Quail*	pastel
82	*Quail in the Rockery*	pastel
83	*Vantage Point*	pastel
86	*Trailing Twinflower*	pastel
89	*California Poppy*	pastel
91	*All that Grass and Sheep in the Road*	serigraph
92	*Delicious Hangout*	serigraph
94	*Orchard Tree*	serigraph
96	*Blue eyed Grass at Iceberg Point*	serigraph
98	*Hellebore and Snowdrops*	pastel

100	*Pacific Wren with Snowdrops*	pastel
102	*Nuthatches in the Pines*	pastel
103	Sketch Book Entry - Hawk	
104	Sketch Book Entry - Kinglets	
106	*Spotted Towhee with Primulas*	pastel
107	*Anna's Does His J Loops*	pastel
107	*Anna's in her Hideaway:* *Winter Blooming Jasmine and Honeysuckle*	pastel
108	*Ceanothus Silk Moth*	pastel
110	*Rufous Male*	pastel
111	*Climbing Treasure Trove*	pastel
112	*Hummingbird Moths*	pastel
113	*Visitation*	pastel
114	*Painted Ladies Cross the Channel*	oil on panel
114	*Contemplating the Void*	pastel
116	*The Brick Walk*	pastel
117	*Summer in the Rock Garden*	pastel
118	*Madame Alfred Carrière*	pastel
120	*Stargazers*	pastel
122	*Hope for Another Season*	pastel
125	*Dahlias on Placemat*	pastel
126	*Plums and Blue Tile*	pastel
127	*Moonlit Lilies*	pastel
130	*Beach Logs*	serigraph
132	*Nighthawks*	pastel
132	*Another Solstice Celebrated*	pastel
135	*Félicité et Perpétue*	pastel
136	*Through Columbine Meadows*	serigraph
138	*The Zen Garden*	pastel
140	*The Circle of Life*	pastel
142	*Great Horned Owl with Aurora*	pastel
144	*The Strawberry Fox*	pastel
145	*Spiranthes Orchids in the Meadow*	pastel
146	*Baby Barn Swallows*	pastel
148	*Snow Geese Overhead*	pastel
149	*One Day Out of the Blue*	pastel
150	*Clouds Across the Water*	serigraphs

Unlisted are photos, photo collages and portions of artwork used as dingbats.

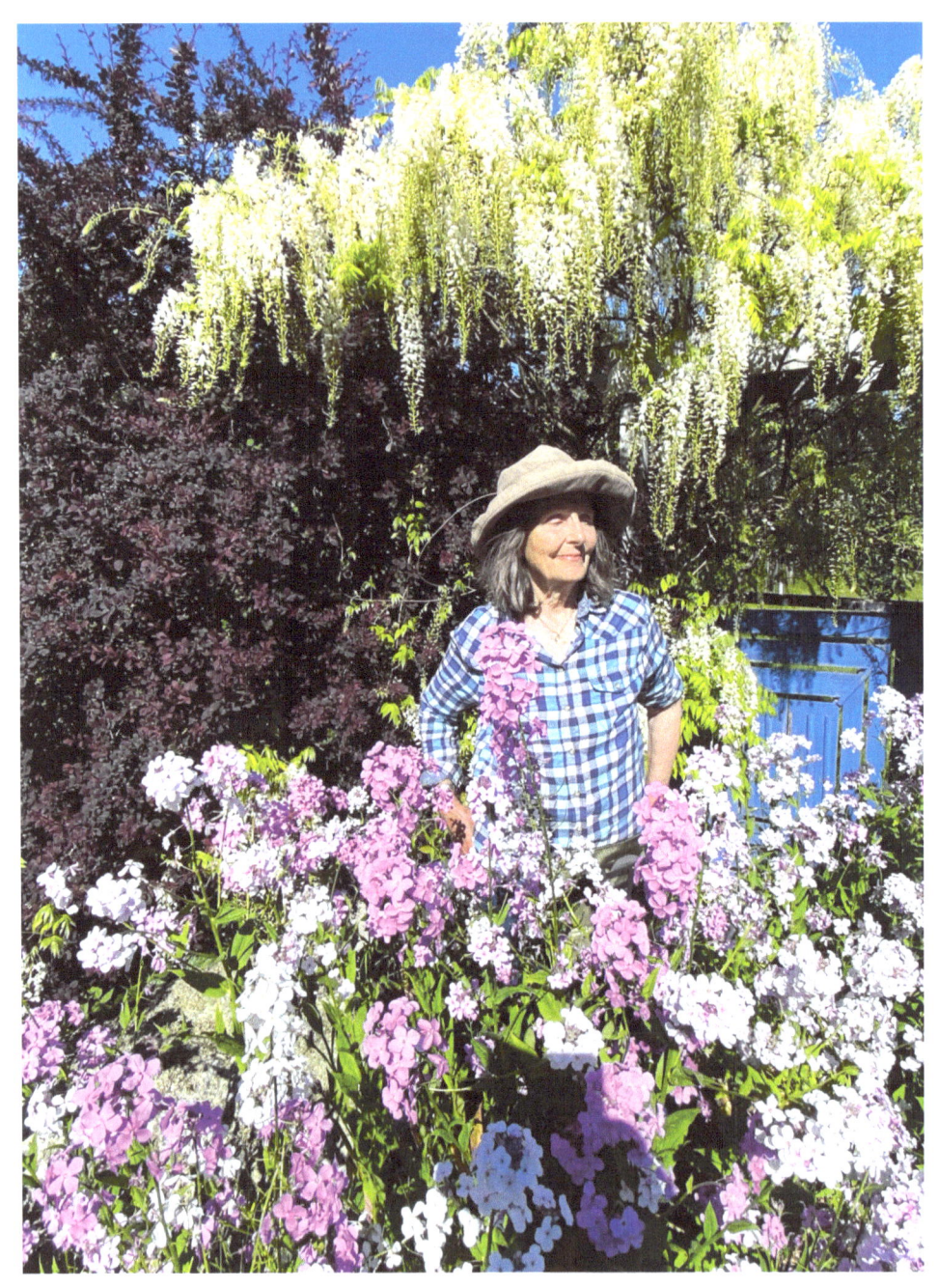

Nancy in Her Garden

About the Author

Nancy Spaulding has been a professional visual artist for over forty years, working primarily as a printmaker, and later as a pastelist.

Life's unpredictability changed the path she had intended to follow. Rather than complete a degree in art education she left college with only one semester left to be completed and joined Volunteers In Service To America, the Domestic Peace Corps, during the momentous sixties. She and her husband Lewis served for two years, living first on the Seneca Nation in upstate New York and and then on the Olympic Peninsula with the Skokomish tribe and low income families working in the timber industry there. With academia behind her, she dove into independent studio work.

After VISTA , the couple became avid hikers and she became a mother. All the while, art remained her passion and means of connecting with the world around her.

She has been part of the arts community on the island where she lives since making her home and studio there.

Coming from a family of journalists and letter writers, she has always kept a "log" of her experiences. *Home in an Island Garden* is her first book.

Acknowledgments

This book would not have come into being without the absolute and wholehearted support of my husband Lewis or the continued encouragement from my daughters, Laurel and Heather.

Neither would it have been possible without my book designer W. Bruce Conway, with his expertise in graphic arts and publishing. His enthusiasm and knowledge of the arts have guided me as we have worked on the concept I envisioned, and his skills have kept me on course.

I have appreciated the editing help from Emily Geyman more than I can ever say. Her encouragement kept me going as I worked and reworked the chapters. She often checked with me socially by phone to see how I was doing which was always a boost just when I needed it.

The editing skills of my journalist daughter Heather have also been deeply appreciated, especially with her perspective of living this story. Lively discussions together awakened many memories.

To my friends and island neighbors who proofed chapters and sections, I thank you with all my heart for your willingness to share your knowledge and your time. Many thanks to Thor Hanson, Susan Vernon, Kathleen Foley, Laura Norris Crawbuck and from further afield, Cara Hochhalter.

I have great appreciation for my writers' group who listened to my first drafts and offered support, encouragement and friendship. To this group I add Judith Azrael whose writing workshop was the origin of our group's formation. Judith has been a sweet voice of support from the very beginning. And I thank you, Tara MacMahon, as an invaluable member of the group, for your ongoing encouragement with all creative endeavors.

For the many islanders we have come to know over the years, those I mention in the book and also those left unmentioned, you have added a rich dimension to our lives with your unique and colorful lifestyles, your accomplishments, inspirations and enthusiasms shared.

I give special thanks to all my final readers...

Finally in memoriam, I thank my parents Robert and Alice McDonnell who encouraged us as we made our unconventional choices and who never stopped believing that we could make it all work. That made all the difference.

www.ingramcontent.com/pod-product-compliance
Lightning Source LLC
Chambersburg PA
CBHW051147220526
45473CB00003B/680